GOD AND COUNTRY

GOD AND COUNTRY

AMERICA IN RED AND BLUE

Sheila Kennedy

BAYLOR UNIVERSITY PRESS

© 2007 by Baylor University Press
Waco, Texas 76798

All Rights Reserved. No part of this publication may be reproduced, stored in a retrieval system, or transmitted, in any form or by any means, electronic, mechanical, photocopying, recording or otherwise, without the prior permission in writing of Baylor University Press.

Cover Design by Cynthia Dunne

Library of Congress Cataloging-in-Publication Data

Kennedy, Sheila Suess.
  God and country : America in red and blue / Sheila Kennedy.
      p. cm.
  Includes bibliographical references and index.
  ISBN-13: 978-1-932792-99-7 (pbk. : alk. paper)
  1. Polarization (Social sciences) 2. Religion and politics--United States. 3. Paradigms (Social sciences)--United States. 4. Pluralism (Social sciences)--United States. 5. Social conflict--United States. 6. United States--Politics and government. 7. United States--Social conditions. I. Title.
      HN90.P57K46 2007
      306.60973--dc22
                                                            2007009738

Printed in the United States of America on acid-free paper with a minimum of 30% pcw recycled content.

CONTENTS

Acknowledgments   vii

Part I
What is a Paradigm, and Why Does It Matter?

1   Habits of the Mind—Thinking in Red and Blue   1

2   America's Religious Roots   21

3   A New Paradigm   37

Part II
The Democratic Dialectic

4   Conflict and Change   57

5   The Culture War Considered   83

Part III
Paradigm and Policy: Now You See It, Now You Don't

6   The Usual Suspects   105

7   Religion, Wealth, and Poverty   125

8	Religion, Science, and the Environment	147
9	Sin and Crime	163
10	God and Country, Us and Them	181

Part IV
Living Together

11 Living Together	209
Bibliography	233
Index	247

ACKNOWLEDGMENTS

I was aware when I began to write this book that I had set out across an intellectually treacherous terrain. An exploration of religious influences on American policy required not only a careful review of American historical and religious experience, but also at least a superficial familiarity with the scholarly literatures of several discrete policy fields. Even summoning all of my personal hubris, I knew I could never accomplish my goal without significant assistance from people with expertise in these areas.

The friends and colleagues I approached for suggested reading materials, disciplinary "roadmaps," and later, to read drafts and provide feedback, responded with unbelievable generosity. There is no way this book could have been written without their advice and counsel, and I am immensely grateful to all of them. Whatever errors remain are entirely the fault of the author!

My most constant support, as usual, came from my best friend, Jan Rubin. She read drafts, asked pertinent questions, made excellent suggestions, and was a model of patience and encouragement.

The Very Reverend Robert Giannini read every word of the manuscript, shared his own copies of books I had missed, and offered appropriate cautions and less deserved plaudits. Similarly, Steve Sanders took a lawyer's eye to the first draft, and made invaluable suggestions for reorganizing, emphasizing, and tightening the arguments. John Clark brought his historical and foreign policy expertise to his review, and the Reverend John Hay Jr. helped ensure accurate representation of his Evangelical tradition. Rabbis Aaron Spiegel and Dennis Sasso offered valuable insights and suggested further readings. My colleague Tom Stucky patiently explained criminal justice theory and pointed me to appropriate resources, while Miriam Langsam brought a prodigious knowledge of American history and historical literature to her review.

Arthur Farnsley, Philip Goff, and Jan Shipps—all noted religion scholars—took time they didn't have to tutor me in that literature, review portions of the manuscript, and offer immensely helpful guidance. Other scholars affiliated with the Center for the Study of Religion and American Culture at IUPUI—Pat Wittberg, David Craig, and Tom Davis—also offered valuable suggestions and feedback, as did Brian Bex at the Remnant Trust.

I owe an immense debt of gratitude to all of them, and—especially, and as usual—to my patient and long-suffering husband Bob, who puts up with me during the frenzied and overwhelming process that is (at least for me) involved every time I write a book.

Last, but most definitely not least, I must acknowledge our five children and four grandchildren, who are the living, breathing reasons I keep trying to clear a path through the past and present to a more thoughtful and accepting future.

PART I

What is a Paradigm, and Why Does It Matter?

Chapter 1

HABITS OF THE MIND— THINKING IN RED AND BLUE

Is America coming apart? If you turn on a "public affairs" television program, listen to talk radio, or attend a lawmaker's "town meeting," you are likely to witness the increasing stridence and incivility of what currently passes for democratic discourse. Our elected officials seem unable to engage with each other in anything approaching a productive and mutually meaningful exchange. Cyberspace is filled with blogs where ordinary citizens post frustrated, angry commentaries. Worse, Americans seem increasingly to be talking past, rather than to, each other. We seem increasingly unable to agree about what it means to be an American.

On one hand, it is important that we not overreact to contemporary divisions, and that we place our current "red state/blue state" hostilities in perspective. This country has seen periods of very significant conflict before—the Civil War, Prohibition, the civil rights movement, and the various dislocations that we collectively refer to as "the sixties," to name just a few—and many of those conflicts have been ferocious. It is equally true that those who bemoan the loss of a former civility are indulging in a rather selective look backward; a glance at the rhetoric used during Thomas Jefferson's campaign for president, to note just one example, will confirm that nastiness and "the politics of personal destruction" are nothing new. Nevertheless, the radical pluralism that characterizes modern life—and the new technologies that bring a certain "in your face" quality to that pluralism—pose challenges that are arguably unlike those of past times. It is not hyperbolic to say that the rifts in our body politic are deep, and their potential consequences serious.

The thesis of this book is that much of what divides Americans these days is rooted in our particular religious histories, and that our seeming inability to address our differences constructively is exacerbated by a profound misunderstanding of the ways in which those religious roots manifest themselves. The religious roots of many conflicts are obvious, of course; as this is being written, members of the Missouri legislature are preparing to pass a resolution "protecting the majority's right to express their religious beliefs" and making Christianity the state's official religion. The State of South Dakota has recently outlawed abortion, and state bans on same-sex marriage continue to receive extensive debate and media attention. But with many other issues polarizing contemporary America, the religious dimensions of our differences are equally significant but far less obvious. The Iraq war has exposed our very incompatible ideas about America's role in the world, and the different standards we employ to determine whether any particular war is just. Ongoing policy arguments about everything from the North American Free Trade Agreement (NAFTA) and the Central American Free Trade Agreement (CAFTA), to the drug war, to drilling for oil in Alaska, to the proper role of government and even our definitions of liberty, all have a basis in religion. Nevertheless, notwithstanding the mountains of scholarly and popular commentary on religion, religion and politics, and the nature of public and private morality—and despite the fact that we do see and recognize the more explicitly religious dimensions of policy conflicts in areas like church-state relations or abortion—most of us consistently misinterpret and underestimate the influence of culturally embedded attitudes that originated with religious beliefs. Americans will not be able to begin a genuine conversation about our differences, and about what it means or should mean to be an American, until we recognize that we are operating out of different paradigms, different frameworks of meaning.

Most of us do recognize that the labeling and insults that increasingly dominate our media and politics are not communication. While communication is not the absence of argument or disagreement, it does require that we actually hear each other, that we argue from the same basic premises, and that at some level, no matter how minimal, we be able to acknowledge what it is the other person is saying and understand the basis upon which that person is saying it. In other words, effective argumentation and democratic deliberation require a shared reality. While it is perfectly possible to have a genuine argument about values, for example—to disagree about which values are sound, or how particular values ought to apply in a particular situation—the term has become shorthand for a far different phenomenon. Even the term *values* means different things to different people; for many, it is a euphemism for arguments over religious doctrine. But the much ballyhooed values debate is not a conflict between people who are religious and people who are secular, nor is it a struggle between those who hold to different religious beliefs. It is an argument between people operating out of different and largely inconsistent worldviews, or paradigms.

These differences can be seen in a number of policy contexts. For example, President Bush has often asserted that Americans value a "culture of life." Yet citizens who would readily agree with him that government policies should respect the sanctity of life hold—and act upon—very different conceptions of what a culture of life is, and what that respect entails. Does support for embryonic stem cell research violate respect for life by destroying the human potential the embryo represents? Or does the failure to engage in such research, with its potential for lifesaving medical breakthroughs, violate that respect? Is the death penalty inconsistent with a genuine respect for life, or does insistence upon the ultimate punishment affirm such respect by sending a signal that we will not tolerate the taking of human life? Does respect for life require the continuation of life support for individuals in a persistent vegetative state, or does it require that we honor an individual's previously expressed desire to have artificial support removed in such circumstances? We need only turn on our televisions and listen to our lawmakers debate these issues to hear people talking past each other.

This inability to engage in genuine communication is seriously threatening our ability to govern ourselves, to construct a workable *unum* out of our *pluribus*. Left unaddressed, it will prevent the construction of a social order capable of dealing with the significant challenges that characterize contemporary American life. We need a truce, based upon terms that will allow us to live with a measure of civility despite our deep and inevitable differences—terms that can be accepted as fair and legitimate by most elements of our polis even when some of those terms do not favor their worldview. That is a tall order, but I will argue that it can be done. However, we cannot begin to fashion that truce or those rules unless and until we truly understand the nature of the conflict.

THE ROOTS OF THE PROBLEM

No matter what our conscious beliefs or lack thereof, all of us have mental frameworks, views of the nature of reality that have been shaped in significant part by religious cultures. Those frameworks are what we call normative concepts, and they dictate our definitions of public virtue and private merit, as well as our attitudes toward work, family, and community. Theologically shaped worldviews—whether or not recognized as religious by those who hold them—frame our individual and communal approaches to issues of race, economic behavior, poverty, social justice, education, crime and punishment, philanthropy, bioethics, and just about everything else. Many of our most contentious public arguments are rooted in differing normative concepts, or realities, that are grounded firmly in religious explanations of reality into which participants in the debates have been socialized. Sometimes the religious dimensions of a public policy debate are obvious: arguments about abortion, prayer in school, or same-sex marriage are often quite overtly sectarian. Both the religious dimensions of those issues and their use as "wedge issues" by people whose real motives are economic or political have been widely noted. Less obvious examples of religious influences include ostensibly secular arguments about responsibility for poverty, the appropriate role of the state, the meaning of law, our responsibility for the natural environment, and the role of the United States in international affairs.

A concrete example of what this all means may be illuminated by a personal story. When my middle son was eight or nine, he asked me the sort of question that makes parents' heads hurt. "Mom," he began, "I say the sky is blue. You say the sky is blue. But how do we know that we are both seeing the same color? Maybe the color I see is what you call orange, and I call orange blue because I've been taught that blue is what we call the color of the sky. How can we ever know whether what you call blue and what I call blue is really the same color?" Indeed. I have frequently pondered that—largely unanswerable—question in the context of the increasingly impassioned, vitriolic pronouncements about what we euphemistically call "social issues," most recently, the rhetoric surrounding withdrawal of artificial nutrition from Terri Schiavo.[1] It would not be accurate to characterize most of the opposing public utterances around these issues as a "debate." In order to debate, we need the ability to actually hear each other. We need to share a paradigm.

This book is ultimately an effort to identify the outlines of a paradigm that most Americans can—and perhaps already do—share. But before we can sketch out the elements of that overarching paradigm, or determine its sufficiency, we need to understand where we are and how we got here. We need to uncover the buried roots of our clashing policy commitments.

[1] Terry Schiavo was a Florida woman who had been in a persistent vegetative state for fourteen years. Her husband wanted to discontinue artificial nutrition and hydration, claiming that Terri had clearly expressed the wish that she not be kept alive under such circumstances. Her parents insisted that she showed signs of cognition, and that life support should be maintained. The Florida courts held multiple hearings on the dispute between the husband and parents, and the constitutionality of efforts by the governor and legislature to pass special legislation annulling the court's determination favoring the husband. When the parents had exhausted all state court appeals, Congress passed, and President George W. Bush signed, "Terri's law" to prevent the withdrawal of nutrition. (The majority leader, Bill Frist (himself a doctor), claimed he had "diagnosed" Ms. Schiavo by viewing a videotape of her, and that she clearly retained some cognitive functions.) Rallies were held outside her hospital. When she was finally allowed to die, an autopsy revealed that most of her cerebral cortex had liquefied and that no cognitive functioning had occurred for some time.

AMERICANS' CONTENDING WORLDVIEWS

Jonathan Gold has described the process by which religious cultures change in response to encounters with different belief structures, a process called a dialectic: "Religions do not have unchanging natures. They are (among other things) complex social organisms that exist in history. Thus, while they are molded by that history, they mold back in turn. When we focus on social forces that affect the development and transformation of peoples, therefore, we always remember that religions are a crucial part of that causal story" (2001, 1). In the United States, that dialectic has been dominated by two major and opposing worldviews, one that incorporates and reflects our Puritan heritage and one that began with the Enlightenment. Chapters 2 and 3 detail the genesis and contours of those worldviews. For purposes of this introductory discussion, it will suffice to say that they rest upon profoundly different conceptions of the essential nature of human beings and thus the purposes of their governing institutions. The Puritan view of human nature is grounded in the essential sinfulness of man and the centrality of the Fall. The post-Enlightenment or modernist view is that people are born innocent—the human baby as blank slate, or tabula rasa—and their subsequent development is influenced heavily by the environments within which they are raised. One consequence of these differences can be seen in the respective approaches to governing institutions and policies of Puritans and modernists. Religious conservatives (in my shorthand formulation, *Puritans*) tend to focus more on individual character and universal moral values, while secular and religious liberals (*modernists*) emphasize the importance of culture and social structure.

The struggle between these two incompatible ways of structuring reality is, of course, more complicated than this description would suggest. For one thing, very few people have worldviews that fall entirely within one neat category or another. As we shall see, the dialectic process that has characterized American social history is replicated, to a greater or lesser degree, within each of us. For another, virtually all cultures are constantly being transformed by their encounters with new and emerging realities, although the process through which such transformations occur, and the new worldviews that emerge, will be heavily influenced by that culture's antecedent folkways and institutions. The most determinedly orthodox or fundamentalist adherent of a religious tradition today bears little resemblance to the orthodox practitioner of that same religion even a hundred years ago; instead, he is a product of the encounter between the older orthodoxy and subsequent social history.

Nevertheless—however tortured the lineage of contemporary Puritans and modernists—in their purer forms they hold significantly different worldviews, inhabit significantly different realities, and are engaged in a poorly understood struggle to control the dominant social narrative, if not through persuasion, then through political coercion. This dynamic can be vividly seen in our more extreme public rhetoric; as many observers have noted, current participants in public discourse hardly bother to pretend that they are responding to opposing views; instead they concentrate on mobilizing their supporters with emotional, rather than persuasive rhetoric. Rousing the base is a means to an end, and the end is the power to determine whose reality will control the social agenda.

DEVELOPING "HABITS OF THE MIND"

Understanding the nature of the conflict requires that we define our terms. Saying that religion is often at the root of our public conflicts is to introduce what lawyers would call a preliminary question, namely, what do we mean by religion? That is not as easy a question as one might think. As a book reviewer for the London *Guardian* (February 7, 2002) once noted, not entirely tongue-in-cheek, "Any argument about religion, whether conducted in the seminar room or the saloon bar, is likely to hit the buffers not just because people hold different religious beliefs, but because they disagree about what should or should not be counted as an instance of religion in the first place." In *The Sacred Canopy*, sociologist of religion Peter Berger wrote, "Every human society is an enterprise of world building. Religion occupies a distinctive place in this enterprise" (1967, 3). Berger defines religion as a "humanly constructed universe of meaning" (175), and he explains, "Worlds are socially constructed and socially maintained." That is, their power to describe reality depends upon their ability to be seen as self-evident, in other words, upon their nature as "taken for granted" attributes of the real world—what Berger called their "plausibility structure" (45). When social changes or world events threaten the self-evident nature of an accepted reality, or undermine its plausibility structure, trouble arises.

In the following pages, I use the term *religion* to refer to the "humanly constructed universes of meaning" around which substantial numbers of Americans have organized their understandings of life's purpose—systems that provide individual adherents with a meaningful framework for understanding the world, establish rules governing ethical personal and social behavior, define the individual's place within society, and legitimize social policies and institutions. The definition I use encompasses such readily recognizable "life-organizing belief systems" as Christianity, Judaism, and Islam, but will also include non-Abrahamic religions like Hinduism, nontraditional religions like Wicca, and nontheistic religions like Buddhism. It is important to be clear at the outset about the way I am using the term, because one's choice of a definition will always affect the nature of the conclusions to be drawn. One reason social scientists get inconsistent empirical results when they study religious outcomes (the effect of religion on health, longevity, or subjective well-being, for example) is that they often begin with quite different ideas about what religion and religiosity are (Hackney and Sanders 2003).[2]

The religious roots of our contemporary conflicts are not traditional doctrinal disputes. The mere fact that you and I attend different churches, synagogues, or mosques, or identify ourselves as members of religions holding different doctrines, does not equate to the holding of different worldviews, and does not account for our civil divisions. Ecumenical civility has largely (although certainly not entirely)

---

[2] Sociologists often divide definitions of religion into two types, functional and substantive. I am employing a functional definition.

replaced purely sectarian disputes like those that led the Puritans to leave England, Roger Williams to found Rhode Island, or Catholics to form their own schools. Today, interreligious difficulties most frequently arise when we simply do not realize that we are operating out of a particular set of assumptions about the nature of reality that may not be shared by others.

We can see the nature of such assumptions when we examine various definitions of religion. Winnifred Sullivan reminds us that "[t]he traditional American evangelical Protestant definition of religion as chosen, private, individual and believed" now shares space in a pluralist culture in which many other traditions define religion as "given, public, communal and enacted" (2004, 257). The facile references to a "Judeo-Christian" Americanism that characterize current discourse ignore or trivialize those profound and still salient distinctions. A case in point is the terminology employed to describe recent government efforts at outreach to religious social service organizations (President Bush's "Faith-Based Initiative"). The term faith-based, undoubtedly chosen rather than religious in an effort to be ecumenical and inclusive, is based upon a narrowly Protestant conception of religion—a conception and a terminology that equates religion with faith, and thus excludes (albeit unintentionally) traditionally works-based religions like Judaism and Catholicism. Similarly, people who consider themselves entirely secular and nonreligious often share significant worldviews with adherents of some religions, and virtually none with adherents of others. Religious worldviews have left indelible imprints on even the most secularized human cultures and worldviews. In *Sacred and Secular: Religion and Politics Worldwide,* Pippa Norris and Ronald Inglehart tell us "distinctive worldviews that were originally linked with religious traditions have shaped the cultures of each nation in an enduring fashion; today, these distinctive values are transmitted to citizens even if they never set foot in a church." To illustrate, they repeat a telling exchange with an Estonian colleague who was explaining the cultural differences between Estonians and Russians. "We are all atheists; but I am a Lutheran atheist and they are Orthodox atheists" (2005, 17).

Religious worldviews inform culture, and culture tells us what behaviors are acceptable; it establishes collective authoritative norms. A culture "nurtures predictability in social relations" by making and then propagating assumptions about human nature, prescribing norms for appropriate social conduct, establishing identity, and maintaining boundaries (Leege and Kellstedt 1993, 8). As Clifford Geertz explains, culture is an "acted document"; it consists of "socially established structures of meaning" (1973, 12). It is public, because meaning is public.

There are, of course, many economic, environmental, and situational factors that interact to shape human cultures. That said, the influence of religion on culture (even on seemingly nonreligious subcultures) has been profound. The religious underpinnings of a culture exert a far-reaching influence upon the life conduct of very heterogeneous people, and particular beliefs and rituals have different cultural consequences; as we shall see, the Catholic doctrine of sacrament, the Lutheran belief in justification through faith, and the Calvinist belief in predestination have each had far-reaching results for the fashioning of a practical way of life.

Individuals' worldviews are the mental frameworks that develop as a result of their encounters with culture and cultural norms, frameworks which we use to filter and sort our encounters with external stimuli. We might call these mental frameworks "habits of the mind" (distinct from, although related to, the "habits of the heart" made famous by Robert Bellah and his colleagues in their book of the same name). Our habits of the mind are just that: habits. Much like a path worn through the grass on a well-traveled shortcut, or ruts on a dirt road left by countless wagon wheels, our mental habits are the cognitive mechanisms through and around which each individual human learns to define and travel the way forward. Our habits describe the "path" of our perceived realities. Worldviews—our mental paths, or paradigms—result from the interaction of the public "reality structure" of the culture with the capacities and experiences of unique individuals.

Another word for these worldviews is *paradigm*, a term that owes its current popularity to Thomas Kuhn. Kuhn was a physicist who—in the course of research for his dissertation—picked up Aristotle's *Physics* and found that it made no sense to him. Since Kuhn assumed that neither he nor Aristotle was stupid, he concluded that they were operating from such different, and incommensurable, realities that communication simply was not possible, and he proceeded to write a book about the meaning and use of these conceptual frameworks and the way science adapts or shifts its paradigms (1962). Other scientists have demonstrated that anomalies—facts falling outside one's paradigm, or frame of reference—are simply unseen. That is, if a fact is encountered for which there is no place in one's conceptual framework, that fact will not be willfully disregarded; rather, its existence genuinely will not be recognized. The way paradigms operate can be seen in the old story of the blind men and the elephant: one blind man feels the tail and says an elephant is a type of snake; one of the others encounters the animal's broad side and says it is a kind of wall, and so forth. We all use our existing frameworks to make sense of the phenomena we encounter, because they are the only tools we have. If we have no frame of reference for a whole elephant, we will not—arguably cannot—see a whole elephant.

Paradigm theory is a useful way of thinking about the normative belief structures that help humans make sense of reality. Such paradigms, or worldviews (I am using the terms interchangeably), need not be rigid, or even coherent, to perform this interpretive function; with respect to worldviews, evidence suggests that the filtering effects of normative paradigms incorporating religious ways of seeing reality persist in individuals who no longer consciously embrace (or are even familiar with) the theological propositions that originally shaped them. In other words, religious or secular, we have all been socialized into cultural and conceptual social norms that were originally based on religion and religious ways of understanding the world, and those norms continue to shape our personal worldviews. Furthermore, since "every theology embodies, either implicitly or explicitly, a *mythos*, a vision of how human communities ought to be organized" (Bell 2004, 423), our theologically based worldviews are inevitably political.

My son learned early in life that the color of the sky is called blue. Like all children, he has—as Erich Fromm might put it—soaked up society's "givens" with his mother's milk. The cultures into which we are socialized provide the guidelines we use to categorize external realities; culture is the reason Americans regard gerbils as pets but mice as pests, the reason we eat cows but shudder at the thought of eating dogs. We acquire habits of mind, habitual ways of processing reality, that dictate what we regard as fact and what as fiction, what we designate as "public" and what as "private," what we consider relevant or irrelevant, what we think of as "natural" and what we reject as "unnatural" (Zerubavel 1997, 67).

There is lively and ongoing debate about the extent to which our individual human behaviors are biologically encoded or "hard wired" and the extent to which they have been culturally transmitted. Despite these scientific disputes over the relative contributions of nature and nurture, however, there is widespread agreement (confirmed by a variety of failed experiments in social engineering) that socialization does not and cannot produce cultural "clones"—that individual differences and experiences will always shape the ways in which individuals appropriate and employ cultural symbols and conventions to make sense of the world and to develop habits of the mind.

For much of human history, children were socialized into quite homogeneous cultures. More recently, due to modern transportation and communication media, immigration, intermarriage, and other phenomena of modernity, we experience far more cultural and cognitive pluralism. One need not accept Samuel Huntington's "clash of civilizations" thesis to recognize that increasing pluralism creates conflict; it threatens the *taken for granted* nature of our mental frameworks. As James Davison Hunter has written, the stridency of much contemporary debate is "inspired more by doubt than confidence, more by fear than by trust and settled conviction. The loudness of the voices is, in some ways, an attempt to drown out the droning noise of uncertainty" (2005, 3). The assault of pluralism and social change on our settled mental "habits" also threatens our ability to govern ourselves.

> The existence of alternative social paradigms may result in problems of communication and understanding of such magnitude they threaten

the legitimacy of the political system. It is because protagonists to the debate approach issues from different cultural contexts, which generate different and conflicting implicit meanings, that there is mutual exasperation and charges and countercharges of irrationality and unreason. What is sensible from one point of view is nonsense from another. It is the implicit, self-evident, taken-for-granted character of paradigms which clogs the channels of communication. And, where the belief in the reasonableness of the political system, and its openness to reasoned argument and debate, break down, the normal channels of petition, protest, and pressure group tactics come to be seen as inadequate. (Cotgrove 1982, 82)

Examples supporting Cotgrove's observations are all around us. In 1996, Alan Miller published a study on the influence of religious affiliation on social attitudes. As part of that study, he examined the ways in which members of different religions initially approached certain issues. Miller discovered that Jews and Christians in his sample classified several issues differently; for example, Christians addressed homosexuality as a moral issue. Different Christians resolved that moral issue differently, but most approached it through the lens of morality, placing it in the same category as atheism and communism. Jews, on the other hand, tended to classify homosexuality as a type of sexual orientation. To use a currently popular phrase, they framed the question differently. As a consequence of these differences in initial classification, Jewish attitudes toward gays did not demonstrate a relationship with their attitudes about drug abuse or pornography, as Christian attitudes did. Miller concluded that these were not mere differences of opinion, but rather "differences in the way these issues are organized in a broader cognitive framework" (Miller 1996, 230). This is a crucial insight.

The fact that people hold to what I have called incommensurate worldviews is a widely recognized phenomenon. Best sellers proclaim that "Men are from Mars, Women are from Venus." A widely distributed business training video some years back used the experience of Swiss watchmakers to drive home a lesson about "thinking outside the box." According to the video, the original inventor of the digital watch was Swiss, but when he tried to convince Swiss watch manufacturers to produce digital watches, they found his design incomprehensible. Watches have mainsprings. Your invention does not have a mainspring; ergo, it isn't a watch. Today, the digital watch industry is dominated by Japanese manufacturers. American history is replete with examples of mutual incomprehension. George Marsden nicely captured the nature of one "incommensurable universe" in a passage describing the famous conflict between William Jennings Bryan and Clarence Darrow at the Scopes trial: "Each considered the other's view ridiculous, and wondered aloud how any sane person could hold it" (1980, 213).

It is important to underscore the independence of these mental frameworks from conscious acceptance of particular religious beliefs. Worldviews are mental habits; they are unrelated to explicit acceptance or rejection of any particular dogma or belief system. Robert Bellah has described them as "cultural codes" (2002, 13). But our cultural codes are, as Bellah and others have also noted, very largely derived from religious belief. It is in this sense that we must understand the United States as a Christian—or more accurately, Protestant—nation. (In America, as the saying goes, even the Catholics and the Jews are Protestants.) Arthur Schlesinger Jr. has wryly noted that assaults on Western tradition by minorities, academics, and others are "conducted very largely with analytical weapons forged in the West" (1991, 72). We are all products of the cultures that create our worldviews; that is what we mean when we say that certain belief systems are hegemonic.

Cultures and the cognitive paradigms they shape do change and evolve, albeit slowly and at times, painfully. Because we take our worldviews for granted, because they describe "the way things are," we rarely doubt or question them. When discrepancies do arise between our observations or experiences and our mental frameworks, we behave much like the blind men with the elephant—we try to "shoehorn" the anomalies into our existing paradigms, and to ignore the inconsistencies that result. Sometimes, however, the discrepancies are too big or too numerous to ignore, and despite our intense resistance to change, our paradigm does shift, transforming the way we see the world. As Olsen,

Lodwick, and Dunlap have noted, however, the new paradigm that emerges will not only be fundamentally different from the old one, it will often be incompatible with it, making rational debate between those holding inconsistent paradigms impossible. As more and more people shift their paradigms, the dominant worldview prevailing in a culture will change; over time, in some cases, that change is so radical that it will represent "an entirely new view of reality" (1992, 2).

> [W]e argue that new social paradigms normally emerge unintentionally, are incompletely and vaguely expressed, and only gradually gain adherents as increasing numbers of people become aware of the anomalies within the old social paradigm. The tendency for adherents of competing scientific paradigms to "talk past" one another and hence fail to communicate in any meaningful way is even more pronounced with social paradigms. (1992, 10)

We may be experiencing such a paradigm shift now.

RELIGIOUS HISTORY AND CHANGING WORLDVIEWS

Ironically, many contemporary scholars believe that the secularization that so offends contemporary Puritans is an all-but-inevitable outcome of Protestantism, with its new emphasis upon the individual—that a paradigm shift occurred once it was no longer necessary to have an ecclesiastic authority mediate the relationship between the individual and the sacred. As C. Wright Mills has described the consequences, "Once the world was filled with the sacred—in thought, practice and institutional form. After the Reformation and the Renaissance, the forces of modernization swept across the globe and secularization, a corollary historical process, loosened the dominion of the sacred" (1959, 32–33). The Reformation, and later the Enlightenment, ushered in new ways of thinking about science, the nature of reality, and the authority of governing institutions. The Industrial Revolution also brought major social changes. Emile Durkheim argued that industrialization brought plurality and *functional differentiation* in its wake—the separation of areas of authority and expertise that characterize modern societies. When a citizen of a modern country breaks a leg, he is likely to call the doctor, not the priest or rabbi; when a student wants to become an engineer, she studies science at the university rather than religious texts at a monastery; when a businessperson wants to know whether patent laws will protect his company's new invention, he consults lawyers, not spiritual advisers. Religious authority has become steadily less extensive; at the same time it faces increasing competition from other centers of authority and from other systems of belief and religion. Mills and others believed that the eventual result would be a world that is more and more secular—a world in which the impact of religion would steadily diminish. More recently, other scholars—including several who originally agreed with this secularization theory—have challenged that inevitability, pointing to the reemergence of religion as a major factor in world affairs. Still others have refined the theory. Pippa Norris and Ronald Inglehart argue that the importance of religiosity persists most strongly among vulnerable populations. They believe that fear—feelings of powerlessness and vulnerability—are the key factor driving religiosity, and they use evidence from the massive World Values Survey to argue that inhabitants of the Western industrialized nations, whatever their professed beliefs, behave in a way that demonstrates the waning influence of religious doctrine and sectarian sensibilities. They predict that affluent and industrialized nations will continue to see a decline in the influence of religion, while poorer, developing countries—with their more vulnerable populations and higher birthrates—will continue to be highly religious.

Whichever view is correct (and that is an argument for a quite different book), it is clear that America is an outlier. As we shall see in chapter 4, the historic process of secularization has changed the American civic and religious landscape in very important ways. In America, however one understands the process of secularization, there has been no steady movement from religious passion to secular rationality. Instead, American history is characterized by periods of declining religious authority alternating with periods of renewed religious zeal. Even during periods of significant religiosity, however, the sources of explicitly moral and religious authority in our highly diverse country have become less monolithic. As our planet shrinks and our pluralism grows, a considerable amount of cultural synthesis is inevitable—especially in a nation where people prize their autonomy and ability to decide for themselves how their lives should be lived. As we shall see, capitalism has encouraged a market ethic that now extends from our selection of neighborhoods, foods, occupations, presidents, and mates to our choice of religious beliefs. While many of us find that autonomy liberating, and others criticize it as "consumerist mentality," we enjoy individual choices on a scale unimaginable to prior generations. And our choices in all categories, including religious ones, are continually expanding. The contemporary American religious marketplace is a veritable smorgasbord of beliefs from which religious consumers can pick and choose. The degree to which we make choices that alter traditional worldviews (or the degree to which altered worldviews permit us to consider a wider range of choices) depends on many factors. Some individuals feel empowered by the range of options available; others feel threatened. But choice is both a consequence and an engine of change in modern capitalist societies.

OUR MODERN DILEMMA

One result of living in a society with competing (and sometimes irreconcilable) worldviews is conflict. In 1980 Charles Kraft, a conservative Christian who was also an anthropologist, wrote a perceptive essay addressing the conflict in worldviews between his own two life commitments: science and religion. He identified several sources of that conflict, including differences over the nature of ultimate authority, the source of Truth (biblical or empirical), and conflicting conceptions of human nature, among others. Furthermore, as Kraft noted, both the scientist and the believer are involved in a struggle to define the nature of reality and control our common civic narrative—a struggle for the right to set the agenda and construct the dominant worldview. This helps to explain why passions are so engaged in public policy arguments revolving around those agencies of society believed to have the most power to set the American agenda: government (especially the Supreme Court), the media, and the schools.

In a political community where people hold incompatible worldviews, the critical question is the extent to which a functioning polity depends upon cultural consensus and shared worldviews. It is often said that government cannot legislate morality; but it is also a truism that democratic government depends upon a moral citizenry—or at the very least, a citizenry that shares some minimal common definition of morality. And if it is essential that we have a moral citizenry, is morality possible without traditional religion?

Rodney Stark has argued that religion is only capable of sustaining a moral civic order when that religion is based upon a belief (presumably a widely shared belief) in a "powerful, active, conscious, morally-concerned God" (2001, 619). In addition to excluding the Buddhists and Freethinkers among us, such a conclusion raises the real possibility that the consensus America requires may be unachievable.[3] This belief in our need for a specifically god-centered consensus has been a staple of American history. (President Eisenhower is said to have remarked, "Our government makes no sense unless it is founded in a deeply felt religious faith—and I don't care what it is.") While the United States has never been a "Christian nation" institutionally, for most of our history, it has been a "Protestant nation" culturally. That overwhelmingly Protestant character of American culture is rapidly diminishing. The question we face is whether the lack of cultural hegemony that characterizes contemporary American life implies a corresponding diminution of our ability to forge a civic consensus on what it means to be an American. This is the question that prompted this book.

---

[3] A consequence that does not trouble him, as Stark's most recent book— *The Victory of Reason: How Christianity Led to Freedom, Capitalism, and Western Success* (2005)—makes abundantly clear.

FORGING A CIVIC CONCENSUS

I believe that a civic consensus does exist and that Americans do share enough of a reality to make governing ourselves possible. If we are to set our civic house in order, however, we need first to understand our disputes—we need to recognize the roots of our disagreements and the effect of our inconsistent worldviews on the public policies we debate. In what follows, I trace the origins of our "habits of the mind," the history of the dialectic through which those habits have evolved and changed, and the influence of religiously rooted worldviews on policy preferences in four highly contentious policy areas where those influences are underappreciated: economic policy, the environment, criminal justice, and foreign affairs.

I also consider, in chapter 5, the hotly debated *culture war* thesis. There is a vociferous—and occasionally nasty—scholarly dispute over the nature and existence of an American culture war. The argument—and acrimony—is reminiscent of the old story (a favorite of mine) about two businessmen who take a quarrel to the village rabbi. He listens to the first man tell his side, and says "Yes, you are right." The second man then gives his version of the affair, and once again the rabbi says, "You are right." At that point, an onlooker protests, "They can't both be right!" to which the rabbi responds, "Ah yes. You also are right." Proponents of the culture war thesis point to the significant differences in Americans' worldviews and fundamental commitments, and those differences are quite real. Critics of the thesis point to polls and surveys demonstrating a stable and overlapping cultural terrain characterized by a number of core, shared values. They are both right.

Yes, Americans occupy incommensurate realities—but we also share a number of common values and areas of agreement. The pertinent question is: are the values that we share enough? I believe the answer is yes, that with sufficient political will to bridge our differences, with a better, more textured understanding of the nature and roots of our differing perspectives, and with appropriately realistic expectations, we can emerge whole from our current impasse. In the last chapter, I suggest how this might be accomplished.

Chapter 2

AMERICA'S RELIGIOUS ROOTS

Listening to some of the "talking heads" who increasingly dominate broadcast media, one might be forgiven for assuming that Americans are engaged in unrelenting religious warfare. Citizens wishing each other "Happy Holidays" are accused of anti-Christian bias. National tragedies are explained as God's vengeance for (other) Americans' departure from godly ways. Objections to government endorsements of religion are countered by angry assertions that America is, after all, a Christian nation—often with the none-too-subtle subtext "and if non-Christians don't like it, they can leave."

One of the difficulties with the recurring debate over whether America is a Christian nation is that, as Richard Holloway has noted (2003), Christianity is not and never has been a single thing. Within white Protestantism alone, there are multiple religious traditions (some counts put the current number of distinct denominations at nearly two thousand), of which two general categories are dominant: mainline and evangelical.

> Denominations are part of larger religious traditions with well-elaborated sets of creeds, teachings, rituals, and authority structures. These dimensions of religious culture shape member's nonreligious attitudes for well-grounded historical reasons.... Mainline denominations have

typically emphasized an accommodating stance toward modernity, a proactive view on issues of social and economic justice, and pluralism in their tolerance of varied individual beliefs. Evangelical denominations have typically sought more separation from the broader culture, emphasized missionary activity and individual conversion, and taught strict adherence to particular religious doctrines . . . [H]istorical trajectories account for the complex but socially significant differences between the two wings of white Protestantism. (Steensland et al. 2000, 293–94)

A 2003 study focusing on the attitudes of clergy from various denominations underscored the salience of these historically rooted differences. Evangelical clergy, asked to describe their "social gospel," identified America as a Christian nation, and believed capitalism to be the only economic system compatible with Christianity. They overwhelmingly believed that American religious values were under attack, and that the government has an obligation to protect the nation's religious heritage. This willingness to employ the authority of the state on behalf of moral concerns has long characterized conservative Christianity. (As James Morone has convincingly demonstrated [2003], despite the popular perception that those on the religious and political Right are anti-big-government, the growth of the federal governmental apparatus has been greatly facilitated by their willingness to enlist the power of government—first local, then federal—to combat perceived moral threats.) Evangelical respondents believed that only one Christian view on most political issues is possible, and doubted that liberals could truly be Christian. Mainline clergy, on the other hand, described their social gospel in terms of support for issues of social justice—amelioration of economic inequities and poverty, and support for human rights. They focused less on issues involving family arrangements. And they were significantly less likely to be politically active. Black Protestant clergy, as might be expected, did not fit neatly into either category, nor did Catholics (Smidt 2003).

Research confirms the sectarian roots of these differences: in 1997, in an article titled "The Christian Left: Who Are They and How Are

They Different From The Christian Right?" Charles Hall reported on research attempting to account for the differences among subjects who considered themselves Christian. He found that demographic differences alone could not account for the differences between the Christian Left and Right, and concluded that religious doctrine, not structural location, was the basis for the variation. He also noted that there was much greater variety of belief within the Christian Left; that is, those on the Right tended to be much more similar in their attitudes than those on the Left.

These contemporary divisions within white Protestant Christianity are outgrowths of America's earliest (overwhelmingly Protestant) beginnings, and in order to understand them, we must look to the religious history of the colonial period—the period stretching from the arrival of the first explorers to the new continent to the founding of the United States. Only by understanding the legacy of those formative years will we be able to make sense of the ways in which those earliest traditions shaped, adapted to, or resisted their successive encounters with newer entrants to the American religious landscape, and to the secularization of modern life.

IN THE BEGINNING

As the noted religious historian Sidney Ahlstrom reminds us, church history in America began in 1492, when Columbus discovered a new world that he named San Salvador—meaning Holy Savior—and claimed that New World for Spain. Columbus's journal entries upon meeting the native inhabitants of this new land reflected his confidence that "they would easily be made Christians"—a confidence that was shared by the Spanish churchmen who followed him to New Spain. "A medieval civilization, revering intellectual and spiritual as well as political authority, acquired a new lease on life and became the heritage of modern Hispanic America" (Ahlstrom 1972, 39). The religion and culture in those parts of the United States that were originally under Spanish domination—primarily New Mexico, Arizona, Texas, and California—were characterized by close identification of church and state, and by missions intent upon converting the native populations. As Ahlstrom summed up the significance of the Spanish presence,

> The final and most enduring consequence of Spanish exploration and settlement for American religious history was that it spurred France and England to increasingly vigorous imperial activity. Quite aside from its internal qualities, the mere existence of the Spanish empire became a stimulus to nations which were already profoundly affected by the Reformation. French Catholics, once their domestic religious wars were over, saw an opportunity to regain in the New World what they had lost in the Old; while England saw on distant shores a New Canaan that must be made safe from the encroachments of Popery. (52–53)

French settlement in the New World was also primarily Catholic—in this case Jesuit—giving "the faith and institutions of the Roman Church . . . a centrality and importance that was equaled in no other empire, not even New Spain" (61).

English colonization efforts got off to a later start. It was 1607 when three ships carrying 105 colonists arrived at the mouth of the James River in what is now Virginia. Establishment of Jamestown was followed by Pilgrim settlements in New England. The Pilgrims were extremist, Separatist adherents of Puritanism who had been promised freedom from molestation by James I. They believed that Christians should separate themselves from the world, hence the label. Other Separatist principles, while not so universally held among them, included separation of church and state, and even separation from other religious communities. Most U.S. history books give short shrift to the Spanish and French presence prior to the Pilgrims' landing; this is understandable, since we tend to trace the origins of the country—especially the cultural origins—to the British. But the earlier colonization had important roots in both the European Reformation and European imperial designs, and as a consequence, an enduring legacy of the competition between English Protestantism and French and Spanish Catholicism would be a persistent strain of anti-Catholicism in the

United States. Richard Hofstadter called anti-Catholicism "the pornography of the Puritan" (1964, 21).

COLONIAL DIVERSITY

The early Pilgrims were soon followed by nearly a thousand Puritans, led by John Winthrop, and by colonists bringing a variety of other religious traditions to the New World. New England would continue to be largely dominated by various strands of Puritan belief, although a number of its early communities were founded by religious dissenters who had been expelled from established colonies for their nonconforming opinions. Among the most notable of those was Rhode Island, established by Roger Williams. From its inception, Rhode Island separated church from state (Roger Williams is thought to have coined the term "Wall of Separation" some 150 years before its more famous appearance in Thomas Jefferson's letter to the Danbury Baptists.) As a result, Rhode Island became a haven for Baptists, Quakers, and other nonconformists. German refugees settled along the Hudson River Valley. Savannah, Georgia, was colonized by Lutherans fleeing persecution in Austria. The Quakers used William Penn's "Holy Experiment" as their model for Pennsylvania—as a consequence, in that colony, although Quakers were accorded preferential treatment, freedom of worship and toleration were extended to all who believed in God. Virginia took a less tolerant road; it established the Church of England in 1619, and in 1641, barred Catholics both from holding public office and from proselytizing on behalf of the Catholic faith.

Despite their significant doctrinal differences and uneven religious passions, all of these early settlers were to some extent products of the Reformation, with its new emphases upon the here and now—man's life on earth, not merely as a prelude to a heavenly hereafter—and the increased importance of the individual. In particular, the European antecedents of American Puritanism—a significant, although certainly not solitary influence on the later American character—contained two important strands that must be recognized in order to understand the

Puritan worldview: an abiding anti-Catholicism, and Calvinism. Calvin taught that God alone was sovereign, and that he had chosen certain people for salvation and others for damnation. Calvin also fashioned what has come to be called a "Presbyterian" model of church governance, in which individual congregations elected delegates to a presbytery, or governing body—a democratic organizational model that has also influenced later American attitudes toward the structures of authority. Calvinism in its various manifestations has been an important influence on American culture.

Another Puritan theme that would recur through American history was a preoccupation with sin, and a conviction that society was falling into sinful ways.

> A synod of Puritan ministers met in 1679, reviewed stacks of contemporary sermons, and published the classic of the [jeremiad] genre: the ancient tenets and taboos were all cracking, reported the ministers. They saw sloth, heavy drinking, bastardy, and rampant sexuality. . . . Public schools were failing, businesses ruthlessly chased profits and lawsuits had gotten out of hand. These sins all sprang from even deeper trouble: permissive parents and their pampered kids. The evils that afflict our society, summed up the synod, flow from "defects as to family government." (Morone 2003, 14)

The Puritans conceived of America as "the Shining City on the Hill." John Winthrop had preached that God had made a covenant with the early American settlers, and later religious figures would reinforce the insistence upon America's special relationship with the deity. That concept of a covenantal relationship, and the Puritan belief in American exceptionalism, would become an indelible part of the American psyche. The American nation was called to be an exemplar, an ideal, a light to other nations. But in order to fulfill our destiny, we all had to live up to God's plan. (As Morone has noted, such a belief virtually requires that we meddle in the behavior of our neighbors.)

Americans are fond of noting that the Puritans came to the New World for religious liberty, but what constituted religious liberty for the

Puritans is something other than our contemporary understanding of that term. As Richard Hughes has reminded us, freedom as they envisioned it was very different from freedom as conceived by most Americans today. "The Puritans sought freedom for themselves but for no one else" (2004, 28). As he explains, "In the Puritan imagination, England became Egypt, the Atlantic Ocean became the Red Sea, the American wilderness became their own land of Canaan, and the Puritans themselves became the new Israel. . . . If one imagines one's tribe or clan or nation a chosen people, then it is also clear that others are not" (30). The worldview that developed out of this Puritan distinction between the elect and the damned, between "us and them," and good and evil, continues to shape American public policy in numerous ways, as we shall see in part 3.

As important as the Puritan influence has been, and however vigorous the worldviews it engendered, it is also important to recognize the presence of what Ahlstrom has described as the numerous "countercurrents" to Puritan thought—religious leaders with more aristocratic leanings, the many settlers who opposed Puritanism and its ideals, the early Quakers, and the nonconformists who joined Roger Williams, Anne Hutchinson, and others in Rhode Island, to identify but a few. Nor were the countervailing currents necessarily religious or doctrinal; economic interests led early merchants to question whether the Bible "made adequate allowance for the exigencies of a healthy commerce" (Ahlstrom 1972, 161), and Enlightenment thought (discussed in detail in chapter 3), later reflected in Deism and Unitarianism, further challenged the Puritan consensus. The institution of slavery had fateful consequences, both for those colonies whose economies depended significantly upon slave labor and those whose religions taught that it was abhorrent (beliefs that would eventually lead them to actively oppose it). Treatment of Native Americans also generated theological disputes, although few challenged the propriety of proselytizing by "God's chosen people" or questioned the morality of taking Indian land. (One of the few who advocated greater respect for the lands and rights of Native Americans was Roger Williams.) And the very diversity of opinion that characterized the colonial period encouraged the formation of a tolerant approach to religion, a "live and let live" ethic that is also, often paradoxically, deeply embedded in our national psyche. (William Hutchison has noted that this toleration for differences in beliefs, however real, rarely extended to toleration for aberrant or heretical behaviors.)

In addition to differences in religious doctrine, religious fervor also varied substantially across the colonial landscape. Virginia was relatively unaffected by the Puritan ethic. Maryland welcomed Roman Catholics (many of whom had been expelled from Virginia), and gradually became identified with Anglicism. Virginia's laws against "nonconformity" also sent Baptist and Quaker dissenters into what are now North and South Carolina. The southern colonies in colonial times were relatively "unchurched," and religious differences tended to reinforce social status distinctions. Perhaps most religiously diverse were the middle colonies—New York, New Jersey, and Pennsylvania. As we shall see, these regional differences all contributed to the development of the distinctive political cultures and worldviews that continue to characterize the larger American polity.

THE GREAT AWAKENING

Also leaving an indelible imprint on American culture and worldviews was the series of religious revivals that (depending upon one's definition) began in the 1730s and continued through the 1740s, known as the Great Awakening. The Great Awakening was described in quite different terms by those who lived through those tumultuous times. To Jonathan Edwards, it was a work of "God's special grace"; to less positive commentators, it was "a confusion that produced 'enthusiastic heat' and 'commotion in the passions'" (Mathisen 2001, 83). The character of the Great Awakening—and even the reality of that phenomenon—have been the subject of considerable debate; one historian, Jon Butler, has called it an "interpretive fiction" (1990), and another, Frank Lambert, has labeled it a historical invention (2003). Other religious historians consider the Great Awakening to be the first unifying event of colonial experience, and attribute the origins of the American evangelical tradition to the influence of its "anti-authoritarian and republican rhetoric" (Mathisen 2001, 84); still others emphasize its relationship to a contemporaneous international Protestant upheaval. There were, as one would expect, significant regional variations:

> In New England, [the Great Awakening] was an apocalyptic outburst within the standing order, a challenge to established authority. Everywhere it went, it extended the range of gospel preaching; in the South, it brought personal religion to the slaves for the first time. Everywhere, it brought rancor and division along with popular enthusiasm and new theological depth. Everywhere it went, it rejuvenated the politically potent elements of the Puritan ideology. (Ahlstrom 1972, 263)

The Great Awakening was in significant part a response to the large and growing numbers of colonists who were both unchurched and impious, and to the conviction among religious believers that the souls of the younger generation were at risk. There were growing numbers of out-of-wedlock births, and other blasphemous behaviors signaled a worrisome loss of moral fiber in the young. To add to these woes, Enlightenment thought was introducing an ethic of moralist individuality and challenging the taken-for-granted nature of religious authority. In such a context, preachers with plausible diagnoses of these civic ills and ready prescriptions for curing them found a grateful audience. The revivals and general religious fervor that constituted the Great Awakening underscored the growing fault line between reason and emotion that characterized the turbulence of these times. (This fault line could be seen even in the most explicitly religious figures of the time. As Ahlstrom has noted, Cotton Mather's endorsement of inoculation against smallpox, and his defense of the new science, undermined the belief that pestilence was to be understood as a sign of divine wrath.) The Great Awakening also brought women into active religious participation in a manner and on a scale that had not previously been seen, setting the stage for later confrontations over gender roles and religious authority.

Cedric Cowing has written that the theological underpinnings of the Great Awakening owe much to Calvinism's stress on God's sovereignty and the "terrors of the law." As he explains, "Presented in the right way, the authoritarian idea of God's sovereignty could appear equalitarian. All men were worms dependent upon God's mercy, incapable of understanding life's higher meaning. . . . The proud and the complacent as well as the overtly sinful were in danger. No one was secure" (1971, 67). The Great Awakening was testimony to the power of personal evangelism and charismatic leadership. Preaching and praying, Bible reading, and personal outreach by believers all increased significantly; experiential faith—frequently manifested by fainting, crying, or other physical responses to revival preaching—challenged the staid rituals of more established churches. Church membership soared, especially among Baptists, whose theology was particularly attuned to the new emphasis upon personal conversion. At the same time, critics expressed concern about the emotional excesses and extravagant behaviors displayed by preachers and converts alike.

Emotional excitement is usually unsustainable, and the passions engendered by the Great Awakening eventually subsided. When the tumultuous revivalism abated, however, the religious landscape had been changed. The legacy of the Great Awakening included "an intensified religious and moral resolution" and a new emphasis on evangelism and the missionary spirit. The old Puritan concept of America as a "Redeemer Nation" was reinvigorated. The seeds of later doctrinal controversies between liberal and conservative Protestants could also be located within the varying reactions and responses to the whole phenomenon (Ahlstrom 1972, 288). David Lovejoy has argued that "a peculiarly American brand of subversion emerged from it which tended to disturb established colonial customs such as the enslavement of blacks and prejudicial treatment of the Indians" (1985, 198).

These legacies would affect different colonies in different ways, thus contributing to the regional idiosyncrasies that have characterized American political culture. In New England, it gave impetus to the establishment of new institutions of higher education, and the propagation of Jonathan Edwards' New Divinity, an effort to meet the challenge of "new science" concepts which has been described as an effort to defend Calvinism in a new, more rational, way. In the South, particularly in the "back country," the Great Awakening was essentially a missionary effort, bringing the unchurched to belief. The chief beneficiaries of the Great Awakening in the South were the Baptists, although Methodism also prospered.

THE AMERICAN REVOLUTION

Religious motives for the American Revolution are challenged by those who ascribe it to more political and economic motivations. Whatever the comparative contributions of British royal intransigence, the indignities of general or warrantless searches, or the burdens of taxation without representation, the growth of revolutionary sentiment was clearly aided and abetted by the identification of America as the "new Israel" and the belief that Americans were a Chosen People. As Robert Mathisen notes, that identification had continued unbroken for a century and a half:

> According to Charles Chauncy of Boston on the eve of the American Revolution, as the founding fathers of New England had been rescued by God from tyrannical England many years after God had saved his people from Egypt and delivered them to their Promised Land, so now New England had been relieved from the oppressive Stamp Act, even as the Jews had been protected from the destruction of Ahaseurus. To reassure his audience of this in 1770, he contended that "perhaps, there are no people, now dwelling on the face of the earth, who may, with greater pertinency, adopt the language of king David, and say 'Our fathers trusted in thee; they trusted, and thou didst deliver them.'" (2001, 119)

Such rhetorical connection of the American cause with God's plan, and similar invocations of the special place of America in the biblical scheme, were common. The essential justice of the colonists' complaints and the superior morality of the revolution were the subject of both religious and secular arguments. Theological liberals like Jonathan Mayhew argued on scriptural grounds against the notion of "hereditary, indefeasible, divine" right of kings. Thomas Paine, one of America's earliest Freethinkers, based much the same argument on reason, in his enormously influential *Common Sense*. While both religious and secular opinions were divided, and many Tory sympathizers would actually leave the colonies for Canada or England, the revolution was widely supported by religious bodies, and its aspirations became wedded to religious language and themes.

> Contemporary historians have been fascinated with this theme as a way of understanding the pervasive identification of the destiny of the American republic with the course of redemptive history. . . . America was to be "both the locus and instrument of the great consummation." This millennial persuasion, buoyant with the civil and religious ideals of the young republic, functioned as a primary idiom of that distinct form of evangelic civic piety that historians have called a "religion of the Republic" or an American civil religion. (Hatch 1977, 128)

As we will see, this notion of "civil religion," this belief that there is a necessary and important connection between national purpose and a common or shared religious conviction continues to inform social commentary and deeply affect attitudes about public policies. The revolution strengthened the conviction that, as Hatch has put it, the kingdom of God and the virtuous republic had become one and the same empire.

One consequence of this insistence upon a common core of religious belief was a renewed search for those common elements that lurked beneath the surface denominational differences of a diverse citizenry. "Americans began to grope for a communal identity to which they could assign an ultimate and inclusive function. That institution was, or became, the nation" (Hatch 1977, 129). This search for a common religious core was made more urgent by the fear that growing denominationalism and the emergence of Enlightenment skepticism and rationalism would tear the new nation apart, and that Americans would simply not have enough in common to see themselves as members of a unified polity. Civic religion and expressions of civic piety were thought to be a necessary "civic glue," and the churches were responsive to that perceived necessity. As Hatch explains,

> Overriding civic concerns led New England ministers to recast the major strains of their traditional eschatology. By bringing to the heart of redemptive history the republican values of civil and religious liberty, ministers articulated a civic theology that gave a profoundly new religious significance to the function of man as citizen, to the principles governing the civil order, and to the role of nations in bringing on the millennium. . . . The prospect of sharing the political ideals of the Revolution with all mankind became, in this climate of opinion, not only the clergy's fondest hope but also a necessary prerequisite for spreading the Christian message. (1977, 131)

In a very real sense, the struggle between good and evil had become a political struggle, with America at its center. Millennialism thrived.

The American victory left other legacies in its wake: a renewed optimism, and a strengthening of the American conviction that a successful government requires a virtuous people. These sentiments did not rest only upon religious beliefs. The impact of the Enlightenment, as we shall discuss in much more detail in chapter 3, was enormous; as Jon Butler has noted, the views of such revolutionary leaders as Franklin, Washington, Jefferson, Madison, and Hamilton were far different from those of the Congregationalists, Baptists, Presbyterians, and Episcopalians who had supported the revolution. "Even John Adams, the 'Puritan' revolutionary, believed that the argument for Christ's deity was 'an awful blasphemy,' best discarded in a new, enlightened age" (1990, 215). But the impact of religion and religious belief in revolutionary times—and the influence of the American Revolution on subsequent American religious beliefs—have been considerable. As Mark Noll has observed, the later disestablishment of state religions and the growth of denominationalism and religious diversity have altered the confidence in a special relationship with God that had characterized Puritan New England, but the American practice of civil religion has continued to flourish, and a crusading zeal has continued to motivate a wide variety of believers to pursue social and political changes demanded by their understandings of Christian principles. As he observes,

> In sum, the Revolutionary period provided an opportunity for a modified Puritan synthesis to retain its viability in America. No longer adhering to the express tenets of Puritanism, American Christians after the Revolution nevertheless worked to maintain personal religion and a comprehensive Christian community. At least partially as a result of the war, American society in general replaced the church as the locus of communal Christian values. (1977, 165)

While it is important to recognize the continued influence of religious beliefs on government and policy, it is equally important that we understand the significant influence of the new American political ideals on religion. The idea of the social contract, the new emphasis on rights, the conception of those rights as something appertaining to individuals rather than groups, and the strongly libertarian character of the new philosophy operated to modify popular religion—and especially Calvinist theology—in a number of significant ways. Mark Noll has suggested that the revolutionary generation came to see freedom as primarily freedom from state authority and the arbitrary exercise of power, while freedom in the earlier, Puritan sense of the word had implied freedom for something, namely, for doing the will of God.

LOOKING FORWARD, LOOKING BACK

Despite the presence of Catholics, Quakers, Deists, Shakers, and even Freethinkers and a few Jews, in these early days of America's history, the term *religious diversity* referred primarily—if not exclusively—to denominational differences within white Protestantism. Pluralism meant Baptists, Congregationalists, Presbyterians, and Episcopalians. In chapter 4, we will consider how that original Protestant "establishment" has affected, and been affected by, successive waves of immigrants who brought with them a dramatically expanded meaning of pluralism.

If, as legend has it, geographic and doctrinal differences caused John Adams to have great difficulty in understanding the preaching of John Witherspoon, what has been the effect on later generations of the American culture and worldview that emerged after the Revolutionary War? William Hutchinson quotes Horace Kallen to the effect that, despite their surface differences, "Americans at the time of the Revolution were prevailingly like-minded. They were possessed of ethnic and cultural unity; they were homogeneous with respect to ancestry and ideal" (Hutchinson 2003, 20). Hutchinson reminds us that America's religious origins were well over 95 percent Protestant, and at least 90 percent Calvinist (rather than Lutheran) Protestant at that. Indeed, 85 percent had been English-speaking Calvinist Protestants. Out of the thirty-two hundred or so congregations in the colonies by 1780, only six hundred were or had been non-English-speaking. Fifty-six were Catholic; even Methodists could count only sixty-five. Other dissenting sects—Moravians, Mennonites, Dunkers, Shakers, and the like—had far fewer. Although there were five Jewish congregations, none yet had a rabbi. It is not difficult to connect certain persistent American tendencies to those common cultural origins—Hutchinson lists legalism, moralism, biblical literalism, and religious activism.

The cultural transmission of religious worldviews has clearly contributed to the salience of religion as a persistent feature of the American experience. Despite the religious fervor of the Great Awakening and the explicitly religious ideology expressed through the revolution, at the time of the nation's founding, only 17 percent of Americans were actually members of any church. Despite this low level of actual religious affiliation, the then prevailing cultural worldviews rooted in religion have shaped later Americans attitudes in numerous ways. Richard Hughes (2003) has identified five elements of an "American Creed" in *Myths America Lives By*: the myth of the Chosen People; the myth of Nature's Nation; the myth of the Christian Nation; the myth of the Millenial Nation; and the myth of the Innocent Nation. As we have seen, the foundations for several of these enduring beliefs about America and the American character had already been laid by the end of the revolutionary period. As we shall see, those elements of our national self-image have had an enormous impact on public policies ranging from public welfare to foreign policy.

It is also important to recognize that evidence for the continuing salience of religious culture is not limited to overarching themes of national ideology. We bring a largely unconscious cultural lens to far more prosaic elements of public policy and our civic life. A case in point: Arthur Farnsley (2003) has noted that organizational differences between state governments tend to reflect the structures of the state's dominant religious communities. In Massachusetts, where a large portion of the population is Catholic, the organization of state government has become increasingly hierarchical. (Massachusetts does not even have functioning counties; most decisions are made at the state level.) In contrast, North Carolina, a state dominated by Baptist congregations, devolves significant responsibility to counties and other local government jurisdictions. Catholic authority structures are centralized and hierarchical; Baptist congregations exercise substantial autonomy. It is highly doubtful that these differences were conscious, intentional responses to external, objective inconsistencies, and much more likely that, over time, they simply came to reflect different cultural perspectives on what *authority* looks like.

In the foregoing discussion, I have alluded only briefly to the impact of science and Enlightenment philosophy on American religious thought and the institutions of the new republic during these formative experiences. That influence was enormous and will be explored more fully in the next chapter. For now, it may suffice to note one of the major effects of religion's encounter with the Enlightenment's dramatically new paradigm for understanding the world: the conflict between those whose worldview is based upon a conviction that Truth is revealed, knowable, and immutable, and those (especially academics) who believe that Truth is elusive, and that human knowledge is inevitably tentative and subject to reconsideration in light of new evidence.

Chapter 3

A NEW PARADIGM

In his introduction to *The Founding Fathers and the Place of Religion in America*, Frank Lambert captures in a few brief paragraphs the enormous disparity between the religious worldviews of the early Puritans and those of the nation's Founders. Those paragraphs are worth quoting, because they illuminate both the genesis of our warring political and historical perspectives and the fault lines that continue to make civic consensus so difficult to achieve.

> In 1639, a group of New England Puritans drafted a constitution affirming their faith in God and their intention to organize a Christian Nation. Delegates from the towns of Windsor, Hartford and Wetheresfield drew up the Fundamental Orders of Connecticut, which made clear that their government rested on divine authority and pursued godly purposes.
>
> One hundred and fifty years later, George Washington took another oath, swearing to "faithfully execute the office of President of the United States," and pledging to the best of his ability to "preserve, protect, and defend the Constitution of the United States." The constitution that he swore to uphold was the work of another group of America's progenitors, commonly known as the Founding Fathers,

who in 1787 drafted a constitution for the new nation. But unlike the work of the Puritan Fathers, the federal constitution made no reference whatever to God or divine providence, citing as its sole authority "the people of the United States." (Lambert 2003, 1–2)

The Continental Congress had drafted, and the legislative bodies of the several colonies had ratified, a Constitution for the new nation that would have been incomprehensible to their Puritan antecedents, the religious dissenters that Lambert dubs "Planting Fathers" to distinguish them from the Founding Fathers. A religious and intellectual paradigm shift had moved the country's predominant—but by no means exclusive—worldview from that of a Christian nation to that of a secular republic in a mere 150-year period. The change owed a great debt to the intellectual ferment caused by the new ideas coming from Europe, collectively called the Enlightenment; but in a very real sense, it was also a product of the politics and religion of America before and during the colonial period. When Enlightenment philosophy knocked, the particularities of their circumstances, beliefs, and experiences ensured that Americans were prepared to open the door.

THE NEW LEARNING

As Sidney Ahlstrom has observed, the search for Enlightenment origins can lead to an infinite regress. Beginning with late medieval and Renaissance intellectual stirrings, natural philosophers had made successive efforts to explain the physical world. The accepted cosmology had been radically altered when Copernicus and Galileo demonstrated that the earth circled around the sun rather than the other way around, challenging the older notion that the earth was at the center of the universe. Descartes had pictured the natural world in mechanistic rather than miraculous terms, writing persuasively about matter in motion, mass, and velocity.

When Francis Bacon insisted that laws governing the material world could be inferred through careful observation (a notion that, for contemporary Americans, is an unremarkable commonplace), it had enormous implications for the existing, traditional, deductive methods of understanding reality. The old learning had begun with an a priori given: the Bible, the absolute truth of which was unquestioned. The primary goal of Puritan education was thus directed at biblical understanding; one began with the text and learned—deduced—how to interpret it. Proper interpretation required the application of time-tested methods of exegesis and analysis, and instruction in historical context and meaning (mostly, what important theologians of the past had decreed to be correct understandings and approaches). One started with Truth, and education was the process of learning to apprehend and defend that Truth.

Bacon changed the fundamental order of things by teaching that education must begin with observation of natural phenomena. From those observations, if sufficiently numerous and careful, a general explanatory theory would be drawn. That explanatory theory, in turn, would be tested against additional observations. Robert Boyle, often called the father of modern chemistry, "envisioned matter as made of minute particles that could arrange themselves into specific patterns" (Durbin 2004, 300). Isaac Newton, building further upon Bacon's work, declared that insurmountable and uniform universal laws capable of mathematical expression governed the physical world. Newton himself discovered the first such uniform, universal law—the law of gravity.

The influence of the scientific method introduced by Bacon, Newton, and others can hardly be overstated. It was also enormously consequential, because it not only changed the way people approached the learning process, it also vastly expanded the subject matter to which that learning process might be applied. Educated people began to believe that human reason could be applied to unlock the mysteries of the physical world. Natural philosophy opened new fields of inquiry and fired the imaginations and ambitions of new generations. Where the old learning had consisted of parsing the enduring truths that had been handed down by God, the new learning encouraged students to find new truths, to question and test, to rely upon their own powers of observation, and (perhaps most significantly) to reject assertions that could not be validated through the exercise of reason.

It was inevitable that this new emphasis on reason and scientific method would be extended from questions about the physical environment to questions about the nature of man and the proper form of his governing institutions. As Isaiah Berlin once wrote, "The frame of ideas within which, and the methods by which, various thinkers at various times try to arrive at the truth" is the history of philosophy (1956, 12). It was inevitable that these new tools for understanding the nature of reality would be employed in the search for truth.

> While Newton mapped nature's laws, John Locke examined the power of human reason to understand those laws. His *Essay Concerning Human Understanding* (1690) began with the Baconian rejection of innate ideas, arguing instead that the human mind is a tabula rasa (a blank tablet) that absorbs information derived from the senses. It is from these simple impressions that all human knowledge is constructed. Thus Locke concluded that human reason created knowledge out of the world itself, and that people should be wary of claims of sacred truth implanted on the human heart. (Lambert 2003, 166)

The *Essay Concerning Human Understanding* is generally considered Locke's greatest work. It was his *Two Treatises of Government*, however, that left an indelible imprint on the U.S. Constitution. Locke spent much of the first treatise demolishing arguments that had been advanced to justify the institution of monarchy; in the second, he dealt with "life, liberty and property." Locke asserted that men are born free and equal, that they are entitled to the ownership of what they create (whatever man mixes his labor with is rightfully his property), and that a social contract is the true basis of legitimate government. A government based upon such a contract will necessarily have limited powers, Locke explained, because government's primary purpose—the purpose that induces free individuals to enter into the contract in the first place—is to protect the liberty and property of its citizens. Its rightful powers will be limited to those necessary to achieve that purpose. In his *Letters on Religious Toleration*, Locke spelled out what the limited nature of government authority should mean for religion. "The business of laws," he wrote "is not to provide for the truth of opinions, but for the safety and security of the commonwealth." In an argument remarkably similar to one advanced by John Milton in *Aereopagetica*, he concluded, "If truth makes not her way into the understanding by her own light, she will be but the weaker for any borrowed force violence can add to her" (Locke 1689).

The intellectual revolution ushered in by these and other Enlightenment scientists and thinkers (notably Hobbes, Montesquieu, Hume, Voltaire, and Rousseau) was reinforced by yet another movement that was gaining currency in the colonies: Common Sense Realism. Common Sense Realism or, as it was often called, the Scottish philosophy, was a product of the Scottish renaissance of the eighteenth century. Its first significant exponent in the new world was John Witherspoon, who came to the colonies from Scotland to become president of Princeton University. Adherents of Common Sense Realism were, like other Enlightenment figures, scientific and empirical. But they concentrated their empirical efforts on "clarifying the nature of man's faculties" (Ahlstrom 1972, 355). They emphasized the agency of man; that is, they held that man is possessed of a rational freedom that empowers him to act (and not just be acted upon). The Scottish philosophers produced what Ahlstrom called the kind of apologetic philosophy that Christians in the Age of Reason needed, "providing philosophical support for the most influential thinker of the century, Adam Smith" (Ahlstrom 1972, 356). Adam Smith's *Theory of Moral Sentiments* and especially his *Wealth of Nations* were immensely popular in the colonies. Smith's theory of markets, especially, bolstered the new emphasis upon the individual and justified the importance of private property by demonstrating the connection between personal incentives to productivity and the contribution of that productivity to the common good. His "invisible hand" legitimized the competition that had long characterized commercial life and (especially during the Great Awakening) had come to characterize religious life as well. Smith advocated a free market in goods, and a free market in ideas, religious ideas included. In a country characterized as much by dissent as by orthodoxy, it is not surprising that such ideas found a willing audience.

The Enlightenment was not in any sense a unitary phenomenon; it included literally hundreds of other thinkers, scientists, political economists, and philosophers, many of whom considered themselves staunch defenders of the established faith. It was certainly not a doctrine, nor a set of agreed-upon principles; rather, it was a new way of conceiving reality, based on science and reason. It nurtured a new worldview and contributed importantly to what came to be called "the new learning." As Peter Gay (1969) has noted, it also required the ability to live with a certain level of uncertainty and ambiguity. As that new learning spread within the educated segments of colonial society, it generated genuine intellectual excitement, and a rising optimism about man's potential to achieve and to control his own fate.

FERTILE GROUND

The impact of the Enlightenment cannot be understood as a one-way encounter between new ideas and a static colonial culture. As we have seen, Americans had been living in a culture that—while overwhelmingly Protestant—was nevertheless characterized by far more pluralism than existed on the European continent. As one historian of American Freethought has illustrated,

> The proliferation of religious sects, and a hands-off policy toward religious pluralism on the part of many of His Majesty's governors, was a conspicuous feature of colonial society. Any pope or church-sanctioned king would have been taken aback by the thanksgiving services held in August, 1763 in New York City to commemorate the British victory in the French and Indian War. There is of course nothing unusual in the annals of human conflict about the victorious side thanking God. What was unusual, indeed unprecedented in a world of unquestioned union between church and state, was the religious diversity in evidence on the day of thanksgiving proclaimed by His Majesty's colonial governor. The services were held in Episcopal, Dutch Reformed, Presbyterian, French Huguenot, Baptist, and

Moravian churches. Even more extraordinary was the participation of Congregation Shearith Israel, representing the city's small community of Sephardic Jews. (Jacoby 2004, 14–15)

Jacoby notes that the existence of many religions, "unchecked by the inquisitor's rack and pyre," tends to call into question the claims of any one religion to possession of absolute truth (15).

Furthermore, Protestantism itself encouraged a greater emphasis on the individual and the "here and now" than Catholicism had. Several reasons for this have been mentioned: the Reformation had broken with the Catholic belief that morality is nurtured collectively, within the family and especially within the church; instead, Protestantism encouraged the radical new notion that every man was his own priest. This spiritual individualism reinforced a still potent strain of Renaissance humanism that had emphasized intellectual individualism. Because Protestantism also had deeply anticlerical roots, seen especially in its rejection of popery, it was congenial to the growth of a much broader antiauthoritarian spirit. Substantial support for the Reformation by the newly vigorous burgher class had reflected the merchants' growing impatience with religious constraints on competition, trade, and commercial activity. All of these elements of the Reformation foreshadowed the competitive pluralism that would later thrive in the colonies, half a world away from the conformity-enforcing presence of kings, popes, and cultural traditions.

As we have seen, pluralism and individualism gained further impetus from the Great Awakening. Religious newcomers and itinerant preachers "brought their new ideas and ways into a given colony, challenging existing laws and structures" (Lambert 2003, 13). This new religious marketplace further empowered individuals, who reveled in their newly expanded ability to choose from among competing sects and traditions based upon their own inclinations. These early evangelicals were "largely united in their insistence on liberty of conscience, disestablishment of religion, and separation of church and state" (Witte 2000, 28). Evangelicals placed a high priority on the religious rights of both individuals and groups, and wanted to prohibit all religious establishments.

Witte quotes from a speech by the fiery Baptist preacher John Leland, in which Leland proposed amending the Massachusetts Constitution:

> To prevent the evils that have heretofore been occasioned in the world by religious establishments, and to keep up the proper distinction between religion and politics, no religious test shall ever be requested as a qualification of any officer, in any department of the government; neither shall the legislature, under this constitution, ever establish any religion by law, give any one sect a preference to another, or force any man in the commonwealth to part with his property for the support of religious worship, or the maintenance of ministers of the gospel. (29)

The concept of freedom that animated Leland and other evangelicals had changed considerably from that embraced by the Puritan settlers who had preceded them. Evangelical religion was also more vigorous in the colonies than in England; as a result, "the heroes and leaders of the radical opposition in eighteenth century politics—John Milton, Algernon Sidney, John Locke, John Trenchard, Thomas Gordon, James Burgh—gained a vastly stronger following in America than in England" (Ahlstrom 1972, 362). As a result, by the time the revolution dawned, both religious colonists and their more secular counterparts were much less likely than their forebears to think of human liberty as "freedom to do the right thing," and much more likely to accept the Enlightenment belief that liberty was the right to act upon the basis of one's individual conscience, free of the interference of government—at least so long as one did not thereby harm one's neighbor.

RELIGIOUS CHANGE AND THE FOUNDING FATHERS

The growth of literacy in the colonies, and the burgeoning interest in science and the "new learning" (at least among members of the more privileged classes), led to the emergence of new religious thought, reflected in Deism, Unitarianism, and even Freethought, the latter best reflected in the works of such revolutionary heroes as Thomas Paine and Ethan Allen. Lambert notes that "[a]lmost without exception, the Founding Fathers were educated in the New Learning."

For example, James Otis, John Hancock, Joseph Warren and John and Samuel Adams, leading radicals in the American Revolution, studied the political theory of Jean-Jacques Burlamaqui at Harvard. His *Principles of Natural Law* was the standard text when they were students. Burlamaqui defined what he meant by natural law: a law that God imposes on all men, and which they are able to discover and know by the sole light of reason. (Lambert 2003, 167)

The important Founders were not only well educated, they were men of considerable intellectual gifts and accomplishments. In addition to his other formidable talents, Benjamin Franklin was a noted scientist, whose discovery that lightning was electricity that could be diverted by the simple expedient of a lightning rod was only one of a number of discoveries (like the vaccine for smallpox) that recast the way the colonists perceived natural phenomena—not as acts of God, but part of an increasingly explicable, natural world. Franklin's well-known, unorthodox religious beliefs were centered on questions of morality and virtue, rather than theology. In this, he was similar to Thomas Jefferson, who denied the deity of Jesus and produced his own version of the Bible, edited to exclude everything but Jesus' moral teachings. Jefferson was a Deist (or, as his political opponents preferred to describe him, an infidel and godless atheist) who wrote in his *Notes on the State of Virginia* that "the legitimate powers of government extend to such acts only as are injurious to others. But it does me no injury for my neighbor to say there are twenty gods or no God. It neither picks my pocket nor breaks my leg." It is a mark of the temper of the colonies at the time that the *Notes* circulated for some twenty years without causing any particular stir; it was only during Jefferson's later campaign for the presidency that his infidelity became an issue.

James Madison was an even more passionate advocate of religious liberty than Jefferson. Madison believed that religion and government were separate realms, with separate jurisdictions—that religious observance and belief must be free of government interference, and that government must be equally free of religious interference. In a famous passage, he wrote,

> If Religion be not within cognizance of Civil Government, how can its legal establishment be said to be necessary to Civil Government? What influence in fact have ecclesiastical establishments had on Civil Society? In some instances they have been seen to erect a spiritual tyranny on the ruins of Civil authority; in many instances they have seen the upholding of the thrones of political tyranny; in no instance have they been seen the guardians of the liberty of the people. Rulers who wish to subvert the public liberty, may have found an established clergy convenient auxiliaries. A just government, instituted to secure and perpetuate [liberty] needs them not. (1788; 1965, 62)

In 1791, Madison proposed that the Bill of Rights specifically prohibit states from passing any law interfering with freedom of conscience—an extension of the application of the First Amendment that would not become a reality until passage of the Fourteenth Amendment applied the Bill of Rights to the states.

Perhaps the most radical of all the Founding Fathers was Thomas Paine. During his early years as a tax collector in England, Paine had argued that forcing Jews to pay taxes while depriving them of the right to vote violated the natural rights of man—a highly unorthodox position—and lobbied Parliament for salary increases for his poorly paid fellow tax collectors. Not surprisingly, he was fired. Benjamin Franklin convinced Paine that the colonies would be more receptive to his ideas and helped Paine resettle in America, where his very first publication was a denunciation of slavery. *Common Sense*, with its attack on monarchy and its argument for American independence, made his reputation; *The American Crisis* ("these are the times that try men's souls . . ."), written during the war, was used by General Washington to rally the dispirited troops. To suggest that *The Rights of Man*, and *The Age of Reason*, published after the revolution, were less well-received would be a considerable understatement. *The Age of Reason* in particular created many enemies for Paine; in it, he attacked all religious beliefs that could not be justified through science and reason.

The founder who left the least evidence of his religious predilections was George Washington. Historians have noted the almost complete absence of any references by Washington to religious matters in general, or Christianity in particular. Although he attended church occasionally during his presidency, he rarely did so otherwise. An entry in Jefferson's journal made shortly after Washington's death may be as illuminating as anything else.

> Feb. 1. Dr. Rush tells me that he had it from Asa Green that when the clergy addressed General Washington on his departure from the Government, it was observed in their consultation that he had never on any occasion said a word to the public which showed a belief in the Christian religion and they thought they should so pen their address as to force him at length to declare publicly whether he was a Christian or not. They did so. However, he observed, the old fox was too cunning for them. He answered every article in their address particularly except that, which he passed over without notice. . . . I know that Gouverneur Morris, who pretended to be in his secrets and believed himself to be so, has often told me that General Washington believed no more in the system (Christianity) than he did. (1800, 284)

Sydney Ahlstrom has written that "only an extensive essay could clarify the religious differences of the major Founding Fathers," and that what all shared was confidence in man, education, and political institutions (1972, 368).

The views of these Founders certainly did not reflect those of a majority of the colonists, although Deism and similar heretical beliefs like Unitarianism were far from unusual. On the other hand, their views on the necessity of separating church and state were widely shared by devoutly religious evangelicals and other Dissenters, although for very different reasons. What may seem surprising is that the omission of any mention of God from the Constitution apparently occasioned little or no controversy at the Constitutional Convention. Two politically persuasive reasons have been advanced for this relative lack of concern: first of all, the new constitution did not interfere with the existing religious establishments of the various states; and secondly, the drafters were preoccupied with the need to deal with the highly contentious issues of slavery.

The one proposal about religion to receive support was offered by Charles Pinckney, who suggested the phrase that eventually became part of Article VI, "but no religious test shall ever be required as a qualification to any office or public trust under the authority of the United States." This suggestion was seen as a statement of the obvious; as Witte has noted, "Only one delegate objected to the motion—not because he favored religious test oaths, but because he thought it 'unnecessary, the prevailing liberality being a sufficient security against such tests.'" (Witte 2000, 63).

The issue of the Constitution's *godlessness* did arise during the subsequent state legislative debates over ratification, and the drafters were roundly criticized both for the omission of any reference to God and for the prohibition of religious tests for public office. A speaker at the Massachusetts convention warned that unless the president was required to take a religious oath, "a Turk, a Jew, a Roman Catholic, and what is worse than all, a Universalist, may be President of the United States" (Jacoby 2004, 29). Nevertheless, efforts to amend the Constitution by adding religious references failed, and the Constitution was ratified subject only to the promise that the first session of the new Congress would prepare a Bill of Rights.

The congressional debates over the language of what is now the First Amendment of the Bill of Rights, especially the religion clauses, included consideration of at least twenty drafts, and the recorded discussions make it clear that, whatever ambiguities remain in the final version, the intent was to remove religious matters from the jurisdiction—or as Madison might have put it, the *cognizance*—of the federal government. Drafts stating simply that there would be "no state Church" were thus deemed inadequate.

The determination to place religion beyond the scope of the new government's powers was undoubtedly based upon the delegates' genuine conviction that such a separation was in the best interests of both church and state. But there were equally compelling political reasons for omitting religion from the new nation's governing document and for excluding religious establishment from the new government's powers. It is important to remember that the Founders were not a group of elitist intellectuals who somehow became entrusted with devising the constitution of a new country. However educated, propertied, and privileged the majority of them may have been, most were also seasoned and savvy politicians, aware of the immense difficulties of unifying the colony's contending philosophies, factions, and interests into a single nation. Religion was a divisive issue; any position adopted to mollify some would incur the enmity of others. "Fractured by pluralism and enflamed by sectarianism, Americans were unlikely to agree upon any federal establishment, no matter how broadly stated" (Lambert 2003, 14). The Founding Fathers embraced Locke's theory of limited government not because they were persuaded of its philosophical superiority, although most undoubtedly were, but also because it seemingly solved the central political problem of pluralism. A government limited in scope to those issues that absolutely had to be decided collectively was a government least likely to incur the hostility of citizens who deeply disagreed about those matters of ultimate concern addressed by religion.

SEEDS OF DISCORD

The solution adopted by the Founding Fathers was consistent with their liberal democratic worldview. By limiting government to secular, civic concerns, and prohibiting its interference with individual beliefs, they *privatized* religion. Such privatization did not remove religion from the public square, but it did remove it from the jurisdiction of the public sector—that is, government. (Churches and other voluntary associations, however public, are part of the private sector.) The adoption of a secular constitution had three notable consequences for religious expression in America.

Conflict

The liberal democratic solution was based firmly on an Enlightenment worldview; however, a significant number of Americans had not adopted that worldview then and have not done so since. A number of others adopted selected aspects only. A constitutional system that separated church and state thus set up a conflict that continues to this day between the Puritan and Calvinist impulses of the "Planting Fathers" and the libertarian principles of the Founding Fathers. The Puritans believed that building the "City on the Hill" required the support of civil authority, and many Christian denominations have continued to embrace all or part of that Puritan paradigm, although several scholars argue that even the most fundamentalist do so through a distinctly modernist and post-Enlightenment lens.[1] Many others—especially the liberal denominations—incorporated or embraced Enlightenment worldviews and adapted their theologies accordingly.

Any effort to understand later American public policy disputes must recognize the particularities—and peculiarities—of the constitutional system devised by the Founders, a system in which the role of the state and the scope of state power are central constitutional concerns. Public policies in the United States are constrained by foundational, normative assumptions (worldviews)—built into that Constitution, but never universally held—about individual rights and the authority of government. Primary among those assumptions is the belief that rights are negative; that is, unlike most other Western democratic countries, the American legal system has never guaranteed so-called affirmative rights. Any entitlement of citizens to health care, adequate housing, education, or social welfare is a creation of statute (or occasionally, state constitutional provisions) subject to revision by a simple act of Congress. Instead, fundamental rights are understood in the classic Enlightenment construct, as limitations on the reach of the state. The Founding Fathers who crafted our constitutional framework "saw constraining discretionary power of

---

[1] In *The Heart of Christianity: Rediscovering a Life of Faith*, Marcus J. Borg argues that, "[a]n emphasis upon the literal-factual interpretation of the Bible is also modern, a reaction to the Enlightenment. Prior to the Enlightenment, it was not the literal meaning of the Bible that mattered most for Christians, but its 'more-than-literal' meaning. . . . But the Enlightenment largely identified truth with factuality. In our time, if someone asks 'Is that true?' we are likely to assume that they are asking 'Is that factual? Did it happen?' Truth and factuality go hand-in-hand. And so for the earlier paradigm, defending the truth of the Bible meant defending its literal-factual truth" (2003, 12).

government officials—the central focus of the rule of law—as essential to the society they hoped to create" (Cass 2001, xii).

The early arguments between the Federalists and Anti-Federalists over the necessity of a Bill of Rights had nothing to do with the importance of individual rights, nor with this particular understanding of the nature of those rights. Both the Federalists and Anti-Federalists argued from Enlightenment worldviews. The dispute was tactical: Federalists believed that, since the government they had created had only the powers specifically delegated to it by the Constitution, it lacked any power to infringe upon the inalienable rights of its citizens. Federalists like Alexander Hamilton also argued that an enumeration of rights would be dangerous, as any right not included might be deemed to be unprotected—an objection that prompted the inclusion of the Ninth and Tenth Amendments.[2] The Anti-Federalists believed it was in the nature of governments to acquire powers not originally contemplated; they therefore felt it prudent to spell out specific limitations on the jurisdiction of the state. The vast majority of the colonists agreed with the Anti-Federalist argument, and the Bill of Rights was ratified in order to function as a libertarian "brake" on the power of popular majorities to authorize actions by government that would infringe upon individual rights. This Enlightenment focus upon the proper role of a limited state runs headlong into more Puritan desires to ensure the morality of one's neighbors.

The passage of the Fourteenth Amendment, in the wake of the Civil War, profoundly changed the way in which America defined these constitutional principles (Amar 1998). The Fourteenth Amendment extended to the inhabitants of the states the "privileges and immunities"

---

[2] The Ninth and Tenth Amendments spoke to both rights and powers. The Ninth Amendment provided that the enumeration of rights in the Bill of Rights should not be taken to *disparage* others; that is, that the omission of a particular right was not to be considered evidence that the people had not retained it. The Tenth Amendment reiterated the Founder's belief that they had constructed a government of delegated powers; it provided that powers not expressly given to the federal government remained with the people and/or the states.

of citizenship, and prohibited the states from denying to persons within their respective jurisdictions "the equal protection of the laws." The equality protected by the Fourteenth Amendment is narrower than equality as described by most political philosophers; consistent with the original constitutional architecture, it is limited to the right of similarly situated citizens to be treated equally by their government. Scholars—perhaps most notably Theodore Lowi—have argued that the passage of the Fourteenth Amendment and the ensuing application of the Bill of Rights to state and local government ignited a widespread conservative revolt against liberal Enlightenment principles. So long as local communities had been able to use state law to validate their religious worldviews, the rules governing a largely distant federal government were not particularly troublesome. Once those rules prevented them from imposing their beliefs about the proper order of things through their local laws, however, their outrage generated a significant political backlash.

Clashes between what I have called the Puritan and Enlightenment worldviews also intensified as governments at all levels increasingly expanded their scope into areas that were previously entirely private. As government agencies become more pervasive, the way in which those agencies conduct business, the ways in which they use their power to shape law and institutionalize value judgments, becomes subject to divisive and polarizing debate.

Voluntary Religion and Religious Vitality

One feature of the Enlightenment emphasis on markets and individual autonomy has been enormously beneficial for American religion—the voluntary nature of affiliation, and the encouragement of a religious marketplace, has contributed substantially to the vigor of American religiosity. (America is an outlier among Western industrialized nations with respect to the levels of religious belief and denominational affiliation.) As previously noted, membership in a church (or synagogue or mosque) stood at less than 17 percent when the Revolutionary War ended, and some estimates put it considerably lower. In the nearly two and a half centuries since, the proportion of Americans who formally affiliate with a religious community has risen steadily. Religiously affiliated voluntary groups are prominent in the nonprofit sector. Americans self-report high levels of belief in God, prayer, and other indicators of religious salience. The importance of religious constituencies in politics is the subject of academic dissertations and talk-show shouting matches. Whatever else one might say about America and religion, it would be hard to argue that religion has become irrelevant.

The voluntary nature of American religion has also enabled the enormous religious pluralism that is perhaps the most significant feature of our religiosity. If religious expression in the United States is robust, it is anything but monolithic. The earlier diversity within Protestantism discussed in chapter 2 has become diversity characterized by thousands of different sects and religious traditions from all over the world. As a result, contemporary differences in worldviews are not between "people of faith" and secular Americans, no matter how insistently some conservative religious spokespeople make such an assertion. The American religious marketplace is just that—a marketplace, characterized by a multitude of religious beliefs, cultures, and traditions that often conflict. If a large majority of Americans are religious—and that certainly seems to be the case—it is equally true that no majority exists for any particular religious doctrine or worldview. The vitality and multiplicity of beliefs and practices that describe American religion in the early twenty-first century are to a significant extent a product of the eighteenth-century Enlightenment constitutional system bequeathed to us by America's Founding Fathers.

Patriotic Piety

Finally, it is important to reiterate that the Puritan belief in covenant—the identification of America as the New Israel—persisted even among the Founders. Richard Hughes reports that, when Congress appointed Franklin, Jefferson, and Adams to a commission charged with designing a seal for the new nation, the suggestions all revolved around this theme.

> Franklin suggested a seal that would portray Moses lifting his hand and the Red Sea dividing, with Pharaoh in his chariot being over-

whelmed by the waters, and with a motto in great popular favor at the time "Rebellion to tyrants is obedience to God." . . . Jefferson suggested a representation of the Children of Israel in the wilderness, led by a cloud by day and a pillar of fire by night. (Hughes 2003, 34)

As Ahlstrom described the same phenomenon, a patriotic spirit "pervaded every aspect of the country's thought and feelings."

With this sublimely confident and optimistic principle the Federal Union entered upon its destiny—a beacon to all peoples and a refuge for the oppressed. With the passing years a new kind of national feeling came into existence. The Union became a transcendent object of reverence, a stern author of civic obligations as well as a source of faith and hope. Americans became stewards of a sacred trust, while the country's statesmen, orators, and poets gradually brought a veritable mystical theology of the Union into being. (Ahlstrom 1972, 383)

H. Richard Niebuhr would later write that the old idea that American Christians were chosen people called to a special task had become the idea that America was a nation chosen by God for special favor. Richard Hughes points out that the myth of the Chosen Nation has been a powerful theme in American life, a theme that has served constructive purposes but that has also justified oppression and exploitation of those deemed outside the circle of that covenant. In Hughes' view, "The myth of the Chosen Nation . . . had its roots in the particularities of Israel's past and the English Protestant experience. In the context of the early national period, however, chosenness became a self-evident truth that helped to undergird the doctrine of manifest destiny." (2003, 46). It is impossible to understand contemporary American policy debates without recognizing the conflicting Puritan and Enlightenment worldviews that shaped our earliest history, worldviews that continue to shape our contemporary policy debates in important and varying degrees.

PART II

The Democratic Dialectic

Chapter 4

CONFLICT AND CHANGE

If our contemporary civic battles were simply a result of inconsistent, Puritan versus Enlightenment worldviews, the outlines of our disputes would be clearer, but our prospects for a shared civic ethos would arguably be dimmer. Fortunately, cultures are not static; they change and are changed by historical experience. American history since the Revolutionary War has been an ongoing process of encounter—confrontation with national growth and world events, with new immigrants and their cultures, with science, technology, and modernism—all within the context of a constitutional framework meant to sharply limit central government power. America has added territories, fought wars, experienced economic and social upheavals, and become steadily more diverse. Along the way, religious, cultural, and political worldviews have synthesized, polarized, and changed. Even those Americans who have responded most negatively to these historical encounters are indisputably products of the modernity they reject. Alan Wolfe (2001) has noted that in its quest for popularity in a democratic society, Puritanism lost its harshness. Much the same phenomenon has modified and tempered other movements and "isms" over time.

Any effort to sketch an inclusive or even minimally adequate picture of the encounters between American's diverse religious worldviews and our collective history would occupy volumes. There are a number of excellent histories that do just that, and many of them address these issues perceptively and in depth.[1] This chapter makes no pretense at duplicating those efforts. It will necessarily omit many significant elements of our democratic dialectic and gloss over many more; the intent is to provide a broad, albeit superficial, context for understanding the reciprocal influences that have changed both American religions and American culture since 1787.

THE POST-REVOLUTIONARY PERIOD

As we have seen, the United States emerged from the Revolutionary War with an unquenchable optimism about the future, fed by a conviction that it was the "New Israel." The City on the Hill continued to be a national metaphor, carrying with it what Jeffrey Alexander has called a predilection for "binary thinking"—good versus evil, us versus them (Alexander, 2004). As James Morone has noted, the result has been a nation consumed by successive moral conflicts, intensified by radically opposing views about the nature of morality and moral responsibility. "Puritans bequeathed America two different answers to that bottom line: Who do we blame for trouble, the sinner or society?" (Morone 2003, 13). In 1827 Lyman Beecher would deliver a sermon capturing perfectly the tenor of the times saying, "I shall submit to your consideration . . . that our nation has been raised by Providence to exert an efficient instrumentality in this work of moral renovation. The origin and history of our nation are indicative of some great design to be accomplished by it" (Mathisen 2001, 151). Just as religion—or to be more precise, Protestantism—left an indelible imprint on American institutions, democratic processes have exerted an enormous effect upon American religious worldviews. After the revolution, millennialism flourished, not only in the standard Christian aspiration to make the world ready for Christ's kingdom, but often in a quite secularized form:

---

[1] Among the most prolific and perceptive of these has been Martin Marty, who has chronicled American religion in a virtual mountain of books over some half a century.

the United States leading the world to peace and plenty. The religious millennialism of this period already demonstrated the impact of the American experience; it was strikingly different from its more passive predecessors. Before the American Revolution, millennialists generally believed that they had to patiently await the destruction of an evil world, after which Christ's kingdom would be established. In the early 1800s, however, Americans were much more optimistic about their ability to bring about the changes needed to usher in the Millennium. During the Second Great Awakening, shortly after the end of the revolutionary period, revivalists urged people to work against social evils. "The moral fervor, the expectancy, and the intense devotion to mission rooted in millennialist ideas inspired early-nineteenth-century efforts at reform and allowed different kinds of reformers to work together" (Mintz 1995, 16). That was fortunate, because different groups had decidedly different ideas about what to reform.

Quakers were the first to prohibit slaveholding among their members. Quakers also organized efforts to ameliorate poverty and encourage temperance and worked to improve the treatment of Native Americans. The newly formed American Unitarian Association adopted as its slogan "Deeds not Creeds" and emphasized human reason and the brotherhood of man. As Mintz reports, despite harsh criticism of Unitarianism from more traditional religionists, Unitarians such as William Cullen Bryant, Henry Wadsworth Longfellow, James Russell Lowell, and Francis Parkman exerted a profound influence on American intellectual life, and the denomination also produced a number of prominent reformers: Dorthea Dix, a crusader on behalf of the mentally ill; Samuel Gridley Howe, a staunch advocate for the blind; educational reformer Horace Mann; and Joseph Tuckerman, one of the nation's first advocates for the urban poor. The Declaration of Independence, with its stirring language about equality and natural rights, contributed a powerful secular impetus to reform efforts. So did Enlightenment philosophy, not only by offering the prospect that humans might use science to control nature, but even more subversively, by encouraging reexamination (or outright rejection) of the notion of original sin. If men were born good, and corrupted by unwholesome environments, efforts to improve those environments made more sense than efforts to save individual souls. Much as devoutly religious evangelicals and Enlightenment Deists had united in support of church-state separation for very different reasons, religious and secular social reformers drew similar conclusions from distinctly different premises.

Several cultural shifts occurred during the post-revolutionary period. Calvinist beliefs about predestination and innate human sinfulness lost ground to considerably more optimistic views of human perfectibility. The Second Great Awakening, itself a reaction against the emergence of more liberal, intellectual approaches to Christianity, encouraged individualism by offering people a broad choice of affiliations available from the growing religious marketplace. (There were other religious parallels to market economics. One of the most successful of the revival preachers, Charles Finney—sometimes called the "father of the Second Great Awakening"—frankly promoted religious marketing techniques that he called "new measures," based upon his own psychological theories.) The Holiness movements emerged, and allowed women a significantly expanded role in religious matters. Feminist groups began demanding the right to vote. (Finney added his voice to the movement for women's emancipation; the New York Female Moral Reform Society was founded in his church.) Elsewhere, the Women's Temperance Union and the New York Anti-Slavery Society were founded, the former in 1826 and the latter in 1833. In 1830, Joseph Smith published the *Book of Mormon*. Democracy and mobility gave people previously unimaginable choices. Social protest and change were everywhere.

The American West was an enormously important element of this climate of change and renewal. It has been suggested that the key to understanding religion in the west was the land itself (Szasz and Szasz 1994). The same might be said for understanding the American character. Certainly the existence of vast expanses, uninhabited except for the Native Americans (whose claims were recognized by very few), encouraged a spirit of adventurousness and independence—not to mention acquisitiveness—and reinforced the already potent belief in America's manifest destiny. As the population surged westward, Dissenting churches in particular flourished. So did voluntary associations, necessary mechanisms for mutual aid in the nation's less populated, less socially organized regions.

In the west, the ethic of religious choice flowered: any group of like-minded pioneers could form a congregation, and thousands did. If internal disagreements arose within a particular church, the dissenters often simply left to form another. The Western culture, and the availability of seemingly unending territory, encouraged such solutions. The West was a metaphor for new beginnings: an ongoing invitation to start over.

Another aspect of the self-reliance and independence fostered by the West's wide-open spaces was a decidedly antiauthoritarian and anti-intellectual bias which found considerable support in the churches. Located far from the governing institutions of their denominations, local congregations were largely self-regulating. Dissenting denominations frowned upon invidious distinctions (except race), and their proclaimed faith in the common man usually led them to oppose professional prerequisites to ordination. Western life required a strong work ethic, and religious institutions obliged with theologies that focused increasingly on this-world duties and the importance of labor. In an environment where production was an imperative, diatribes against business and materialism were largely absent. Intellectual and cultural pursuits, on the other hand, diverted energies better spent on material labor, and were viewed with suspicion or outright hostility. Schooling was important for teaching a trade, and for imparting practical information necessary to make one's way. Scholarship or art not geared to such practical ends was viewed as a distraction (Miyakawa 1964).

The western ethos that developed varied considerably with geography and with the cultural backgrounds of the people who settled in the various territories. California and the Pacific Northwest, in particular, developed highly distinctive political cultures. Religiosity dropped off sharply the farther west one went; in the nineteenth century, a common joke was that "the Sabbath shall never cross the Missouri." Religious pluralism, and the West's comparative openness to diverse religious expression (or the lack of such expression), undoubtedly facilitated the extraordinary success of western Jewish immigrants.

> In the 1850s, Jews composed perhaps 10 percent of San Francisco's merchant community. Relying on a credit network that included family members and coreligionists, Jewish families provided vital economic services, both in rural areas such as New Mexico, and urban centers, such as San Francisco, Portland, Los Angeles, Denver and Seattle.
>
> Contemporary visitors marveled at how well the western Jews had succeeded. In the Los Angeles 1876 centennial celebration, a young Jewish woman portrayed the "Spirit of Liberty" while a rabbi helped preside over the festivities. In San Francisco's first *Elite Directory* (1870–79), Jews composed over one-fifth of the city's "elite." The historians Harriet Rochlin and Fred Rochlin have counted over thirty nineteenth century western Jewish mayors, plus countless sheriffs, police chiefs and other elected officials. . . . California's failure to produce a "religious mainstream" allowed all faiths to flourish. (Szasz and Szasz 1994)

SLAVERY, CIVIL WAR, AND THE BLACK CHURCH

Throughout the post-revolutionary period, the issue of slavery—the issue that had consumed so much of the constitutional negotiators' energies—continued to fester. In a country that had expressly committed itself to the proposition that all men were created equal, inequalities of many kinds remained glaringly obvious. As James Morone has noted, however, slavery was inequality of a different magnitude. "Americans have been furiously assigning one another to balconies since the seventeenth century. We sort each other by religion, ethnicity, gender and bank account. But nothing marks American differences quite like race" (2003, 119).

By the 1830s the energies of the moral reformers—reinvigorated by the Second Great Awakening—had largely converged on opposition to slavery. Once they focused their efforts on abolition, they benefited greatly from institutions and networks originally created for other *moral campaigns*. In the 1820s, when the U.S. Postal Service introduced Sunday mail delivery, religious leaders had organized a huge campaign to stop what they saw as desecration of the Sabbath. Their rallies, petitions, and tracts failed to persuade Congress to cease Sunday mail, but later reformers used the infrastructure created during that campaign to mail "great piles of abolitionist propaganda" into the slave states (Morone 2003, 25). Southerners, including Southern churches, reacted predictably, with large mobs burning the mail and creating other disturbances—and doing so, it should be noted, with the encouragement of the then president Andrew Jackson. As abolition conflicts polarized North and South, a regional shift occurred that would have continuing consequences for American political and religious institutions. As a number of historians have noted, by the early 1830s, modernism and liberalism had largely moved north and west. Southern religion became increasingly orthodox, and Southern churches lent an important voice to the region's defense of slavery. The towering Southern thinkers and political figures—the men who had earlier authored Virginia's religious freedom laws and figured so prominently during the Constitutional Convention—were gone; their successors would be found in the Northeast and in the western states that were now joining the union.

As many times as the turbulence of the era has been described, it remains difficult for modern Americans to grasp. Lynching of black men in the South, particularly Mississippi, was commonplace, and it was not unheard-of to see lynching of whites suspected of collaborating with abolitionists. Antislavery rallies consumed Northern cities, where sentiment was by no means uniform in favor of abolition and there was considerable sympathy for the economic arguments of the slaveholders. Abolition groups fought among themselves over what role, if any, women should be permitted to play in the movement, and a number of other issues muddied the waters, among them "nativism, temperance, free-labor capitalism" (Morone 2003, 121).

These were formative times, not just for white Americans confronting an institution blatantly inconsistent with an officially libertarian philosophy, but for African-American communities, both slave and free. Until the 1830s, more Africans had crossed the Atlantic than Europeans. Snatched from different parts of the continent, they arrived in the New World with different languages and different religions; even after converting to Christianity, most retained many of their original religious customs. "Precisely because of their adaptability, African religions could embrace new gods and new rituals without losing their fundamental character" (Raboteau 1999, 13). Conversion of slaves to Christianity had begun in earnest during the First Great Awakening, when slaves "encountered a form of Protestant worship that resembled the religious celebrations of their African homelands" (18). Because Baptists and Methodists had issued early condemnations of slavery (later recanted), and because they were willing to license black preachers, blacks gravitated disproportionately to those denominations.

In the North, where growing numbers of slaves had been emancipated and other free blacks had settled, "the black churches formed the institutional structure for the development of free black communities."

> The main public issues that absorbed the attention of free blacks in the North were the social conditions of poverty and illiteracy that afflicted the majority of African-American communities, the continuation and expansion of slavery in the South, the legal and social discrimination that restricted the rights of free blacks, and coming to terms with the troubling existential question, what did the black experience in America mean? As the single institution that black communities controlled, churches played an active role in addressing these issues. (Raboteau 1999, 25)

The centrality of the black church in African-American life continues to the present, a structural reality with political and cultural as well as religious significance.

Characteristically, when the Civil War began, both North and South saw their side as the cause of God. As Robert Mathisen has written, "Religious rhetoric claimed divine support for the direction each side took before, during, and for decades after the war" (2001, 269–70).

In the South, "the symbiotic relationship between religious and political discourse in the antebellum South consisted of the adapting of ideas and rhetoric from religion to politics, while at other times the interplay between Southern religion and politics resulted in their convergence and mutual reinforcement" (279). It is impossible to overstate the influence of race and racial politics on the American character. If the Civil War was a wound, it has yet to fully heal; we continue to deal with the innumerable structural, psychological, economic, and religious consequences of slavery. Americans often celebrate the role of religious conviction in ending slavery, and that role was important. But we also tend to gloss over and minimize the extent to which many religious institutions provided support and justification for the practice. Then as now, there was no such thing as a singular religious voice, no such thing as a unified or monolithic *people of faith.*

THE FOURTEENTH AMENDMENT

The Thirteenth and Fourteenth Amendments were passed in the aftermath of the Civil War. The Thirteenth Amendment wrote emancipation into the constitutional fabric. The Fourteenth Amendment required state governments to extend the "privileges and immunities" of citizenship and the "equal protection of the laws" to all citizens within their jurisdictions. The precise language of the first section reads:

> All persons born or naturalized in the United States and subject to the jurisdiction thereof, are citizens of the United States and of the State wherein they reside. No State shall make or enforce any law which shall abridge the privileges or immunities of citizens of the United States; nor shall any State deprive any person of life, liberty, or property, without due process of law; nor deny to any person within its jurisdiction the equal protection of the laws.

The Fourteenth Amendment was ratified in 1868, finally accomplishing what James Madison had proposed nearly a century earlier, and effecting a significant structural change to America's constitutional architecture. Yale constitutional scholar Akhil Reed Amar has called it a "constitutional reconstruction" (Amar 2000). Ever since its ratification, there have been persistent efforts to undo it, to argue that the amendment has been misconstrued—that it was intended to be applied only to exslaves, that it has never been properly ratified, and that an imperial judiciary has used the language as a warrant for all sorts of unintended mischief. However, a dispassionate reading of the congressional history confirms that the amendment was intended to apply the Bill of Rights to the states. Jonathan Bingham, the Republican legislator and primary sponsor, was explicit on the point. On February 28, 1866, Bingham made a speech to the House of Representatives entitled "One Country, One Constitution, and One People: In support of the proposed amendment to enforce the Bill of Rights," in which he asserted that states had no right to interfere with their citizens' constitutional rights: "The equality of the right to live; the right to know; to argue and to utter, according to conscience; to work and enjoy the product of their toil, is the rock on which [the] Constitution rests, its sure foundation and defense" (Amar 2000). During the ratification process, newspapers and political figures argued for or against ratification based upon their belief that states would thereafter be bound to respect the fundamental rights of their citizens, black or white.

Once the amendment was ratified, the Supreme Court nevertheless took decades to incorporate the protections contained in the first eight amendments—that is, to rule in a series of cases that the Fourteenth Amendment required local governments to respect the fundamental individual rights at issue. The legal changes effected by the Fourteenth Amendment were ultimately transformational, as were the social and cultural consequences of those changes. As Theodore Lowi (1996) has written: rights expanded; rights necessarily involve morality; and morality radicalizes. Lowi has located the beginnings of what we now call the culture wars in the passage of the Fourteenth Amendment. As he argues, conservatism finds expression in the religious and moral beliefs of local communities, with real families, identifiable institutions, and traditions. So while the early national elites, educated in Enlightenment philosophy and devoted to Lockean ideals, were busy shaping national governing institutions, conservatives were content to concentrate their energies on their local communities. What happened in Washington was largely irrelevant to them—one doesn't go to Washington to change laws dealing with divorce, adoption, or custody of children. Congress had no role in public education, regulation of sexual practices or abortion, or determining the status of women. Those were matters of exclusively local concern and control, and so long as local communities remained free to impose their views of morality on their neighbors, they were largely content to ignore the federal government.

The Fourteenth Amendment thus did more than nationalize the Bill of Rights; it nationalized—and radicalized—populist (nearly always religious) conservatism. It is important to recognize that the Fourteenth Amendment did not expand government power. Certain matters had long been subject to local government control. What changed was the identity of those who would have the last word on the propriety of those controls. The Fourteenth Amendment gave federal courts a veto over local government decisions. Over a period of years, the Supreme Court would tell local officials that they could not require children to pray in their schools, could not criminalize birth control or abortion, could not impose a variety of disadvantages on women and minorities, and could not censor books and magazines they found distasteful. The enormous resentment these decisions created was grounded in a Puritan belief that local government should have jurisdiction to dictate the morality of local community behaviors. If the country's territorial expansiveness had seemed to promise unlimited independence from centralized government, the newly intrusive federal rules—together with an assortment of technological and commercial innovations tying the growing American population ever more closely together—were reminders of unavoidable and unwelcome limits on local autonomy.

DARWIN AND EVOLUTIONARY THEORY

The first American review of *The Origin of Species* appeared in 1860. "For men of faith . . . Darwinism represented both opportunity and danger, a powerful natural theory of the origins and development of life that must somehow be reconciled with the traditional explanations offered by religion" (Jacoby 2004, 125). The challenge was particularly critical "in a nation born during the Enlightenment, [where] the reverence for science as the way to understand all aspects of reality was nearly unbounded" (Marsden 1980, 15). Since God's truth was unified, the evangelical Christians who dominated America's informal Protestant establishment had confidently expected that science would proceed to confirm biblical truths. This confidence was already beginning to erode, assaulted by skepticism and rationalism at home and *higher* biblical criticism, questioning the factual truth of biblical accounts, from abroad. As George Marsden recounts, American clergy initially felt confident that such foreign influences would gain no foothold in America.

> President William F. Warren of Boston University told the Evangelical Alliance that "toward the middle of the last century came the fullness of God's time for generating a new Christian nationality." America had seen various forms of infidelity, such as that of Thomas Jefferson, Thomas Cooper, and Thomas Paine, known as the "three doubting Thomases," and then more recently Transcendentalism, Owenist Socialism, Spiritualism, and phrenology, but "none of them were of American origin." The old idea of American innocence versus European corruption still seems plausible. "Thus all these threatening surges of Antichristian thought," Warren told the international audience, "have come to us from European seas; not one arose in our own hemisphere." (Marsden 1980, 18)

That belief in the impregnability of the City on the Hill was shattered by Charles Darwin.

Some evangelical leaders argued that evolution and Christianity could be reconciled, that an all-powerful God could certainly have created evolutionary processes, and that Darwinian natural selection could coexist with faith. For others, evolution was an attack on the literal truth of the Bible, on the nature of reality itself, and the two were therefore irreconcilable. "For most educated American Evangelicals . . . the commitment both to objective science and religion was so strong, and the conflict so severe, that they were forced into one of two extreme positions" (Marsden 1980, 20). Those who held that evolution and the Bible were incompatible would insist that Darwinian natural selection was another form of heresy; they would argue that it was hypothetical, a *theory* only and not really scientific as Bacon had defined science, because it could not be directly observed. Those who chose instead to redefine the relationship between science and religion did so by uncoupling religion's moral and ethical content from literal interpretation. Science would henceforth describe the material world; religion would speak to the heart and soul.

If biblical literalists rejected evolution, others embraced it. Evolution, especially in its Christianized version, fit well with the American belief in science and progress. Freethinkers saw it as a breakthrough, as evidence that science would ultimately displace reliance on supernatural explanations of natural phenomena. More ominously, other religious and philosophical figures used natural selection to justify survival of the fittest (a term coined by Herbert Spencer, not Darwin), social policies that some have described as "naturalistic Calvinism." Social Darwinism was particularly attractive to Gilded Age captains of industry and has had an enormous impact upon American economic policy, as we shall see in chapter 7.

It was largely his fear of social Darwinism that led William Jennings Bryan to fight so ferociously against evolution.

> Had William Jennings Bryan been able to present his speech, written to serve as the closing argument for the state in the *State of Tennessee v. John Thomas Scopes* (1925), historians might have a better understanding of the connection between Bryan's theological conservatism and his economic liberalism. Here Bryan reiterates his critique that the principle of "survival of the fittest" would be used to justify the cruelest social policies. (Walsh 2000, 5)

Darwin's theory was not the only challenge to traditional forms of biblical faith. Between the late 1800s and the beginning of World War I, a number of freethinkers made their own claims to influence in American society. Alongside the growth of American religious institutions was a parallel expansion of religious skepticism, exemplified by such figures as Robert Ingersoll (the "Great Agnostic") and Felix Adler, who founded the Ethical Culture Society in 1876. Freethinkers had widely different ideologies, but they all supported separation of church and state, and most agreed on the importance of free speech and opposition to censorship (especially the then widespread censorship of information about birth control), expanded rights for women, and the importance of public education. Ingersoll, the son of a Presbyterian minister, was the most famous. It is a reflection of the times that his humanist views did not prevent his holding public office—he served as Illinois attorney general—nor, apparently, from being very active politically. He was an accomplished orator whose speaking tours drew large and admiring crowds, and he spoke often on behalf of Republican candidates (including his equally agnostic brother, who was elected to three terms in Congress). An ardent abolitionist, he also supported early congressional efforts to apply the Bill of Rights to the states. Ingersoll was a creature of the Enlightenment; his vision might be summed up in these lines from one newspaper essay, "We are looking for the time when the useful shall be the honorable; and when *reason*, throned upon the world's brain, shall be the King of Kings, and God of Gods" (Ingersoll 1900, 90).

In addition to religious, scientific, and ideological clashes, the period between the Civil War and World War I was roiled by industrialization, immigration, and various crises of urbanization. It was also a period that saw regional differences intensify. The cultural differences between North and South, especially, continued to harden; in addition to the resentments flowing from the Civil War, Southerners increasingly came to see the North as the source of troubling "new ideas" like evolution and women's rights. Thomas Cooper's expulsion from the faculty of the College of South Carolina for heresy in 1832 was part and parcel of a Southern reaction against any sort of change—racial, political, or religious.

THE TWENTIETH CENTURY: CONTINUITY AND CHANGE

It wasn't only science that was challenging the accepted order. The gulf between conservative and liberal religious beliefs was widening, as liberal *modernists* embraced cultural adaptations that conservatives saw as capitulations to secularism. The Industrial Revolution, increasing urbanization, and a constant influx of immigrants brought disorienting changes that further differentiated and secularized American life. Pluralism suddenly meant something other than different kinds of Protestantism, and the metaphor of an American "melting pot" that included Catholics and Jews came into common usage. Any remaining evangelical consensus shattered. Economic disparities were glaring. Predictably, people with different cultural and religious worldviews responded to these new challenges very differently.

One response to the disarray was the Social Gospel—a Protestant-led effort to address the underlying causes of poverty and misery. Such reform efforts ran the gamut from temperance and Prohibition to a renewed emphasis upon Christian obligation to help the less fortunate by eliminating poverty and disease. Often described as the religious expression of progressivism, the Social Gospel was critical of the excessive individualism of the nineteenth century. Adherents of the Social Gospel—and they were a significant percentage of American Protestants—were committed to social justice and economic reform. Leaders of the movement spoke out against political corruption, poor working conditions, and child labor. They supported unionization and challenged many of the most ingrained aspects of capitalist society.

> These social gospel programs and literature reflected an important transformation of Protestant theology. While formal, academic statements of theology did not appear until later in the twentieth century, social gospelers redefined salvation, the nature of God, and religious commitment and in so doing, made an important departure from the Protestantism of the Second Great Awakening. . . . Eschewing the lonely struggle with sin for a sense of individual assurance, social gospelers insisted that salvation was a social matter—that Christians

were responsible for their brothers' and sisters' redemption as much as their own." (Curtis 2001, 365)

This emphasis upon Christian responsibility led both to moralizing campaigns against liquor and prostitution, which drew upon older Puritan themes, and to support of social programs to ameliorate poverty and injustice. The Social Gospel explicitly rejected the Puritan belief that poverty was evidence of personal inadequacy.

Other responses to the insecurities and hardships of these times took very different forms. Nativism ebbed and flowed. Abroad, America engaged in empire building, fueled by belief in the country's "manifest destiny." At home, social Darwinists vigorously contested the premises of the Social Gospel. Andrew Walsh has admirably summarized the Calvinist religious beliefs of the social Darwinists: the Fall necessitates a struggle for survival; the free market is the state of nature, and the invisible hand of the market is the hand of God; wealth is a sign of grace, while poverty is a punishment or test; and the poor are responsible for their own poverty (Walsh 2000). Ironically, social Darwinists were (and are) often found among those who most categorically rejected scientific Darwinism.

Ultimately, however, it was the battle over scientific Darwinism that produced the most enduring divisions among American Protestants. World War I had shaken American culture. On the one hand, it had encouraged interreligious cooperation among wartime agencies such as the National Catholic War Council, the (Protestant) Wartime Commission of the Churches, and the Jewish Welfare Board (Hutchison 2003). On the other, it had raised deeply disturbing questions about civilization, morality, and religion. In this "postwar atmosphere of alarm, 'fundamentalism' emerged as a distinct phenomenon" (Marsden 1980, 6).

Prior to America's entry into the war, fundamentalists and their modernist counterparts exhibited the same variety of opinion as the general American public. George Marsden notes that the two most popular figures connected to fundamentalism, William Jennings Bryan and

Billy Sunday, expressed dramatically different views on the possibility of war, with Bryan going so far as to resign as Wilson's secretary of state. In the prelude to hostilities, and during the war itself, however, another exchange of hostilities, in this instance theological, would have enormous ramifications for fundamentalism. Modernist theologians at the University of Chicago Divinity School authored a series of inflammatory articles arguing that premillenialism, in denying human responsibility for reform and the betterment of society, "strikes at the heart of democratic society." This was accompanied by suggestions that German sources were funding the dissemination of premillenial ideas. Understandably, such accusations (which Marsden characterizes as "wartime paranoia") were met with outrage. Premillenialists responded that it was the modernists who had fallen under German influence, an influence reflected in their acceptance of German scholarship promoting rationalism, evolutionary naturalism, and Nietzschean philosophy. As George Marsden has observed,

> Evolution became a symbol. Without the new cultural dimension, it is unlikely that the debate over Darwinism could have been revived in the spectacular way it was or that fundamentalism itself would have gained wide support. Americans had just fought a war that could be justified only as a war between civilization and barbarism. German barbarism could be explained as the result of an evolutionary "might is right" superman philosophy. (Marsden 1980, 149)

The Fundamentals were published between 1910 and 1915. They were a series of twelve paperbacks, responding to the modernizing theologies of the preceding decades, and arguing that five beliefs were fundamental to Christianity: inerrancy of Scripture; the Virgin birth; Christ's atonement for man's sins on the cross; Christ's bodily resurrection; and the objective reality of Christ's miracles (Armstrong 2000). Armstrong argues that World War I had introduced an "element of terror" to conservative Protestantism that turned it fundamentalist (171); Marsden describes fundamentalism as "militantly anti-modernist Protestant Evangelicalism" (1980, 4). Both note the centrality of the

Scopes trial in cementing the divisions between fundamentalists and other evangelical and liberal Protestants.

Because Darwinism contradicted the literal truth of scripture, "the Scopes trial was a clash between two utterly incompatible points of view" (Armstrong 2000, 176). The trial centered upon accusations that a young science teacher, John Scopes, had violated a Tennessee law forbidding the teaching of evolution in public school classrooms. The "Monkey Trial," as it was called, garnered enormous publicity. Although Scopes ultimately lost the challenge, Clarence Darrow's questioning of William Jennings Bryan during the trial was widely reported, and Bryan—and the creationists—became objects of national derision. In reaction, the fundamentalists retreated into their own communities, where they would proceed to establish a network of Bible colleges and other separatist institutions. While many liberal Christians assumed that the conflict was over, fundamentalists nursed a considerable sense of grievance and a determination to emerge and prevail. "In the intellectual battle between true Christianity and the philosophical materialism of modern life, said J. Gresham Machen, 'there can be no peace without victory; one side or the other must win.'" (Marsden 1980, 4). A 1924 article from *Christian Century* characterized the conflict between modernists and fundamentalists as "Two world-views, two moral ideals, two sets of personal attitudes . . . Christianity according to fundamentalism is one religion. Christianity according to modernism is another religion."

The evolution controversy arose at a time when the availability of new technologies—telephones, radios, movies, automobiles—was changing everyday reality for millions of Americans. Industrialization was transforming the workplace. Women were demanding a voice in politics (in 1920 they had finally won the right to vote). During the 1920s, for the first time in American history, more people lived in cities than in the country. It was getting harder to ignore American differences. The clash over evolution did not occur just because different people held widely different views. That had been the case for some time. What had changed was the social environment, which was making it far more difficult for groups to maintain independence from the broader culture. Mass communication and public education, in particular, made contact inevitable, with the result that confrontation became far more likely. Many of the themes that would later be labeled as "culture war" issues emerged out of this clash: the portrayal of academics as arrogant elitists, regionalism (harbinger of "red state/blue state" rhetoric), anti-Semitism, and hostility to foreigners. As Willard Gatewood has pointed out, fundamentalism had undergone a considerable transformation by 1941, and in the wake of WWII, fundamentalists displayed a renewed militancy (458).

Between the Scopes Trial in 1925 and America's entry into World War II in 1941, however, the major fact of American life was the Depression, an experience which profoundly challenged American optimism. It also called into question the Calvinist insistence upon personal responsibility for one's fate. Here was a situation clearly beyond the ability of individuals to control, or local governments to ameliorate. When Roosevelt was elected, he promised a "new economic constitutional order." In rhetoric that was part social gospel and part modern science, he emphasized that the causes of poverty were beyond the control of individuals and required a systemic response. He elevated notions of shared community over those of rugged individualism, and he instituted social programs and legal reforms that reflected that emphasis. Roosevelt's programs reshaped American attitudes about the role of government, and his rhetoric "submerged the familiar discourse about them and us, about vice and virtue" (Morone 2003, 355).

Roosevelt created a newly muscular federal government, but his response to the Depression was not the only reason federal power increased. James Morone has pointed out a particular irony of the seemingly inexorable growth of centralized government authority; it had been erected on a federal infrastructure created during prior, successive "moral panics" (343). Prohibition had vastly augmented federal police powers. The Comstock Act had given the postal service broad new authority to "fight smut"—primarily racy books and the dissemination of birth control information. In these and similar efforts, Americans' persistent Puritan desire to impose morality had already trumped their devotion to local control. After the Depression, federal growth continued, fueled by challenges individual states could not meet. Technological innovations like the telephone and radio did not respect state borders; increasingly, neither did commerce. Standards for food and drug safety, control of air traffic, provisions for interstate commerce—all required national coordination. By the beginning of World War II, the Bill of Rights had been nationalized, social security and other national social programs had been instituted, and an ever-growing number of federal agencies were intruding on the traditional prerogatives of local governments. The pace and scope of change was dizzying.

World War II affected American culture—and American religious and regional subcultures—in innumerable ways. "Rosie the Riveter" replaced men who had left the nation's factories to fight, giving women a tantalizing taste of independence. The discovery of Nazi concentration camps both reinforced popular belief in American moral superiority and further challenged American theologies. Thousands of soldiers left the farm, saw "Paree," looked at unspeakable horrors, and had their horizons forever changed. For American Jews, the Holocaust precipitated a crisis of meaning—and brought large numbers of foreign Eastern European Jews to America. The obvious need for national coordination of the war effort further centralized authority. When the war was over, the world had—once again—irrevocably changed.

MODERNITY'S ACCELERATING CHALLENGES

Cultural change continued to alter the American landscape in the aftermath of the war. Postwar programs like the GI Bill and low-down-payment FHA and VA mortgages gave returning veterans new career choices and housing options. Suburbanization increased, and with it economic stratification and dependence on personal automobiles. Television brought the news and entertainment to the living room— and showed everyone how "the other half" lived. Advertising and growth in disposable income encouraged consumerism. Women— including those with children at home—entered the workforce in ever-larger numbers. Black soldiers who returned home to find segregation and Jim Crow in the South, and less overt but still widespread discrimination elsewhere, joined a renewed movement for racial equality. Whole books have been written tracing the cultural consequences of each of these, and other, developments.

Earlier in the century, Sigmund Freud had introduced increasingly anxious and uprooted Americans to psychoanalysis, and after World War II, the number of Americans seeing 'mental health professionals' had grown dramatically. The rise of what Bellah and others have called the "therapeutic culture" has been attributed to many things: the increasing professionalization and atomization of postwar life; the fracturing of older familial and community support systems; a growing confidence in the ability of science and medicine; and spiritual emptiness resulting from the loss of the old verities. Bellah and his co-authors note that an attractive feature of the therapeutic relationship was its basis in science, rather than moral judgment. "The therapeutic relationship underscores the intersubjective nature of reality. It alerts the participants to discrepant definitions of the situation stemming from different personal histories. It cautions them against projecting their feelings on others and overgeneralizing their own views . . . " (1985, 122). This reluctance to judge, to apply inflexible moral standards without regard for the particulars of an individual's situation, fit well with earlier American libertarian premises—if you aren't hurting anyone else, who am I to tell you how to live? (That attitude deeply offends equally American, considerably more Puritan, beliefs about community and morality.)

The early twentieth-century popularity of psychoanalysis has been compared to the contemporaneous popularity of Christian Science, a new religion founded by Mary Baker Eddy. Both began by assuming that health and happiness were products of individual effort rather than social or institutional change. Both offered a modern faith in man and reason. And both claimed to be scientific at a time when science was increasingly venerated (Hunsberger 2005). After the Second World War, that "therapeutic ethic" was increasingly attractive—and affordable—to the growing middle class.

The war effort had fostered an ecumenical spirit, and the threat of "godless communism" also brought Protestant denominations together, masking for a time their deepening liberal-conservative divisions. Attitudes toward Jews and Catholics improved as well (although not nearly as much as some of the rhetoric might suggest). During National Brotherhood Week in 1942, the National Conference of Christians and Jews issued a declaration listing "the fundamental religious beliefs held in common by Protestants, Catholics and Jews." It affirmed a belief in "one God" and rejected "all attempts to explain man in merely material terms." It was during this time that *Judeo-Christian* came to be used as "a shorthand term for a worldview, and a set of beliefs, that Jews and Christians held in common" (Hutchison 2003, 198). The term was given further currency by Will Herberg, whose 1955 book *Catholic, Protestant and Jew* pictured America as a (largely benign) "melting pot" of ethnic identities. Churches and synagogues alike flourished in the postwar environment. The melting pot metaphor first gained, then lost popularity as Americans rediscovered—and elected to preserve—their distinctive religious and ethnic identities. At the same time, interreligious marriages became much more common (as interracial marriages would in the latter half of the century), blurring and blending those rediscovered identities.

William Hutchison makes a critical point about the emerging effort to create a civil religion—an effort perhaps best captured by Robert Bellah's famous 1967 essay in *Daedelus*, "Civil Religion in America." Rather than genuine pluralism, Hutchison says, it represented an "'American Way of Life' that was really a sociopolitical surrogate for the principal ideologies of Protestant America . . . this common civic faith may, indeed, best be understood as a secularized Puritanism." Referring to a ubiquitous margarine commercial, Hutchison wryly described the dynamic: "Each time a diner said 'butter,' a polite little voice responded, 'Parkay!' When politicians and others boasted about a new, more inclusive religious mainstream, anyone paying attention was likely to hear a disembodied but distinct rejoinder: 'Protestant!'" (2003, 209). Beneath the surface ecumenicism, enormous differences in worldviews contributed to continuing tensions over church-state relationships, particularly the 1963 decision striking down required prayers in public school, and Catholic efforts to secure public funding for Catholic schools. New evangelical organizations broke off from the Federal Council of Churches. An American Council of Christian Churches was established in 1942; the National Association of Evangelicals for United Action was formed in 1943. In the 1950s revivalism reemerged, largely in response to Billy Graham's crusades. Liberal Protestant reaction to Graham was mixed. Reinhold Niebuhr described him as "a personable, modest and appealing young man who has wedded considerable dramatic and demagogic gifts with a rather obscurantist version of the Christian faith" (Silk 1989, 561). The late 1950s also witnessed the beginnings of meteoric growth in denominations previously considered marginal: Adventists, Pentecostals, and Jehovah's Witnesses.

In 1954 the Supreme Court decided *Brown v. Board of Education*. The ruling sparked such fierce resistance that President Eisenhower dispatched troops to Little Rock, Arkansas, to protect the new black students from angry white mobs. In 1955 Rosa Parks refused to give her seat on a Montgomery, Alabama, bus to a white passenger, and Martin Luther King Jr. called for the boycott that would ignite the civil rights movement. In 1963, King would direct his famous *Letter from the Birmingham Jail* to antagonistic white clergy and help found the Southern Christian Leadership Conference. Meanwhile, the racist, anti-Catholic, anti-Semitic Klu Klux Klan was operating with impunity throughout much of the South. A series of church bombings and the murder of three young civil rights workers in Mississippi horrified the nation and reinforced the Northern image of the South as a refuge for unenlightened throwbacks—many of whom were quoting Bible passages to justify acts of terror.

Further support for that image came in 1960, when Southern Baptists and other evangelicals (many from the North) formed the "National Conference of Citizens for Religious Freedom" to oppose the presidential candidacy of John F. Kennedy, contending that a Catholic president would be a puppet of the Vatican. In September of that same year, over one hundred liberal Protestant, Catholic, and Jewish leaders had signed a statement affirming their belief that no candidate should be disqualified by virtue of his religion.

The turmoil we refer to as "the sixties" actually lasted well into the 1970s. Its major flashpoints were the struggle for civil rights and the protests against the Vietnam War, but publication of Betty Friedan's *Feminine Mystique* in 1963 also led to a proliferation of "consciousness raising" groups and emergence of a full-fledged women's movement. Universities were under attack by everyone—students protesting the draft, parents horrified by the weird, atheistic ideas their children were suddenly spouting, and various defenders of the American way of life convinced that *academic* freedom was a liberal, elitist defense of communist propaganda in the classrooms. Protesters at the 1968 Democratic Convention were clubbed in the streets by Chicago police on national television. Students participating in an antiwar demonstration were shot and killed by National Guardsmen at Ohio's Kent State University. President Kennedy, Martin Luther King Jr., and Bobby Kennedy were all assassinated. The Civil Rights Act of 1964 was passed. Black separatists and Black Power advocates spurned King's nonviolence, while Students for a Democratic Society and the even more radical Weathermen engaged in everything from civil disobedience to robbery and murder in the name of radical ideologies. In 1969 New York police raided the Stonewall Inn, a gay bar, in what was a fairly common incident of official harassment of gays; this time, however, the gays and lesbians fought back—and gave birth to the gay civil rights movement.

Constant confrontation and disorder shattered the complacency that had characterized so much of middle-class life in the fifties. Television news and an evermore ubiquitous popular culture forced Americans to confront divisions and issues they preferred not to acknowledge. They did not need Bob Dylan to remind them that "the times they are a-changing."

> The high tide for liberalism and privacy came with *Roe v. Wade* in 1973, when the Supreme Court struck down state laws forbidding abortion. . . . With Roe the court had almost fully dismantled the

Victorian sexual regime—and roused a completely new era of hellfire politics. The long socially progressive swing ended, and the political pendulum headed back toward the politics of personal morality. (Morone 2003, 444)

The scene was set for the confrontation between Puritans and modernists that some call the *culture wars*.

Chapter 5

THE CULTURE WAR CONSIDERED

In 2003, when federal courts required the removal of the five-ton granite stone displaying the Ten Commandments erected at the Alabama Supreme Court by Judge Roy Moore, supporters rallying in support of Judge Moore were interviewed by television reporters. Virtually all of them denounced the removal of the monument as an infringement of their religious freedom. Lawyers and civil libertarians found this claim ludicrous; they saw Judge Moore as a theocrat attempting to use the authority of the state to endorse a particular religious perspective at the expense of all others—the antithesis of religious freedom. Few on either side were pandering or dissembling. They looked at the same basic facts—a five-ton stone with a carved replica of the Ten Commandments, located at the entrance to the State Supreme Court, and a federal order to remove it—but they interpreted what they saw in radically different ways. Both genuinely believed the other side was willfully ignoring plain truths: Moore's supporters were angry that federal courts would not recognize the fact that the United States was a Christian nation. Civil libertarians found Moore's position incredible in the face of the First Amendment's clear prohibition of religious establishments—a clarity which, needless to say, eluded Moore's defenders.

Such conflicts have become quite common, if not yet unremarkable. One reason is that by the end of the twentieth century, religious pluralism had come to mean something other than the essentially Protestant denominationalism that had made America seem so diverse a century earlier. The country had changed in many other ways as well. It was more densely populated—home to more than 281 million people, including nearly 35 million African Americans, 2.5 million Native Americans, over 10 million Asian Americans, and 15 million individuals of other, unspecified races. Nearly 7 million people checked the new census form box next to *multiracial*. Thirty-five million people, representing a variety of races, were ethnic Hispanics or Latinos. Forty-six million spoke a language other than English at home. Ninety-eight percent of all homes had at least one television set, 51 percent had a computer, and over 40 percent had Internet access. More people lived alone. The average household size had declined to just over two and a half persons, and the average family size to just over three. The population was also aging as a result of both longer life spans and fewer children. Americans were more mobile than ever. And while the census bureau does not collect information on citizens' religious affiliations, the American landscape in 2000 was overflowing with megachurches, cathedrals, mosques, synagogues, and temples. Diana Eck (2001) begins *A New Religious America* with descriptions of a mosque outside Toledo, a Hindu temple near Nashville, a Cambodian Buddhist temple near Minneapolis, and a Sikh gurdwara near Fremont, California.

Also much in evidence by the century's end was an ongoing debate over the causes and consequences of continued partisanship and rancor among policymakers, and increasing gridlock in Congress. The polarization of the American electorate was vividly displayed in the 2000 presidential election: Al Gore won the popular vote but George W. Bush—after an indeterminate Florida result followed by a month of political and legal wrangling culminating in a Supreme Court decision—won the electoral vote. The campaign had to a large extent been fought over a complex set of issues and attitudes that Americans had come to call the culture war.

NEW WORLDVIEWS ON THE BLOCK

Whatever the sources of an individual's framework of meaning, the social environment of the late twentieth century challenged them. It was no longer possible to withdraw into a remote community with like-minded companions and simply ignore those who were different. They lived next door, even in gated communities, and even if they lived half a globe away, television brought them into the living room. Unfamiliar music and a suggestive popular culture dominated an ever-more pervasive entertainment media. Government's growth and extended reach meant that congressional actions and Supreme Court decisions affected people in small towns and large metropolitan areas alike. Immigration and mobility meant that the farmer down the road in the most remote part of the heartland was as likely to speak with a foreign accent as a nasal twang. Americans had little choice but to confront "the other." Many found the process exhilarating; they embraced new foods, adopted new ideas, and welcomed new friends. Others found the changes disorienting, the new ideas troubling or terrifying, and the new people threatening.

Any discussion of the much debated culture war thesis has to begin with a reminder that "some twenty-first century Americans discuss Christian theology on Sunday morning and manipulate New Age crystals on Friday night" (Weaver-Zercher 2004, 34). In our typically American tendency to think in bipolar terms, to assign labels allowing us to establish neat, mutually exclusive ideological categories, we fail to appreciate the far more ambiguous and complicated realities of ordinary American lives. We also need to remind ourselves that, as important as the role of religion is and has been in the construction of our individual worldviews, "Not all cultural values, Durkheim notwithstanding, are religious values, and not all social groups can be defined by religious values" (Leege 1993, 10).

The current use of the term culture wars to describe Americans' divergent worldviews dates from 1991, when James Davison Hunter published *Culture Wars: The Struggle to Define America*. The book was billed as an effort to make sense "of the battles over the family, art, education, law and politics." In it, Hunter marshaled an impressive array of evidence of religiously rooted, incompatible worldviews, which he characterized as follows:

> I define cultural conflict very simply as political and social hostility rooted in different systems of moral understanding. The end to which these hostilities tend is the domination of one cultural and moral ethos over all others. Let it be clear, the principles and ideals that mark these competing systems of moral understanding are by no means trifling but always have a character of ultimacy to them. They are not merely attitudes that can change on a whim, but basic commitments and beliefs that provide a source of identity, purpose and togetherness for the people who live by them. . . .
>
> The divisions of political consequence today are not theological and ecclesiastic in character but the result of differing worldviews. That is to say, they no longer revolve around specific doctrinal issues or styles of religious practice and organization but around our most cherished assumptions about how to order our lives—our own lives and our lives together in this society. Our most fundamental ideas about who we are as Americans are now at odds. (Hunter 1991, 42)

Hunter noted that the differences are so profound that they extend to the legal processes Americans have established to mediate and adjudicate those differences—an observation amply supported by the escalating passions over the role of the judiciary and the appointment of judges. He also argued that the arguments over doctrine that had characterized traditional religious divisions had been eclipsed by a new alignment. The contenders in the culture wars were no longer Catholics versus Protestants versus Jews; rather, the orthodox members of each of these traditions were increasingly arrayed against the liberal and modernist adherents of those same traditions.

Hunter's thesis triggered its own war, albeit a scholarly one. Robert Wuthnow and David Leege have lent support to many of the book's key points, while Rhys Williams, N. J. Demarath III, and Kevin Slack, among others, have challenged Hunter's conclusions. Alan Wolfe, in *One America After All*, has argued that Americans share more values than the culture war thesis recognizes. Indeed, reading Wolfe's interviews with citizens from around the country, one cannot help but be struck by the number of people whose opinions cannot be neatly captured and categorized, and who hold to an unlikely mélange of cultural assumptions not far removed from the marriage of New Age crystals to Christian pieties. There is significant evidence to suggest that the real conflicts in the culture war are to be found within the psyches of ordinary Americans, who are neither religious fundamentalists nor unambiguous modernists. To the extent that interviews can provide a window into their worldviews, it would appear that the great majority of American worldviews include bits and pieces of different and often quite inconsistent perspectives. Americans have been deeply influenced by the antiauthoritarian "live and let live" ethic of the American Constitution. At the same time, a significant number also remain heavily in thrall to the nation's early Puritan moralism. The two traditions often coexist (more easily than we might imagine) within a single worldview.

To say that most of us are not culture warriors "suiting up" to fight for a rigid and all-encompassing ideology is not to negate the explanatory power of Hunter's conclusions, however. (In fairness, Hunter himself never suggested such a thing.) What most critics of the culture war thesis miss is the impact and true nature of Americans' conflicting conceptual paradigms. Hunter clearly understood that the attitudes he was describing were deeper than mere social and political opinions. Ironically, the very arguments offered by Hunter and his critics provide an excellent example of the paradigm phenomenon: by framing the inquiry in a particular way, each finds evidence supporting his hypothesis. This is emphatically not a criticism of any participant in this (or any) debate; it is an inevitable consequence of the way human cognition functions. (There is an old bit of folk doggerel that is particularly apt: "T'wixt optimist and pessimist, the difference is droll. The optimist sees the doughnut, the pessimist, the hole.")

The culture war thesis is essentially correct in describing profound differences that are politically and practically consequential. Those divisions are not differences of opinion, although they frequently lead to different opinions, and they are not simply the result of conflicting, conscious, and considered values. In much the same way that the Jewish and Christian respondents in the Miller study referenced earlier conceptualized the nature of homosexuality differently, partisans in the culture wars use different cognitive frameworks to organize reality, and they thus perceive and classify information differently. Examples are everywhere. In addition to the story about Roy Moore's supporters with which this chapter began, we might consider a much-discussed incident in the wake of the devastation in New Orleans following Hurricane Katrina. In two separate reports, television cameras caught individuals—in each case, a man and a woman—wading through waist-deep water holding food and water taken from a nearby convenience store. One couple was white, the other black. The voice-over described the white couple as desperate residents who had managed to forage food; the description accompanying the footage of the black couple described them as looters. It is possible, but unlikely, that the disparity in perception was a consequence of intentional, conscious racism. It is much more likely that the description of the black couple as "looters" was the result of those deeply embedded habits of the mind we call conceptual paradigms—"pre-judgments" based upon the perceived nature of reality.

If we believe, with the Puritans, that religious freedom means freedom to do what is right, we will see one reality. If we believe, with the Founders, that freedom is the right to choose our own moral ends free of government interference, we will see another. If we occupy a reality within which humans are innately sinful, we will worry about public policies that are too lenient; if we see poverty as evidence of moral dysfunction, we will evaluate social welfare programs from that perspective. These attitudes may or may not be explicit—even to the person holding them. (Racial stereotypes are notorious in this regard, as any pollster will attest.) We are rarely aware of the framing and filtering effects of our own cultural and religious assumptions, and we are generally astonished to encounter people who don't see evidence that we see so plainly. As a result, it is easy to believe that they are simply lying—or in the case of political candidates and elected officials, pandering.

AMERICAN POLITICAL CULTURE(S): VARIATIONS ON A THEME

The term *culture war* has become a convenient shorthand for these conflicts precisely because the differences we are fighting over are embedded in our cultures. Cultures are enormously complex, protean constructions, and it would be impossible to catalog all of the influences—economic, technological, and prudential, as well as religious—that shape their development over time. To complicate matters further, culture, like politics, inevitably "plays out" differently in different places. Despite our vastly increased mobility and interconnectedness, America shows no sign of developing a homogenized, unitary political culture any time soon. Regional, ethnic, and socioeconomic differences matter.

The term political culture can mean many things. Perhaps the most useful theoretical and descriptive analysis was constructed by Daniel Elazar in *The American Mosaic: The Impact of Space, Time and Culture on American Politics*. Reminding readers that political culture is by its nature fluid and evolving, a product of particular times, places, and cultures, Elazar painstakingly traced the movements of native and immigrant populations over the country's geography and history. He also mapped the substantial regional distinctions that remain. Elazar demonstrates that each of the three distinct subcultures he identified—Individualistic, Moralistic, and Traditionalistic—has remained tied to specific geographic regions of the country. It is important to note that, as he uses them, these descriptive terms do not translate into the conservative-moderate-liberal framework used in popular media, although there are some parallels, and that they also do not correspond to the distinction between Puritan and Enlightenment influences that were the subject of part 1 of this book.

An individualistic political culture, in Elazar's formulation, sees the polis as a type of marketplace. Individualistic cultures emphasize the centrality of private concerns, look askance at most government interventions, and see political activities primarily as transactions. Political success is achieved by mutual accommodation; the art of politics consists in giving the "buying public" what it wants. Political party regularity is highly valued, and the politics of the subculture are characterized by what Elazar calls a "quid pro quo" mentality, in which patronage is considered a natural attribute of political life.

Moralistic political cultures, on the other hand, see political activity as one of the ways in which communities attempt to construct the social good. Politics is considered noble, a *calling* rather than a job, and holding political office is viewed as public service, not as simply another way to make a living. In moralistic cultures, government is considered a "positive instrument" through which communitarian goals can be met, and party affiliation and regularity are accordingly less important than in individualistic states.

Traditionalistic political culture, in Elazar's formulation, is "rooted in an ambivalent attitude toward the marketplace coupled with a paternalistic and elitist conception of the commonwealth" (1994, 235). It functions to confine power to a relatively small group of people, and one's place in the power structure is determined through family and other ties to the elite. In traditionalist cultures, political systems tend to be dominated by a single party, and political leaders play a "conservative and custodial" role. (Elazar notes that traditionalist political culture, which was largely an outgrowth of the southern agrarian plantation system, has diminished and can be expected to continue to diminish.) While most states have elements of more than one political culture, Elazar finds predominantly moralistic cultures in the Northwest and several Western and upper Midwestern states (Utah, Oregon, Colorado, North Dakota, Minnesota, Michigan). States having a primarily individualistic character are relatively few and Midwestern (Illinois, Indiana, Ohio, Pennsylvania). States with traditionalist cultures are all Southern (Arkansas, Louisiana, Alabama, Mississippi, Tennessee, Georgia, South Carolina, Virginia). Other states exhibit varying mixtures of these three.

Elazar is focusing on political subcultures, albeit subcultures heavily influenced by religious migration patterns. But an analysis of purely religious regional differences finds a strikingly similar pattern. As Philip Goff has written,

> Despite the growing diversity of faiths, a stable regional map of religion marked the late twentieth century. If one looks at the largest religious groups (those with more than a million members) in the United States in 1990, a clear picture develops: eight "national religious families" (to use the terms of scholars William Newman and Peter Halvorson) dominate the three thousand or so Counties in the nation, and a second stratum of eight families exhibit regional strengths without the same national force. (2004, 355)

Goff has created a table showing the distribution of the national and multiregional religious families: America's 53 million Catholics are fairly evenly distributed among the four regions of the country (the Northeast, Midwest, Southeast, and West). Eleven million Methodists are also quite evenly distributed. Southern Baptists, numbering nearly 19 million, are present in 71 percent of the counties in the Northeast, 60 percent of those in the Midwest, 91 percent of those in the West, and in every single county in the South. None of the other national families—Evangelical Lutheran, Presbyterian (U.S.A.), Episcopalian, Assemblies of God, and Churches of Christ—are nearly as sizable as these top three; the next largest are the Evangelical Lutherans, with slightly over 5 million adherents (Goff 2004).

Other large religious groups tend to be strong in some areas of the country, and scattered—if present at all—in others. Although there are nearly 6 million American Jews, for example, there are synagogues in only one-quarter of the nation's counties, primarily in the Northeast. Mormonism is growing, but Mormons are still far more of a presence in Utah than elsewhere. And so on. Goff hastens to remind us that lack of substantial presence does not necessarily equate to lack of cultural impact.

> Likewise, there are culturally influential religious groups whose numbers do not grab the eye of researchers or the public. For example, even though the numbers of Hindus and Buddhists in the United States remain small compared with those of the large Christian denominations, many of their practices have entered the vernacular of American life. Often unaware of the roots of such practices, Americans will claim they earned good "karma" with an act of kindness, or learn to control their blood pressure through meditation, or relax driving home from work to the strains of New Age music.... Alongside these mixings, borrowings, and syntheses on the national level exists a curious "hard-shell" regionalism that continues to characterize religion in America. (357)

How does all this affect the broader conflict between Puritans and modernists? Individuals are inevitably influenced by the cultural norms of their immediate communities, whether they adopt or reject those norms. And while differences in regional political cultures result from the interaction of a host of historical, economic, racial, geographic, and other factors, the formative influence of dominant religious beliefs — and the reciprocal influence of political culture on religion — is undeniable. Just as the American historical experience has both shaped religion and been shaped by it, regional cultures both reflect and affect the religious worldviews of the individuals who live there.

Regional subcultures are not the only special environments exerting a significant influence on those who are part of them. Racial and ethnic communities also have cultures that exhibit and transmit their unique histories and traditions. Jews draw distinctive lessons about the importance of civil liberties and the separation of church and state from their historic experience of marginalization and a rabbinic tradition emphasizing ethics and social justice. Latino Catholics are more likely to be

Democratic than other Catholics, less likely to be concerned with environmental issues, and considerably more likely to believe that government should do more to assist minorities. Among African Americans, the cultural centrality of the black church has produced a subculture that borrows from traditional Protestantism and the larger culture, but is distinctive from both. In order to understand the contemporary policy preferences of black Protestants, especially the hypothesized "growing conservatism" of some black voters, it is necessary to recognize that there are two traditions of black ministry, liberation theology and prosperity gospel. These traditions "have very different notions of Christ, and therefore exert different influences on political action" (Harris-Lacewell 2004, 1). Harris-Lacewell describes liberation theology as a belief in a black Christ, one who is on the side of those struggling against racism and marginalization. In marked distinction to that perspective, she says, the Christ of prosperity gospel is concerned primarily with securing the financial freedom of his people, Christ "as an investment strategy and personal life coach" (2004.) Unsurprisingly, the first view promotes political and social activism, while the second discourages it (and marshals what activism does occur on behalf of different priorities). Through most of African-American history, liberation theology has been dominant, if not hegemonic, in the black community. While the influence of prosperity gospel is growing, it continues to be a distinctly minor thread in the overall black American experience. When political scientists describe the outlier politics of black Americans, they are largely describing the effects of liberation theology.

Researchers have amply documented significant differences of opinion and political behavior between black and white Protestants. Fifty-six percent of white evangelical Protestants (and seventy percent of traditionalist evangelicals) are Republicans, compared to just 11 percent of black Protestants (Green 2004), Twenty-nine percent of evangelical and mainline Protestants support additional government spending, compared to forty-five percent of black Protestants. Twenty-six percent of evangelicals and 33 percent of mainline Protestants support the substitution of life imprisonment for the death penalty; for black Protestants, the number is 49 percent. History and experience matter, theologically and politically. So does geography.

THINKING IN RED AND BLUE

Americans are accustomed to seeing regional political differences reflected in red and blue on televised election-night maps. Political scientists and opinion researchers have mapped similar differences in political and policy preferences of religious adherents. In *The Diminishing Divide: Religion's Changing Role in American Politics*, Andrew Kohut, John Green, Scott Keeter, and Robert Toth examined a wealth of existing polling data in an effort to trace the connections between religious beliefs and political policy positions. In the introduction to their study, they take note of American exceptionalism.

> Whereas most modern, technologically advanced democracies have low levels of religiosity, America is both a highly modern and deeply religious nation. Indeed, since the beginning of its history, America has been defined at once by market economics, technical progress, and religious faith—a peculiar combination. . . . This nexus of faith and freedom has helped sustain a vigorous individualism and moral self-restraint; it has also produced bitter disputes over individual rights. Historian Richard Swierenga captures this aspect of the American ethos well: "People act politically, economically, and socially in keeping with their ultimate beliefs. Their values, mores, and actions, whether in the polling booth, on the job, or at home, are an outgrowth of the god or gods they hold at the center of their being." (Kohut et al. 2000, 12)

While their conclusions provide plenty of evidence that America's religious citizens are anything but monolithic on public policy issues, it was when they looked at so-called social issues—abortion, gay rights, availability of sexually explicit materials, the role of women, and so forth—that they found the greatest disparities among adherents of different religious traditions. Those they categorized as "committed evangelicals" (unfortunately, they did not distinguish between fundamentalist and other evangelical traditions) were "by far the most conservative group in the population" (38). Other evangelicals, committed mainline Protestants, and committed Roman Catholics were also more conservative than the American average. Jews were the most socially liberal group surveyed, although other mainline Protestants and secular respondents were also significantly more liberal than the average American.

> Committed evangelicals are not only more conservative than other citizens with respect to sexual and cultural issues but are also much more likely to say that these issues are important to them. . . . It is the combination of strong conservative opinion and high salience—a strong sense that social, sexual, and cultural issues are important in comparison with other issues—that makes committed evangelicals a powerful political force in the realm of social, sexual and cultural policy. (38)

The conclusions drawn by the authors of *The Diminishing Divide* are consistent with those of other researchers. Other survey researchers, like John Green (2004), have taken the additional step of distinguishing between traditional and more liberal evangelicals, which gives a considerably more nuanced picture of those who make up that category. Evangelicals are by no means as monolithic as popular opinion suggests, and the lack of differentiation in many studies of this sort tends to blur the very real differences among them. It is also important to recognize—and question—the assumptions underlying the definition of religious commitment used by many researchers, including Kohut and his colleagues. In this approach, individuals are deemed to be more religiously committed based upon the frequency of their church attendance, prayer, and other explicitly religious behaviors. It is equally possible, however, that these criteria are evidence of one particular type of commitment, a commitment to traditional religious norms—that is, to a particular idea of what religion is—rather than a measure of the importance or saliency of belief. Nancy Ammerman (1997), among others, has suggested that those less likely to score high on such measures, those she calls "Golden Rule Christians," may be just as committed to their religious perspectives as the more traditional churchgoers are to theirs. Similarly, very secularized Americans are frequently passionate about social or political beliefs that do not appear religious to researchers measuring religious commitment by the frequency of prayer or attendance at religious services.

Americans have a regrettable—and demonstrably inaccurate—tendency to equate religious commitment with orthodoxy and measurable religious activity. But the issue of salience—the degree to which particular beliefs are experienced as vitally important—that Kohut and his colleagues highlight and Ammerman illuminates, is significant, and it points to a problem repeatedly encountered by opinion pollsters: it is relatively simple to measure general public reaction to everything from a policy proposal to a new soft drink. It is much more difficult to measure the depth and intensity of that opinion, the degree to which any particular issue is seen as centrally important, or salient, to the respondent. But without that information, efforts at public information (i.e., "would you support policy X if you knew Y?") or marketing ("be sure to ask for Fizzy Cola") are likely to miss their mark.

In *The Nature of Prejudice*, Gordon Allport noted the importance of salience to prospects for eliminating bigotry. He distinguished between culturally conditioned, widely accepted, "everybody knows" attitudes about minorities—the reflexive expectation that Jews will be sharp businesspeople, or that blacks will be lazy—and the far more visceral hatreds that characterize (thankfully) a much smaller number of people. Allport believed that the former group could be educated to see past their casually adopted, culturally sanctioned attitudes. Those whose worldviews were rigid, however, who were so emotionally invested in a particular view of reality that the loss of any one piece of it would be experienced as a threat to their very identity, were beyond reach.[1] The

---

[1] In *The Paranoid Style in American Politics*, Richard Hofstadter describes just this phenomenon. Differentiating between various nineteenth-century movements and the right wing of his own day, Hofstadter wrote, "The spokesmen of those earlier movements felt they stood for causes and personal types that were still in possession of their country—that they were fending off threats to a still-established way of life. But the modern right wing, as Daniel Bell has

individual who has been socialized into a belief that is accepted but not particularly salient—that is, an individual whose worldview does not depend upon the continued plausibility of that particular belief—will change it in response to sufficient experience inconsistent with its validity. A white person who works alongside blacks comes to realize that black people are pretty much like white ones; men who work with women learn to regard them as friends and coworkers, not just sexual objects or mother figures; parents who discover that their son is gay rethink their attitudes about homosexuality. Individuals for whom such beliefs are central, however, will experience no such paradigm shift. They are more likely to look for, and find, evidence confirming their prior beliefs. Allport was a social psychologist, and he was describing what most of us would consider pathology; nevertheless, his insight into the nature of salience helps us understand not just those on the radical fringes of our political world, but the sometimes bewildering disconnect between what is reported to be majority public opinion and subsequent political action.

Salience also explains why so many people vote in ways that are contrary to their own economic interests. Some rational choice economists may dismiss such behavior as the result of inadequate economic information, but seasoned politicians understand that self-interest involves more than economic well-being. The beliefs that lead people to do volunteer work, to donate to charitable causes, or to work for political change, are rarely explicable solely—or even primarily—in economic terms. Protecting the integrity of our worldviews will generally be more salient than voting our pocketbooks.

POLICY IMPLICATIONS

What does all of this—or any of it—have to do with any specific American policy? How does it help us understand why so many Americans are in prison, or why America withdrew from the Kyoto

---

put it, feels dispossessed: America has largely been taken away from them and their kind, though they are determined to try to repossess it. . . . " (*Harper's Magazine*, November 1964, 77–86).

accords? How do these religious and cultural attitudes manifest themselves in the details of particular laws? To ask that question another way, how do our conceptual paradigms and their saliency translate into legislative and administrative decisions? In part 3, we will examine specific policy areas in an effort to answer that question, but before we turn to those specifics, a few general observations—and cautions—are in order.

It should be self-evident that the worldviews of those individuals we elect or appoint to actually make and implement America's laws will be reflected in our laws. As George Appenzeller has noted, "In a democracy, the context of those in power is the context of policy and policy implementation" (2004). It is arguably the recognition of that fact that leads voters to focus on the character of candidates—what is really important to this person? How does she define the common good? What can we learn about his fundamental commitments from his past activities?

Beyond that obvious connection, and beyond the different policy commitments that arise out of our different views of reality, we need to recognize that our worldviews determine the sorts of political activities we undertake and our methods of engaging the political system and other stakeholders. Research suggests that people socialized into different religious cultures approach the policy process not just with different goals, but with different strategies: some will see it as a bargaining arena, others as an opportunity to co-opt opposing viewpoints, and still others as an opportunity for coalitionbuilding (Kanagy 1992). What we choose to do, and how we choose to do it, are both functions of our cognitive paradigms.

Furthermore, our religiously rooted worldviews shape the context within which we develop particular positions, by determining our attitudes toward the sources and legitimacy of authority, the proper uses of power, the nature of law, and the appropriate relationship between the coercive mechanisms of the state and the behavior of individual citizens. As we have seen, our religious roots affect our definition of liberty; researchers suggest that they also affect our willingness to extend civil liberties to others (Reimer and Park 2001). Our arguments about social justice and inclusion are almost inevitably theological. As one scholar, reflecting on the theological roots of secular policy language, has put it,

> For many groups this commitment to inclusion is not a sign of tepid faith or an unwillingness to disclose one's beliefs to others, but rather reflects a principled point of theology. Though different religious traditions vary in their approach to politics, a common idea behind the commitment to inclusion is that when God created the world and all that is in it, politics and political authority were instituted for the good of all persons, not merely the elect. The domain of politics, both as to goals and practices, is accessible to all persons through reason and worldly prudence, not revelation. Martin Luther perhaps best exemplified this attitude when he claimed it was better to be ruled by a wise pagan than a foolish Christian. (Bailey 2002, 251)

As we explore in part 3 the theologically based assumptions driving specific policy debates, we need to keep in mind Hunter's insight about the non-doctrinal nature of our clashing worldviews. If we look at contemporary political disputes as reflections of a division between religious and secular Americans, we will miss the real nature of these arguments. The most acute political divisions may be those within religious traditions, and those debates are increasingly being conducted in quite explicitly religious terms. A few examples will illustrate this. In June 2005 the National Council of the Churches of Christ sent out a fundraising letter taking to task what they characterized as the "hubris of easy certainty" displayed by fundamentalist Christians, and arguing—based upon "reading the same Bible, studying the same parables and praying to the same God"—for progressive public policy solutions. Former presidential candidate Gary Hart, a graduate of Yale Divinity School and Bethany Nazarene College, wrote an op-ed for *The New York Times* (November 8, 2004) in which he argued for "the duty of Christians, based solidly on Jesus' teachings, to minister to the less fortunate," and asserted that "Liberals are not against religion. They are against hypocrisy, exclusion and judgmentalism."

J. Brent Walker, Executive Director of the Baptist Joint Committee, began an article for *Liberty Magazine* (May/June 2003) by plaintively asking, "Where have all the Baptists gone?" Walker revisited the historic commitment of Baptists to strict separation of church and state, and argued for fidelity to their insights about the nature of religious freedom. He ended the article by regretting that Baptists fighting to preserve that heritage often find themselves battling other Baptists. Indeed, it is virtually impossible to pick up a newspaper or magazine, or turn on a radio, without encountering arguments between Americans arguing for very different policies based upon the same religious—generally Christian and Protestant—traditions.

Just as we should not mistake the conflict between worldviews for a showdown between the believers and the heathens, however, we must not lose sight of the extent to which religiously rooted paradigms and culturally transmitted ways of perceiving reality affect the policy commitments of even the most secular among us. And we must also be constantly mindful of the nonlinear, evolving nature of both our general culture and our religious worldviews. Alan Wolfe reminds us of the reciprocal influence between American culture and American religion. "Religion is not a countercultural force resisting the dominant culture" (2005). In the words of Jonathan Zimmerman, "America's Christian fundamentalists do combine their religion and their politics—and the fusion has made them more humane, tolerant and inclusive." At the very least, they have adopted the language of equal rights and liberties—and language is consequential (2001).

Finally, we must also recognize the importance of what Robert Kuttner has called the "multiple, overlapping communities" that have always characterized America.

> Back in the 1950s, political scientists celebrated America for its "pluralism." That meant people had multiple, cross-cutting identities. Maybe you were a Catholic and also a trade unionist, a sport fisherman, a member of a veterans' group, and an engaged PTA parent in a multi-ethnic neighborhood. No single identity absolutely defined you.

. . . Why was this special? Because it created multiple, overlapping communities and prevented the cultural or political absolutism that plagued most societies. It wove tolerance and political suppleness into the fabric of American democracy. (2004)

Because individual worldviews will ultimately be the product of each individual's intellectual capacities, experiences, hopes and fears, tolerance for ambiguity, and all of the other imponderables that make humans unique, any exploration of the multiple ways in which our religiously rooted worldviews affect our policy choices can illuminate, but never fully explain, that process. With that caveat, we now turn to an exploration of Americans' policy disputes.

PART III

Paradigm and Policy: Now You See It, Now You Don't

Chapter 6

THE USUAL SUSPECTS

Christopher Mooney has offered an insight critical to our understanding of contemporary culture war debates: morality policies are "no less than legal sanctions of right and wrong, validations of particular sets of fundamental values" (2001, 3). He also highlights a factor essential to understanding both the reason particular conflicts emerge when they do and the reason they arouse such passions: it is only when values are threatened that they need to be defended—i.e., codified and thus reaffirmed. It is only when cultural shifts threaten the taken-for-granted nature of their worldviews that people find it necessary to fight for their continued dominance.

> And when threats to basic values do occur, they cut so deeply into the core of a society that their codification appears imperative, literally, to "save the world" as it has been known. These values define not only who each individual is and his or her place in society but also the society itself. If these values change, then society changes. Nothing is certain anymore. It is as if Newton's Third law of motion was suddenly repealed. (4)

In many of the policy debates we will consider in part 3, the ways in which our conflicting worldviews predispose us to support particular policy choices are widely influential, but largely unseen; there is no readily recognizable religious dimension to the questions under consideration. In other areas, however, religiously rooted worldviews are more obvious—sometimes glaringly so—but highly salient to far fewer people. These are the so-called morality or culture war issues—abortion, gay rights, prayer in public school, stem cell research, sex education, the propriety of teaching creationism or intelligent design, alongside evolution in science classes—for some people, even smoking or recycling. These issues engage partisans' passions in ways that economic or environmental debates seldom do. The intensity of these conflicts generates considerable attention from lawmakers and the media, obscuring the fact that the interest groups involved are not representative of the far more complex views on these matters held by most Americans.

Civil libertarians are often bemused by American Puritans' unflagging determination to outlaw sin, and liberal theologians are fond of pointing out that coerced piety is by definition inauthentic. Policy scholars write earnest treatises on the ineffectiveness—and frequently, the counterproductive nature—of attempts to legislate private, consensual behaviors. Lawyers worry that—because such laws are largely unenforceable and widely ignored—the passage of measures that are largely symbolic encourages contempt for the rule of law. However true such observations may be, they miss the essential nature of these conflicts. Rather than efforts to actually control the individual beliefs or behaviors involved, these highly fraught campaigns are best understood as efforts to control the cultural narrative, to ensure that a particular worldview is a privileged feature of America's "legitimizing mythology." In the United States, law has become the preeminent arena for cultural competition (Mazur 1999).

In his classic study of the American temperance movement, Joseph Gusfield noted that policy differences between ethnic and religious groups have assumed a greater importance in the United States than in Europe partly because American economic divisions have been less dramatic. Gusfield characterized those cultural disputes as one way through which a cultural group acts to preserve, defend, or enhance the dominance and prestige of its own style of living within the total society. In the set of religious, ethnic, and cultural communities that have made up American society, drinking (and abstinence) has been one of the significant consumption habits distinguishing one subculture from another. It has been one of the major characteristics through which Americans have defined their own cultural commitments. (1963, 3)

It is the contested nature of these values, the fact that so many Americans do not share them (or even actively oppose them), that creates the urgency, the felt need to enlist the power of the state to affirm them.

This insight helps to explain why antagonists take positions that otherwise seem frustrating, illogical, and inexplicable. When a proponent of legal recognition of same-sex marriages asks opponents for any "real" evidence that such recognition will harm or otherwise affect heterosexual marriages, he or she will be mystified when opponents respond with variants of "It was Adam and Eve, not Adam and Steve." Those who are outraged by the same-sex challenge to traditional marriage see the threat as so self-evident as to require no justification, and are equally mystified that others do not recognize its world-destabilizing consequences. Pointing to the relatively late emergence, historically, of what we now call "traditional" marriage, documenting the prevalence of different familial forms in other societies, or challenging the highly selective nature of the immorality chosen for legal disenfranchisement will all be dismissed as irrelevant—not because these observations are untrue, although their validity may be challenged, but because they are not what the argument is really about.

Nonactivist participants in policy debates over moral behaviors may, of course, have other reasons for preferring one result to another, depending upon the issue, and the particular experiences, interests, and attitudes of the individual. Public policy texts acknowledge the importance of culturally conditioned worldviews, but also recognize a variety of other factors that will affect policy preferences: the institutional context of our constitutional democracy, economic interests, geographic and demographic influences, and of course, ideology. It would be misleading to ignore the importance of such factors, just as it would be inaccurate to suggest that the more extreme positions considered in this chapter represent the views of most Americans. For the "culture warriors," however, what is clearly at stake is the threat to important and highly salient elements of their religiously rooted worldviews.

The nature of religiously rooted paradigms also helps explain the ferocity and corresponding lack of civility that characterize these particular battles. In a recent book, Jonathan Fox (2004) argues forcefully that conflicts involving religion—whether those conflicts occur between religions, or between or within denominations—have a higher likelihood of escalating into quite bruising battles. The particular faith involved did not seem to be a factor; it was the religious character of the conflict that caused the escalation. This conclusion is entirely consistent with what we know of conceptual paradigms and peoples' behaviors when their most fundamental commitments are challenged.

All legal and policy arguments are ultimately disputes over problem identification; it is a truism of legal education that "he who frames the issue wins the debate." Our paradigms dictate the frames we each employ. It is not an exaggeration to say that when worldviews clash the combatants are fighting in different wars. The antichoice demonstrator is engaged in saving innocent lives; the pro-choice activist is fighting for separation of church and state and for women's right to self-determination. The anti-death-penalty crusader is protecting the sanctity of life; the supporter of the death penalty is protecting civilization from predators and reinforcing the morality of personal responsibility. These partisans are not engaged in a policy debate; they are arguing past, not with, each other.

Finally, these disputes are so passionate not just because the perceived threat is to a highly salient aspect of the culture warrior's worldview, but because the terms of the debate are seemingly so simple. Tax policy, monetary policy, environmental policy—these arguments involve the arcana of technical and scientific (or pseudoscientific) disciplines. But everyone can have an opinion on moral issues, and at times it seems as if everyone does. The Protestant Reformation legitimized an unmediated encounter with the biblical text, and the consequence has been at least one nation in which virtually everyone feels competent to interpret its plain meaning. Scholars and theologians may find subtlety and complexity in religious dogma, but they have only the authority they can earn in America's robust religious marketplace, where they must compete with vendors of far simpler (and thus, for many, more satisfying) spiritual goods.

AMERICA'S RELIGIOUS WARRIORS: PRODUCTS OF EVOLUTION

The unfortunate tendency of the media to accept uncritically the claim that people of faith can all be found opposing stem cell research or gay rights does a real disservice to the very diverse religious perspectives involved. The constant reference to those on the traditionalist side of the culture wars as evangelicals is equally unfortunate. While the most conservative religionists may be evangelical, many evangelicals are not religious fundamentalists. Furthermore, not all of America's culture warriors are Protestant—or even Christian. Increasingly, as Hunter noted, they represent the orthodox elements of Judaism and Catholicism as well.

In a recent essay (2005), Arthur Schlesinger Jr. remarked upon a distinction drawn by the great Protestant theologian Reinhold Niebuhr between those who take the Bible seriously, and those who take it literally—a distinction that is particularly apt in this context. Respected religious historian George Marsden has attributed the fracturing of America's dominant evangelical coalition in the early twentieth century to the "vast cultural changes of the era from the 1870s to the 1920s," a period also chronicled by Richard Hofstadter in *The Age of Reform*. The ensuing crisis caused evangelicals to split into two factions, modernist and fundamentalist. "[B]y the 1960s, 'fundamentalist' usually meant separatists and no longer included the many conservatives in mainline denominations" (Marsden 1991, 3). By far the most important cause of this schism was Darwinian evolution, and failure to recognize the centrality of evolution in particular and science in general to the opposing worldviews that emerged is failure to understand the essence of today's culture wars. As Mark Lilla has written, "'Liberal' in the theological sense means several things. It includes a critical approach to Scripture as a historical document, an openness to modern science, a turn from public ritual to private belief and a search for common ground in the Bible's moral message" (2005, 39). In the wake of Darwin, liberal, modernist Christians found that they could integrate science and religion in their worldviews by taking the Bible seriously, but not literally; fundamentalist believers in the literal truth of the Bible experienced science, especially evolution, as an assault on the very idea of God. "The central symbol organizing fears over the demise of American culture became biological evolution" (Marsden 1991, 59). Marsden reports that between 1878 and 1906, nearly every major Protestant denomination experienced at least one heresy trial, usually of a seminary professor. After their humiliation at the Scopes trial, fundamentalists retreated from public visibility, but they did not change their views. They nursed their grievances and regrouped, spending their energies on evangelizing and the building of a formidable grassroots institutional network. In the 1980s, they emerged to engage the secular and modern worldviews that are so threatening to their reality.

While some orthodox Jews and conservative Catholics make common cause with fundamentalist Protestants in this power struggle, the worldviews of many other American religions have not developed within the "either-or" paradigm that creates such a dilemma for literalist Christians. Although Islam betrays many of the same internal divisions that characterize contemporary Christianity, with more modernist adherents accepting biological evolution and fundamentalist Muslims arguing against it, other religions have had markedly less difficulty accommodating scientific discoveries. Judaism has a long history of *pilpul*, or parsing, interpreting, and debating the underlying meanings of texts of holy documents. With respect to Genesis, warnings against literal interpretation go back as far as the twelfth century, when Maimonides published his *Guide for the Perplexed*. While there is no one official Jewish position on science or any other subject, most contemporary rabbis take a position similar to that of liberal Protestantism—that is, science deals with material fact, while religion deals with values.

Buddhism is, if anything, even more open to scientific discoveries; a recent book by the Dalai Lama contains the following observation: "My confidence in venturing into science lies in my basic belief that as in science so in Buddhism, understanding the nature of reality is pursued by means of critical investigation: if scientific analysis were conclusively to demonstrate certain claims in Buddhism to be false, then we must accept the findings of science and abandon those claims" (2005, Prologue). This approach simply does not work for biblical literalists. As one Lutheran pastor has written, "As soon as I read what leading evolutionists actually said, I realized that there is no room for my truce in the world of neo-Darwinian materialism, no matter how many of us think we can be theistic evolutionists" (Mees 2005, 1).

In 1968 some forty years after the Scopes trial, the Supreme Court finally considered whether school boards could constitutionally outlaw the teaching of evolution in public school classrooms. The court unanimously held they could not, in *Epperson v. Arkansas*. The decision held that using state power to advance the beliefs of conservative Christians ran afoul of the Establishment Clause. In response, literalists adopted the language of science and developed a theory they dubbed "creationism" or "creation science." Several school corporations subsequently required that science classrooms offer balanced treatment of the two scientific theories—evolution and creationism. In 1987 the Supreme Court decided *Edwards v. Aguillard*, involving one such balanced treatment law that had been adopted in Louisiana. The Court ruled 7–2 that the law had a religious, rather than a secular purpose, and thus violated the Establishment Clause. (Justices Scalia and Rehnquist, the dissenters, opined that there was insufficient evidence on the issue of intent, and that the question whether creationism was science was for the legislature to determine.)

More recently, the conflict has been recast once again, with an effort to promote the new scientific theory of intelligent design—a theory that most scientists, religious or not, adamantly reject as nonscientific. They ground that rejection in the nature of science. Science—as opposed to art, literature, religion, music, and other ways of understanding the human condition—is based upon testable, empirical evidence. In other words, if something cannot be subjected to experimentation and observation, it cannot be categorized as part of the discipline we call science. Many deeply religious scientists are quick to point out that excluding a theory from the category *science* does not necessarily mean it is less true, or less meaningful. It simply means that, by definition, it is not part of the conceptual paradigm we call science.

Proponents of intelligent design assert that evolution is simply a theory, and they point to examples of things that the theory does not explain as evidence that it is fundamentally flawed. Scientists respond that science (like all disciplines) has its own vocabulary: when scientists talk about the *theory* of evolution, they are not using the term as it is commonly used, to refer to a hypothesis—or educated guess—about the subject. In science, the word *theory* means something else entirely. Science starts with hypotheses, or educated guesses, and after enough facts have been gathered and empirical testing done, those hypotheses are either confirmed or discarded. A framework constructed from confirmed hypotheses is called a theory. Every theory will be subject to "tweaking" as new facts are found and incorporated, and answers to previously unanswered questions are found, but the outlines will remain fixed, because the theoretical framework did not emerge until many original hypotheses had been exhaustively tested and verified. This empirical testing process is the *scientific method*. Evolution is a theory in the sense that it is constructed from hypotheses that have been tested and verified; it forms the conceptual framework that has made genetics, biochemistry, neurobiology, physiology, ecology, and other biological disciplines possible. As one columnist has written, "Without the biological advances made possible by the theory of evolution, diseases would still be treated with leeches and incantations" (Kennedy 2005, 12).

Liberal Christians have resolved the problem of faith coexisting with evolution by altering their conceptual paradigms and categorizing religion and science as separate disciplines addressing different truths. They note that faith is by definition the acceptance of assertions that cannot by their very nature be proved. The fact that God cannot be taken into a laboratory and verified is thus not a statement about the truth or falsity of claims for God's existence but a recognition that such claims are simply not subject to experiment or observation. Like scientists, religious modernists see creationism and intelligent design as religious doctrines. They can be taught in classes on comparative religion, but since they do not fall into the category *science*, they cannot be taught as science—just as the story of David and Goliath can be taught as literature, but not as history. Biblical literalists are outraged by this approach, because their conceptual paradigms do not include separate categories for biblical and scientific truth. In the literalist worldview, belief in God simply cannot coexist with the belief that humans are products of natural selection. They also see labeling only one type of truth as scientific as a way of privileging of that category—as bestowing a social "stamp of approval" on the accepted nature of the facts described. The liberal Christian belief that an omnipotent God could easily have chosen to work through an evolutionary process is not consistent with a literal reading of Genesis, and the suggestion that the latter be taught in comparative religion classes is tantamount to an admission that its literal truth is contested. There is no middle ground. In the words of a popular bumpersticker, "God wrote it, Jesus died for it, I believe it."

If the debate over evolution has been seminal, a survey of other culture war issues gives evidence of the continuing divide between those who might be considered pro-science, Enlightenment modernists and those who are biblical literalists, or fundamentalists. While such a crude division clearly does a disservice to the nuances among members of both categories, it can nevertheless provide a useful insight into the very different worldviews of the combatants. We might think of fundamentalists as the descendants of the Planting Fathers and modernists as heirs of the Founding Fathers.

HOMOSEXUALITY

If Darwinian evolution represents the most unbridgeable fault line between the worldviews of fundamentalists and moderns, attitudes about homosexuality are probably a close second. Arguments over gay rights also offer an example of the interrelated nature of the opposing worldviews involved: those who are members of secular or religiously liberal communities consider evidence of the changing nature of the workplace and the biological aptitudes of men and women, and adjust gender role expectations accordingly. They consider recent scientific confirmation of biological differences between straight and gay men, and between lesbian and straight women, and emerging theories about the genetic component of sexual orientation, and readjust their stereotypes about homosexuality. Modernists evaluate emerging science within the libertarian and constitutional framework of equal rights under the law: if gender and skin color are immutable, if people do not choose their sexual orientation, on what basis does society penalize people for such identities? If competent adults engage in consensual sexual behaviors, they harm no one; there is thus no logical reason to outlaw miscegenation or homosexual sodomy, or to deny gays and lesbians the same civil rights protections against discrimination in housing or employment accorded to women and racial minorities, or to refuse to extend to homosexual couples the legal benefits (1008, by one count) that accompany state recognition of marriage. Despite the considerable and understandable discomfort attendant to any radical social change (particularly acute when the subject involves sexual behavior) a substantial number of mainstream Christian denominations, businesses, and other organizations have concluded that these traditional attitudes are unfair and should be modified. A 2004 poll found that a quarter of straight voters support same-sex marriage and another 35 percent support recognition of civil unions (Egan and Sherrill 2005). Clearly, the taken-for-granted nature of marriage, and the taken-for-granted definition of deviance are undergoing challenge if not redefinition.

At the extremes, fundamentalist Christians have responded to this cultural shift with rhetoric that seems shrill and hysterical to modernist ears. Gays are accused of sin and abnormality, of perversion and pathology. Groups like the 700 Club, the Christian Coalition, the American Family Association, and the Family Research Council fill mailings and Web sites with warnings: all gays are pedophiles, who menace children and want to abolish laws setting the age of consent. The Family Research Council has published a tract claiming that "Militant homosexuality is fundamentally opposed to religion, family and anything that presupposes a natural moral order, a transcendent God or something else higher than ourselves" (Schwalm 1998). Another publication warns that all gays want to outlaw religion. Pat Robertson has accused gays of intentionally giving churchgoers AIDS.

A pamphlet issued by a group called Wisconsin Christians United is particularly interesting, because it directly addresses, in question-and-answer format, the concerns about antigay discrimination that bother many conservative Christians who have adopted elements of the Enlightenment worldview. To the question "Don't individuals have a constitutional right to engage in homosexual practices," the pamphlet answers "No! There is no constitutional right to commit homosexual acts, regardless of what any liberal court might claim." The text proceeds to defend this position with references to "Nature's God"—and assertions that "sodomy and other sexual perversions clearly violate both God's laws of nature and His written law." To the question "Aren't homosexuals born that way?" the response is that every "unbiased" [sic] study says otherwise. The answer to the quintessentially libertarian question "What's wrong with a 'live and let live' attitude" is that "depravity always begets more depravity," buttressed with statistics purporting to demonstrate the overwhelmingly criminal nature of the homosexual population. A particularly revealing passage occurs in answer to the question "I am against the 'special rights' homosexuals demand, but I do not believe that homosexuals should be discriminated against. Isn't that a proper stand on this issue?" The answer: "No. If citizens are not allowed to discriminate in any way with regard to out-of-the closet homosexuals, then there is no basis for denying those involved in sexual perversion the right to adopt and teach children, marry one another, be policemen or medics, serve in the armed forces, be elected officials and judges, work for you and rent from you." As one legal scholar has noted, these arguments result from the use of strikingly different frames of reality. The anti-gay framework begins with the assumption that heterosexuality and homosexuality constitute essential (but not innate) human difference, and incorporate different ideas about God and nature, the family, and the significance of reproduction. The lack of reproductive capacity, in particular, is used to establish the defective and unnatural nature of homosexual unions (Battalora 2005).

The debate over gay rights is very much a part of the Christian nation paradigm that is being challenged from all sides: the dramatic growth in America's religious diversity, the pervasiveness of a popular culture portraying gay citizens and others in ways inimical to fundamentalist values, the increasing number of businesses with explicitly nondiscriminatory employment and benefit policies, the decline of the traditional family (where the male was the breadwinner and the female was the homemaker), and the continued privatization of religious belief. As liberal Christian denominations have moved (often haltingly and painfully) toward greater acceptance of gays and lesbians, other religious traditions have contributed quite different beliefs about the relationship between morality and human sexuality to the debate. While the Dalai Lama has expressed somewhat less accepting views, Theravada Buddhists believe that peoples' sexual orientations, like their races and genders, are innate, and that sexual behavior—heterosexual or homosexual—within committed relationships is moral. Zen Buddhists make no distinction between heterosexual and homosexual behavior, defining morality as nonexploitative, mutually loving, and supportive relationships. Traditional Native American groups hold homosexuals, who often become tribal shamans, in high regard. Unitarian-Universalism and Reform Judaism endorse committed same-sex relationships. On the other hand, the generally proscience Baha'i's condemn homosexuality, and Islam, like Christianity, divides along fundamentalist-liberal lines. America's increasingly "wired" populace and interrelated communications systems have increased general knowledge of these non-

Christian religious positions, further challenging the taken-for-granted nature of fundamentalist beliefs, and the fundamentalist insistence that all genuine people of faith share common absolutes.

CHURCH AND STATE

Inevitably, morality issues lead back to what may be the most profound distinction between the visions of the Planting and Founding Fathers — their diametrically different conceptions of the proper role of government. Put in its most absolute terms, the distinction is between those who view government as a mechanism through which a moral, chosen community builds a "City on the Hill" and those who believe the primary task of government is to ensure a civic order within which individual liberty can thrive. Is liberty the right to do what is morally correct? If so, who gets to decide which behaviors are morally correct? Or is liberty the right to act in accordance with one's individual conscience, free of state interference, so long as one does no harm to the person or property of a nonconsenting other? If that is the proper understanding of liberty, how shall harm to others be defined, and by whom? Ultimately, it is this conflict that plays out in our most passionate political disputes — over abortion, stem cell research, prayer in public school classrooms, and the inclusion of *under God* in recitations of the Pledge of Allegiance. This fundamental, normative division over the role of the state and the nature of liberty is at the very core of Americans' incommensurate worldviews, and it triggers deep divisions over Supreme Court decisions and the selection of judges.

Just as theologically rooted differences motivate support for or opposition to specific public policies, there are deeply held doctrinal differences over the nature and proper role of the state, the nature of law, and the primacy that should be accorded to legal structures and systems. Some religious traditions make law a central religious category; others have defined themselves in opposition to the worldview of law (Dane 1996, 114) Judaism, Islam, and Hinduism are among the former; Pauline Christianity and Confucianism among the latter. Traditions differ also on the relative weight to accord secular authority. "John Calvin argued that civil government was a response to human evil, designed to protect church and society and establish general tranquility." While the Kingdom of God came first, law was a necessity and a close second. Antinomians like Anne Hutchinson, on the other hand, believed that the Gospel freed Christians from required obedience to any law, even scriptural law, and that salvation was to be attained solely through faith and divine grace. Dane suggests that the contemporary disjunction between the letter and the spirit of the law grows out of that antinomian impulse, and that debates between positivists and natural law advocates raise largely religious questions about the existence of "transcendent, normative truths" and their relevance to law (Dane 1999, 114).

Religious worldviews frame legal discussion in a number of ways: questions like: "What is the state, and what is its jurisdiction?"; "From where does the state derive its authority?"; and "How far does that authority extend?" grow out of conflicting beliefs about the source of law's authority, the nature of human community, and, as noted previously, the definition of liberty. The fundamental challenge to liberal democratic regimes—those founded on Enlightenment principles of limited government—comes from citizens unwilling to privatize hegemonic religious ideologies. If the goal of the law in liberal Enlightenment regimes is the achievement of legal neutrality toward differing conceptions of the good, as many political philosophers assert, liberal democracies will be faced with a dilemma: how should the law deal with citizens unwilling to live in a neutral state? What is the proper response to those members of the polis whose worldviews and most fundamental commitments require that their particular views of morality be universally imposed, and who consequently experience equal treatment by government as discrimination? That is the core issue separating today's Planters and Founders.

Incommensurate approaches to the role of the state are at the heart of the impasse over issues like gay rights and abortion. The *Lawrence* case, in which the Supreme Court invalidated sodomy laws as an infringement of the liberty interest protected by the Fourteenth Amendment, was interpreted by fundamentalist critics as endorsement of a right to practice homosexual sodomy. Enlightenment liberals saw the decision as an affirmation of limited government—the right to be free of government as Peeping Tom and moral nanny. Pro-choice advocates typically argue that the state has no right to interfere in the decision of an individual woman to terminate her pregnancy. Many pro-choice individuals genuinely disapprove of abortion; nevertheless, they believe that in a country with considerable moral and religious disagreement over that question, government should abstain from interference with what they see as a profoundly personal moral decision. In that view, state abstention from efforts to outlaw abortion represents prudent governmental neutrality on a highly contested issue: an often-heard expression of that theme is, "If you don't believe in abortion, don't have one." Anti-choice activists see the matter much differently. If the state is not actively discouraging—or preferably, outlawing—abortion, the state is being complicit in murder. The government is failing to endorse and enforce moral behavior, failing to protect the most vulnerable. To use the language of the Planting Fathers, by failing to act, government is betraying the foundations of the Christian Nation and the City on the Hill. In the case of abortion, these conflicting positions are further complicated by religiously rooted beliefs about the nature of human life and when it begins. Government is in an unenviable position; it must deal with irreconcilable absolutes, because genuine neutrality is not possible.

A similar dynamic underlies arguments over the propriety of prayer in public school classrooms or at public school graduation ceremonies. Proponents of school-sponsored prayer see its elimination as hostility to religion, as added evidence that people of faith are subject to official marginalization. Opponents of such devotions, predictably, frame the issue much differently. For them, it is not a question of opposing or supporting prayer; what they oppose is giving an instrumentality of government the right to decide when and how children will pray. These arguments, too, are complicated by deep theological divisions over the propriety of public prayer. In the highly charged atmosphere of the culture war, efforts to craft genuinely neutral moments of silence (as distinguished from efforts to use such devices as a strategy for reintroducing prayer) are generally doomed: for historical reasons, opponents suspect ulterior motives, and because fundamentalists' real goal is visible government endorsement of their particular worldview, proponents find moments of silence insufficient.

Efforts to keep government scrupulously neutral in these debates are not only likely to fail; they arguably misconstrue an essential element of the American legal structure. Achievement of strict neutrality is not what our constitutional architecture was intended to provide. The Establishment Clause—indeed, the entire Bill of Rights—is the product of an Enlightenment worldview and value structure; it clearly privileges certain values over others. The contemporary secular state does not represent an absence of a conception of the good; it represents a choice of one particular conception of the good. The neutrality required by our constitutional system is equal treatment among those willing to accept the Founders' original choice, and willing to operate within the confines of laws that flow from it.

Even those who do operate within the secular, liberal democratic construct, as we have seen, often do so for very different reasons, reasons which in turn lead them to different conclusions about what a proper reading of those laws tells us about the intended role of the state. Howe has reminded us that separation of church and state was the result of two opposing, but complementary, traditions, anticlericalism, which was suspicious of the divisive potential of religion, and radical Baptist theology, which was equally suspicious of the corrupting influence of the state (1965). Dividing jurisdiction of the church from that of the state was thus a common solution to two quite different concerns—concerns that continue to inform political discourse. Liberals, adopting variants of Enlightenment rationalism, tend to view the state as a means to civic peace and order. Accordingly, they believe that the threshold question about the propriety of government action is who decides and how. Puritan and communitarian critics of the liberal democratic construct, many of whom are intellectual heirs of the Planting Fathers, argue that the state should be more concerned with ends. These disputes about the proper role of the state are hardly new. In *City of God*, St. Augustine criticized Rome for its failure to create a *true* republic, on the grounds that it had not established the right sort of human community.

In this instance, the Enlightenment frame is also the practical, political, and inevitable one. After all, in our dealing with one another, decisions about human conduct must constantly be made. Who will have the authority to make those decisions? Shall the state determine the nature of morality, or shall each individual make that determination, consistent with an obligation to respect the equal rights of others to do so?

DECIDING WHO DECIDES

These debates over the proper role of the state also motivate recurrent criticisms of so-called activist judges—a term used by partisans of all stripes to describe judges who hand down decisions with which they disagree—and the institution of an independent judiciary. In 2004 one of the periodic efforts to strip the federal courts of jurisdiction over culture war issues was sponsored by Indiana congressman Michael Pence. The bill purported to deny federal courts jurisdiction over challenges to the 1954 inclusion of the phrase under God in the Pledge of Allegiance. In the course of debate, Congressman Pence specifically attacked the idea of an independent judiciary as undemocratic, and charged that *Marbury v. Madison* had been incorrectly decided.[1] This criticism of an elitist court overruling the will of the people is often leveled by lawmakers whose efforts to enlist the power of government on behalf of particular moral crusades have been thwarted by the courts. The constitution provides for the appointment of judges who serve for life and can be removed only by impeachment. An independent judiciary is thought to be insulated from electoral and partisan pressures; the purpose was to create an environment in which the judge's only fidelity would be to the rule of law.

---

[1] *Marbury v. Madison* was the famous case in which the Supreme Court, under Chief Justice John Marshall, established the doctrine of judicial review. The case arose when newly elected President Thomas Jefferson refused to deliver judicial commissions signed by John Adams as he was leaving office.

Not that the courts have been wholly immune from popular sentiment. Even the Supreme Court clearly takes the likely support for (or resistance to) its decisions into account. The *Korematsu* case is an infamous example, but hardly the only one.[2] In 1940, as much of the world was already fighting what would become World War II, a Jehovah's Witness family sued the Minersville, Pennsylvania, School District over a requirement that all children participate in a morning flag salute—a requirement that violated Witnesses' religious beliefs. Clearly swayed by the widespread patriotic fervor of the times, the Supreme Court ruled that civic obligations outweighed the family's religious convictions. In the wake of that decision, Witness children who failed to salute were expelled from school, sent to reformatories, and physically assaulted; their parents were prosecuted for "causing delinquency." In 1943 the Court took another case, *West Virginia Bd. of Education v. Barnett*, and reversed itself. In a famous passage, Justice Jackson reaffirmed the Enlightenment view of the limited state that had been ensconced in the U.S. Constitution:

> The very purpose of a Bill of Rights was to withdraw certain subjects from the vicissitudes of political controversy, to place them beyond the reach of majorities and officials and to establish them as legal principles to be applied by the courts. One's right to life, liberty, and property, to free speech, a free press, freedom of worship and assembly, and other fundamental rights may not be submitted to vote: they depend on the outcome of no elections.

The decision was a ringing affirmation of Enlightenment principles, and it outraged many legislators who felt that honoring the flag was more important than respecting the religious beliefs of a minority.

If the Court has often been influenced by majoritarian passions, it has more frequently acted as the Founders arguably intended, as a libertarian brake on those passions. In the 1950s, negative reaction to

---

[2] In the *Korematsu* case, the Supreme Court upheld the forced detention of thousands of American citizens and residents of Japanese ancestry during World War II.

Brown v. Board of Education was so intense that President Eisenhower had to send troops to Little Rock, Arkansas, to enforce the Court's ruling that separate wasn't equal. There was much public hand-wringing again in 1965, when the Court ruled in *Griswold v. Connecticut* that legislatures had no business deciding the morality of contraceptive use by married couples. These and many similar decisions would be far less likely in a system of elected, responsive judges. The Founders saw the creation of an independent judiciary as an essential safeguard of the limited government they envisioned—part of the checks and balances necessary in a representative democracy.

Efforts to strip federal courts of jurisdiction, like the highly visible efforts to place so-called strict constructionists on the bench, are part of the ongoing effort to enlist the state in the campaign for a specific vision of Christian morality. (Earlier in 2004, the House of Representatives had also passed a bill denying the federal courts the right to hear challenges to the Defense of Marriage Act.) Thus far, court-stripping bills have failed to pass the more deliberative Senate and have died; even if such a measure were to pass, however, it would undoubtedly be struck down as a violation of the constitutional separation of powers. Futile or not, genuine efforts to change the system or more cynical attempts to pander to a particular constituency, these efforts highlight the persistence and continued salience of very different understandings of the role of the state—and of efforts to control the cultural narrative by controlling agenda-setting institutions.

VALUES IN THE LIBERAL STATE

Contemporary political philosophers often characterize Enlightenment liberalism's "who shall decide?" as a *thin* procedural inquiry, and describe the question posed by Communitarians and Puritans, "what is to be decided?" as substantive, or *thick*—a distinctly unhelpful framework. Labeling one approach as thick and one as thin mischaracterizes these important differences, and fails to recognize that the dispute reflects different, *equally thick*, conceptions of the good. That recognition, unfortunately, brings us back to the continuing impasse between the worldview of the Planters and that of the Founders, and to thorny questions of morality politics and the proper role of the state. If the state is to be the arbiter of personal moral behaviors, how will the character of proper behavior be determined? By majority vote? If we are to be a Christian nation, whose version of Christianity shall we adopt? If our radical diversity makes the Christian nation rhetoric distasteful even to most committed conservative Christians, how will we justify criminalizing sin?

Arguably, the Founders were drawn to the Enlightenment construct of a limited state, and the Enlightenment definition of liberty, in order to remove the state from such decisions. But that conclusion, however warranted, does not guide us in dealing with citizens unable or unwilling to accept that construct—citizens who experience lack of state endorsement of their particular worldview as active hostility to that worldview. Public conflicts over issues of sin and morality highlight that intractable disjunction.

In an odd way, however, these conflicts between relatively small numbers of modernist and fundamentalist absolutists may be easier to understand and resolve than the more complex policy disputes that are the subject of the next four chapters. Culture war issues present us with a rather stark choice, and often the constitution is quite clear in dictating what that choice must be. With religiously rooted beliefs about the economy, or criminal justice, or other ostensibly secular policy areas, the influence of sectarian beliefs is less obvious, even to those who hold them. And unlike the issues inflaming culture warriors, large majorities of ordinary Americans hold strong opinions on those policy issues, and the Constitution has much less relevance to their resolution.

Chapter 7

RELIGION, WEALTH, AND POVERTY

Political scientists have often noted that Jews "look like" Episcopalians, but vote like blacks. That is, while Jews are demographically similar to (historically Republican) Episcopalians, they resemble African Americans in their voting patterns. More recently, Democratic activists have publicly expressed frustration over working-class voting behaviors that seem inimical to the economic self-interest of those voters. "Here we see the impact of a kind of value-based voting independent of social class" (Fowler and Hertzke, in Walsh 2000, 86).

The importance of religious culture in framing economic policy commitments is amply confirmed by numerous studies of political behavior, and by poll results that cannot be explained solely by reference to economic or social status. Scholars have also documented significant policy differences among religious people all of whom are deeply observant—differences that correspond to the theological perspectives involved. One study of the relationship between religious identity and attitudes toward social welfare among American Protestants found that, contrary to the widespread assumption that more religious people are more politically conservative, individuals who demonstrated significant religiosity in their personal behaviors— those for whom religion was most salient—held quite different policy commitments, and those commitments correlated with the individualistic or communitarian orientation of the religious tradition involved. The study defined *individualists* as fundamentalists and evangelicals, and categorized most modernists as *communitarian* (Niles and McCammon 2000). Other studies have found that affluent churches—that is, those with sufficient resources to engage in social welfare ministries—are more likely to undertake such activities if they are theologically liberal (Davidson, Mock, and Johnson 1997).

The Fourth National Survey of Religion and Politics, conducted in 2004, further documented the persistence of policy preference differences between mainstream and evangelical Protestant voters. Respondents holding more traditional religious beliefs were more likely to object to public spending in general, and much more likely to approve of tax cuts, than were respondents holding modernist beliefs. When questioned about social welfare spending, although all groups (with the exception of the most traditional evangelicals) supported increasing such spending, white evangelical Protestants were the least supportive of all those questioned (Green 2004). A number of other studies have yielded similar conclusions.

Despite the strength of the relationship between theological beliefs and economic policy preferences, it is important to emphasize that the reciprocal influences of culture and religion are by no means simple to untangle. The nonlinear nature of the relationship is particularly visible in the case of otherwise very traditional black churches, where history and experience have uncoupled literalist biblical beliefs and economic conservatism, but the phenomenon is by no means restricted to African Americans. In a great many ways, the ongoing dialectic between Americans' Puritan and Enlightenment beliefs have created worldviews incorporating pieces of both. One result is that the behaviors—if not the expressed beliefs—of the majority of evangelical Protestants are indistinguishable from those of the general population. Ron Sider has pointed to some interesting paradoxes: "Divorce is *more* common among 'born again' Christians than in the general American population. Only 6 percent of evangelicals tithe. White evangelicals are the *most* likely people to object to neighbors of another race" (Sider 2005; emphasis in the original). Prominent evangelical liberals like Sider and Jim Wallis argue forcefully that such behaviors, as well as evangelicals' current enthusiasm for a virtually unfettered capitalism and their disapproval of social welfare measures intended to assist poor Americans, represent a serious departure from historic evangelical beliefs.

This intermingling of Enlightenment and Puritan worldviews, and the difficulty in determining the actual genesis of current American attitudes that we categorize as religious, was a theme of "The Christian Paradox: How a Faithful Nation Gets Jesus Wrong." When asked the source of the phrase *God helps those who help themselves*, three out of four Americans named the Bible. The actual source, of course, was Benjamin Franklin. "[N]ot only is Franklin's wisdom not biblical; it's counter-biblical. Few ideas could be further from the gospel message, with its radical summons to love of neighbor. On this essential matter, most Americans—most American Christians—are simply wrong, as if 75 percent of American scientists believed that Newton proved gravity causes apples to fly up" (Henneberger 2005, 3). The confusion is one more example of the peculiar amalgam of American folk wisdom and Christian gospel that characterizes much of contemporary religious discourse.

WEBER AND THE SPIRIT OF AMERICAN CAPITALISM

Max Weber was the most famous proponent of the theory that capitalism and Protestantism developed in a symbiotic relationship, and that Protestantism, in effect, made modern capitalism possible. *The Protestant Ethic and the Spirit of Capitalism* is undoubtedly his most famous book, although he produced a number of other important works. Weber did not suggest that Protestantism "caused" capitalism, but that elements of the new religion interacted with other social and economic changes to create a climate that fostered planning, hard work, and deferred gratification—that complex of behaviors that Weber called the "Protestant ethic" and contemporary observers refer to as the work ethic. Other scholars have suggested that Weber got it backwards; R. H. Tawney, for example, argued that economic change came first and contributed to religious change. Whatever the causal chain, elements of Protestantism consistent with the new economic system of capitalism included the emphasis upon the importance of work and the "rational ethics of ascetic Protestantism." Weber particularly credited Calvinist Protestantism, with its emphasis upon proving one's faith in worldly activity, rather than Lutheranism. Weber theorized that Jews and other national or religious minorities marginalized or subordinated by the dominant social order would be likely to respond to their exclusion from positions of political influence by turning with particular intensity to economic activity, and he speculated that one reason that Catholics had failed to conform to this model in those countries where they were a minority might be that religion's focus on asceticism and the afterlife.

Whatever the criticisms of Weber's thesis, his central point—that religious beliefs affect economic behaviors and policies—seems inarguable. As other scholars have subsequently confirmed, "Religious belief and practice influence virtually every aspect of economic behavior. Religious values shape production by, on the one hand, making labor a sacred obligation and, on the other, demanding periods of leisure for worship" (German 2004, 261). The Protestant Reformation not only brought a new emphasis on the individual, it made productive labor the sacred calling of Christians—especially in its Calvinist forms. These and other aspects of the Reformation brought about a greater emphasis upon the here-and-now and the conditions of life in this world, as we have seen previously. All of these theological changes tended to establish a cultural climate conducive to the commercial activity and trade that characterize capitalist systems. But the theological precept that arguably had the greatest effect on economic activity was the Calvinist doctrine of predestination. According to that doctrine, God had decided at creation the ultimate fate of each person in the afterlife—whether he or she was *elect* and going to heaven, or *not elect*, and thus headed for hell. The doctrine reinforced individualism, since each individual had to walk alone down life's path to meet his or her destiny. Calvinism's emphasis upon the duty to glorify God included the belief that the faithful discharge of one's calling—farmer, laborer, artisan, or housewife—would give evidence of the depths and sincerity of one's faith. This not only encouraged the virtues of diligence and hard work, it also caused work itself to be respected and ennobled.

Belief in predestination could also create a severe psychological strain for believers:

> They could never know for certain whether they were among the "elect" destined for salvation or the "damned" destined for destruction. Nor could they do anything to alter their fate. At best, they could look for signs of God's grace in their lives. Evidence of self-control and self-denial—ceaseless productive labor and the reinvestment of profits—along with the material prosperity that such behavior often provided figured prominently among the "marks" of grace. (German 2004, 263)

This Calvinist worldview has continued to shape a distinctly Protestant approach to charitable and voluntary activities. In the nineteenth century, Catholics and Protestants who may all have agreed with the abstract proposition that true Christian stewards would share their talents and material resources with others to benefit society nevertheless had quite different perspectives on the reasons for stewardship, and significantly different beliefs about what such stewardship entailed. Protestants generally believed that they would be saved through faith, not works; accordingly, they tended to see acts of benevolence not as a way to earn salvation, but as a way to manifest the depth of their faith and to evidence their likely status as elect (Oates 2003). Catholics, on the other hand, had been taught that salvation rested on good works as well as faith, and that charity was a religious duty incumbent on all believers. For them, charitable works were a way to earn salvation, not evidence of its probability.

Scholars have also remarked upon the way in which the doctrine of original sin has shaped economic policy preferences by encouraging the belief that the trials of economic life are earthly tests of sinfulness and virtue. An early corollary to both of these doctrines—predestination and original sin—was the belief that the suffering of the poor must be intended by God as a spur to their repentance, the belief that the poor were poor for a reason, whether that reason was to signal God's disfavor or to encourage conversion. Accordingly, helping them escape poverty would thwart God's will. As one writer has described this perspective, "Poverty was not understood as a problem to be fixed. It was a spiritual condition. Work-houses weren't supposed to help children prepare for life; they were supposed to save souls" (Bigelow 2005, 6).

These attitudes were by no means universal, even within individuals. Scorn for the poor and the belief that material wealth was a sign of spiritual superiority coexisted with early evangelical beliefs in the importance of covenant (the Puritan belief that citizens owed a duty to each other) and with later efforts to ameliorate the social problems created by industrialization, particularly those such as alcoholism and prostitution, that in addition to contributing to poverty, had a distinctly moral dimension. As we have seen, however, as the evangelical movement splintered, different Protestant denominations emphasized and/or transformed different aspects of these early theological principles into the theological and economic positions that characterized the Gilded Age, creating the competing philosophies we call social Darwinism and the Social Gospel—positions that continue to influence economic policy disputes today.

SOCIAL DARWINISM AND THE SOCIAL GOSPEL

The victory of the North in the Civil War had economic as well as social consequences. As German reminds us, the wartime demands for iron, steel, and textiles had done a great deal to promote Northern industry, and the subsequent development of the corporation—a new form of business organization—enabled enterprises to capitalize and grow at a pace not previously possible. "The men who made the Industrial Revolution—including Cornelius Vanderbilt, J. P. Morgan, Andrew Carnegie, and John D. Rockefeller—became new cultural heroes of mythic proportions" (2004, 279). The invention of corporations also led to the development of middle management, a class of individuals who earned salaries rather than hourly wages, and fostered further growth of a professional class. Although poorer wage earners saw an increase in their standard of living, one consequence of this particular set of economic developments was a significant widening of the gap between the rich and poor. Another was a proliferation of material goods and luxuries available to the middle and upper classes that would have been out of the reach of all but the wealthiest elements of previous generations. Historians typically refer to the period as the Gilded Age.

The Gilded Age precipitated a spiritual crisis for many Americans. "Whereas both Christianity and Enlightenment rationalism had linked social and material progress to morality, technological progress seemed amoral" (German 2004, 280). "Isms" multiplied: Darwinism, pragmatism, Andrew Carnegie's "Gospel of Wealth," Dwight Moody's revivalism—all brought different perspectives to an American landscape profoundly changed by immigration, industrialization, and science. Among the worldviews competing to provide new paradigms for understanding the American experience, social Darwinism was a powerful contender.

The two names most commonly associated with social Darwinism are Herbert Spencer and William Graham Sumner. Spencer was an early and enthusiastic supporter of Darwin's science, but he took it a step further; he adapted—or appropriated—Darwin's theory of natural selection to justify an economic position. As Spencer saw it,

> Blind to the fact that under the natural order of things society is constantly excreting its unhealthy, imbecile, slow, vacillating faithless members, these unthinking, though well-meaning, men advocate an interference which not only stops the purifying process, but even increases the vitation—absolutely encourages the multiplication of the reckless and incompetent by offering them an unfailing provision, and discourages the multiplication of the competent and provident by heightening the difficulty of maintaining a family. (Spencer, quoted in Walsh 2000, 6)

Similar sentiments led Americans like William Graham Sumner to dismiss any moral claim on society's resources by those less fortunate.

> But the weak who constantly arouse the pity of humanitarians and philanthropists are the shiftless, the imprudent, the negligent, the impractical, and the inefficient, or they are the idle, the intemperate, the extravagant and the vicious. Now the troubles of these persons are constantly forced upon public attention, as if they and their interests deserved especial consideration, and a great portion of all organized and unorganized effort for the common welfare consists in attempts to relieve these classes of people. . . . Now who is the Forgotten Man? He is the simple, honest laborer, ready to earn his living by productive work. (Sumner, quoted in Walsh 2000, 7)

While later social scientists would conclude that the biological theory of evolution cannot and should not provide a framework for social policy, evangelicals like William Jennings Bryan saw Spencer and Sumner's philosophy as the logical outgrowth of Darwinian biology, and a refutation of the essential philosophy of Jesus' Sermon on the Mount. Bryan's rejection of the biological theory was largely motivated by his conviction that its grounding in natural selection would be used exactly as Sumner and Spencer were using it—to justify harsh and punitive social policies and to undercut the importance of government efforts to address systemic causes of poverty.

The social problems and misery accompanying the dislocations of industrialization evoked a very different response from clergymen like Washington Gladden and Walter Rauschenbusch. Rather than emphasizing biblical justifications for poverty, they stressed the biblical injunction that made man his brother's keeper. They criticized excesses of capitalism and competition and worked to ameliorate the causes and effects of poverty. Their social gospel rejected the notion that the poor were solely responsible for their own misery, and they championed efforts by government to address the structural and systemic forces that prevented the poor from improving their lot. Rauschenberg, in particular, was a pivotal figure in creating and promulgating the Social Gospel; his books—*Christianity and the Social Crisis* and *Christianizing the Social Order*—were broadly influential among mainstream Protestants, and enunciated a philosophy that fit well with the missions of the numerous voluntary organizations being formed as a response to the social problems of the day. As one scholar has characterized him, "Rauschenbusch despaired of individualized attempts at social service because they perpetuated the corrupt social system. Sin was both individual and corporate. Saving souls was important, but so was transforming the social order" (Leonard 1988, 249).

Susan Curtis has described the Social Gospel as the religious expression of progressivism in the early twentieth century and as a departure from the nineteenth-century Protestant emphasis on individualism. "In place of unbridled competition, individual responsibility for success, and government policies of laissez faire, social gospelers proposed cooperation, social responsibility for justice, and an interventionist welfare state" (2001, 363). The Social Gospel thus reflected a significant shift in Protestant theology—indeed, its adherents would eventually redefine the meaning of salvation and the nature of religious commitment. For those who accepted the Social Gospel, salvation became a communal obligation rather than an individual one. It required a concerted attack on the "poverty, vice and filth that prevented many Americans from staying on the road to redemption" (2001, 365).

The Social Gospel appeared at a time when Protestants' nineteenth-century worldviews were under severe strain. The Gilded Age had called their faith into question.

> An increasingly industrialized, bureaucratized, urban economy thwarted the efforts of many an ambitious individual to strive and succeed on his own. The demands of the market along with greater educational opportunities for women brought more women into the workplace as laborers and professionals, thus eroding the domestic ideal. Thousands of Catholic and Jewish immigrants from southern and eastern Europe began to undermine the Protestant majority and its outlook. . . . [B]iblical criticism, Darwin's theory of evolution, and Freudian psychology brought religious certainty under direct attack. Men and women raised to believe in individualism, self-restraint,

domesticity, liberalism and free moral agency found themselves in the late nineteenth century in a world that did not sustain their beliefs. (Curtis 2001, 366)

They needed a belief structure that would reassure them and that would be consistent with the new realities with which they were living. The Social Gospel filled that void.

The God of the Social Gospel was not the angry and judgmental God of the Puritans. This God was immanent, a loving, parental deity who had endowed mankind with moral agency which was to be used to improve the world and make it suitable for his kingdom. This view of God and of man's relationship to him produced a further shift away from concern with the afterlife, and toward much more earthly concerns with the evils of poverty, depravity, and injustice. Those who believed in the Social Gospel rejected the view of the poor held by the social Darwinists; for many of them, their personal experiences and volunteer work had convinced them that individual efforts alone were insufficient to change the conditions of poverty. Social gospelers de-emphasized individual salvation in favor of what might be called *social salvation* or social justice, and the importance of improving the lot of the communities they lived in. Perhaps the most significant element of the Social Gospel was its emphasis on the importance of institutional structures in thwarting or enabling individual efforts. In sharp distinction to the social Darwinists, social gospelers emphasized structural or systemic solutions over personal transformation, and lobbied for communal and governmental solutions to social problems. In the process, they adopted secular language and became closely identified with the secular, Enlightenment values of the broader American culture.

It was not only Protestants who experienced a theological shift in order to deal with the realities of industrialization, immigration, and urban poverty. The experiences of American Catholics in the late 1800s made them receptive to many of the same themes that animated Protestant social gospelers. First of all, a significant proportion of the new immigrants were Catholic. Those Catholic immigrants were disproportionately working class, and thus especially vulnerable to the economic instabilities of the times. The series of massive strikes by laborers in the latter years of the nineteenth century, and the attendant unrest, thus had especial relevance for — and posed a particular challenge to — the Catholic community. Also, in response to the exclusion of Catholic clergy from many public hospitals and other public institutions — orphanages, asylums for the insane or the poor — Catholics had created a system of parallel social services through which the community could be responsive to the church's historic concern for the poor. As the dimensions of urban industrialization and immigration in the last decades of the century made the needs more imperative and visible, and (not incidentally) as more women entered Catholic social service, the character of the Catholic response began to change. The growing concern with the conditions of workers led the hierarchy to abandon its earlier disapproval of labor unions, and to endorse many of the themes that would characterize the Social Gospel movement of the early twentieth century. Catholic women created the settlement house movement, of which Jane Addam's Hull House in Chicago is the most famous example.

THE RESURGENCE OF SOCIAL DARWINISM

While both the Catholic and Protestant versions of the Social Gospel included critiques of unrestrained capitalism, neither version proved immune from the influences of a thriving consumerist, capitalist culture. Industrialization had created social ills, but it had also produced a wide array of consumer goods and a middle class that could afford them. Religious holidays, especially Christmas, became highly commercialized opportunities for consumption. The purchase of Easter bonnets and the exchange of Christmas gifts sacralized the culture of the consumer. By the 1920s the Social Gospel had been eclipsed by easy credit and consumption. Frugality and self-denial were no longer identified as moral behaviors; indeed, in the popular culture, "conspicuous consumption and evangelical Christian virtue went hand-in-hand" (German 2004, 284–85). Moral opprobrium was reserved for drunkenness and other dissolute behaviors, and the moral fervor that had been channeled into efforts to ameliorate poverty was redirected to other causes, notably the temperance movement.

The Depression forced a temporary reevaluation of this growing materialism and allowed Roosevelt to build on the central insight of the Social Gospel—the need for a communal, institutional response to poverty—to create a federal social safety net. Following the Second World War, however, prosperity returned. By this time, Americans' religious worldviews had come to include the proposition that material well-being "was the natural product of political freedom and economic individualism, which in turn were rooted in essentially religious conceptions of the human person" (German 2004, 286). The challenge of communism further solidified an ethic that opposed "godless" communism to an implicitly religious capitalism. The American view of religion became increasingly utilitarian—that is, religious belief, whatever the content, was seen as an important safeguard for democratic capitalism, rather than as an intrinsically valuable system of ethics or belief. When communism fell, and the superiority of a market economy was widely if not universally acknowledged, it was viewed by many Americans—particularly on the far right—as vindication not just of an economic system, but of a specifically evangelical Protestant approach to the economic order.

Mainstream, modernist Protestants have retained a significant amount of the Social Gospel in their worldviews, and have forged considerable common ground with Catholics and Jews in endorsing a role for the state in economic matters. Conservative Protestants and fundamentalists, on the other hand, have combined their continued rejection of biological Darwinism with a newly energized social Darwinism. Fundamentalist economic arguments begin with the Fall, the significance of which is to validate their view of the world as a "dog eat dog" Hobbesian environment in which God has imposed scarcity, and compassion is neither feasible nor desirable (Walsh 2000, 12). The Institute for Christian Economics, one of several Christian Right economic policy organizations, has explained its mission as follows: "The perspective of those associated with the ICE is straightforwardly conservative and pro-free-market. . . . For well over half a century, the loudest voices favoring Christian social action have been outspokenly pro-government intervention. . . . We have to convince the liberal-leaning evangelicals of the biblical nature of the free market system" (quoted in Walsh 2000, 12). The organization not only defends the free market—as most Americans do—it goes further, and opposes not only any form of redistribution through the tax system, but both government welfare programs and private charity. Supporters of ICE, the Christian Freedom Foundation, and similar economic think tanks established by the Christian Right view pure capitalism as the only economic system consistent with the rule of nature. They believe that interference with nature's system of reward and punishment is interference with the world God has created, and that God is the "hidden hand" that works through the free market to reward the righteous and punish the indolent. In this view, there is no systemic or structural component to human poverty: the reason people are poor is because they choose to be poor, or because they are morally defective. The only alternative to a society where the talented and hardworking are rewarded is a society that encourages sloth and inefficiency—and "subsidizing sluggards is the same as subsidizing evil." It is all or nothing. Nineteenth-century economic liberalism—originally an Enlightenment construct—has thus been reimagined as a "secularized and Darwinian version of biblical social ethics" and adopted as a biblical imperative (Walsh 2000, 13).

The beliefs summarized above are held in so stark a form by a relatively small number of the most literal fundamentalists and evangelicals, but thanks in no small part to the number of well-financed think tanks, media commentators, and political activists promoting them, versions of this paradigm influence the worldviews of a vastly larger number of citizens, who identify Americanism with its highly idealized and newly sanctified version of capitalism. Those who hold these worldviews equate taxation—especially progressive taxation—with robbery; like communism and socialism, and (like Robin Hood, a story repeatedly targeted for its *communist message* by fundamentalist censorship efforts) they see progressive taxation as an effort to penalize the diligent in order to "subsidize sluggards." They oppose government regulation of business and industry, because such regulations interfere with the natural order that God has established and that the market represents.

Furthermore they reflexively—and often viscerally—oppose government social welfare programs that benefit the poor.

Political observers often express frustration over the seeming inconsistency between conservatives' willingness to use the power of the state in the service of an enforced morality and their adamant opposition to any governmental role in economic matters. In reality, however, the two beliefs are more congruent than first appears. To the central question of political theory, namely, "What is the role of the state?" the Enlightenment answered, "To enforce civil order and protect individual autonomy." The Puritans, on the other hand, believed government should build the City on the Hill by enforcing biblical morality and constructing God's preferred economic and social structure. God wants the government to punish sin and reward virtue by respecting the inviolability of the market he created. Religious conservatives do not wish to limit state power; they simply want to deploy that power in a manner consistent with their reading of biblical mandates.

THE CASE OF THE FAITH-BASED INITIATIVE

In 1996 Congress passed the Personal Responsibility and Work Opportunity Reconciliation Act, reforming welfare "as we know it." Among the provisions of that bill was a section later dubbed "Charitable Choice," requiring that states contract with faith-based providers of secular social services on the same basis as they contract with other for-profit and nonprofit providers. The bill specified that such organizations were not to be discriminated against; they were to be allowed to maintain hiring policies based upon their religious dictates and (while they were prohibited from proselytizing), they could not be required to divest the premises where services were delivered of religious iconography. Similar provisions have since been attached to Welfare-to-Work (1997), Community Services Block Grant (1998), and Substance Abuse and Mental Health Services Administration legislation (2000). Subsequently, President George W. Bush made a Faith-Based Initiative modeled on Charitable Choice a cornerstone of his domestic agenda, and established a White House Office on Faith-

Based and Community Initiatives with satellite offices in each federal department. The president repeatedly echoed three central assertions made by Charitable Choice supporters: that unduly rigid legal and constitutional interpretations had prevented "Armies of Compassion" from assisting the poor; that faith-based organizations had been subject to discrimination in the award of government contracts and grants; and—most emphatically—that while other forms of social service assistance had proved to be of limited utility, those that are faith-based work.

Soon after assuming his duties as the first director of the new White House Office on Community and Faith-Based Initiatives, John DiIulio wrote an op-ed in the *Wall Street Journal* (February 14, 2001), in which he underscored the president's message.

> The "Charitable Choice" provision of the 1996 welfare reform law changed the federal government's procurement and performance-based contracting rules so that religious organizations that provide social services could compete for support on the same basis as other non-governmental providers of these services, and do so without having to hide their religious basis.

Welfare scholars and people who worked in social service agencies were puzzled by much of this rhetoric, which simply ignored the historic involvement of religious providers like Catholic Charities, Jewish Family Services, Lutheran Social Services, the Salvation Army, and literally hundreds of others. In many communities, the majority of non-profit organizations providing tax-supported social services have for decades been those affiliated with religious communities. The legislation did not define *faith-based*, and neither Congress nor the White House addressed a common question: how are the faith-based providers targeted for outreach and inclusion different from the religious organizations that have been contracting with government for decades?

THE SECULAR ARGUMENTS

Despite the emphasis on faith-based organizations, and arguments over the proper relationship of religion and government, the policy arguments advanced for and against Charitable Choice and the Faith-Based Initiative were virtually devoid of specifically religious content. Supporters insisted that the legislation was simply an effort to ensure that all potential government bidders were treated fairly and equally—a classically liberal argument for extending equal consideration to all providers irrespective of their religious character. They also argued that the unfair exclusion of these providers operated to make government programs less effective because, as "everyone knows," faith organizations do a better job at less cost, and are more successful than government or secular organizations in their efforts to help the poor. Many proponents argued that poverty is largely attributable to the absence of middle-class values, and that religious organizations are better prepared to focus on the difficult task of inculcating those values. They argued that only through an infusion of diligence, thrift, the ability to delay gratification, and other behavioral transformations can welfare recipients achieve self-sufficiency, and they pointed out that religious organizations are in the business of inculcating values. Some supporters also echoed the president's argument that Armies of Compassion would join the effort to help welfare recipients leave the rolls once the barriers to their participation were eliminated.

Opponents focused most on concerns about church and state. Most agreed that religious organizations had a right to be considered on the same basis as secular ones, and pointed out that religiously affiliated nonprofits had always made up a significant percentage of government contractors. But they also emphasized that the existing contractors— even pervasively sectarian ones—were operating under applicable professional standards, and respecting the constitutional boundaries that limit explicitly religious content and proselytizing. In response to the equal treatment argument raised by supporters, they argued that what the Constitution requires is equal consideration of all qualified bidders willing to abide by the restraints imposed by the First Amendment's Establishment Clause; there was no evidence that religious contractors able to perform and willing to play by the rules had been discriminated against. Even Stephen Monsma, a well-regarded scholar and an enthusiastic proponent of Charitable Choice, found little evidence of bias in administration of government contracts with religious providers. In his widely reviewed book *When Sacred and Secular Mix* (1996), Monsma reported on the religiosity of schools and agencies receiving government funds, and the problems they experienced related to their religious expression. While 30 percent of respondents noted that questions had arisen related to religious practices, only 11 percent reported that they had been required to curtail such practices. Furthermore, as Monsma notes, most of those practices involved required religious activities and usually required attendance at church services. Monsma also documented extensive and open religious activity by faith-based contractors, some of which arguably went well beyond what is constitutionally permissible.

Because it was difficult to reconcile the reality of long-standing religious involvement in government social service provision with the assertions of widespread antireligious bias that accompanied passage of Section 104, opponents believed that other motives were really driving the effort to include more faith organizations. Noting that faith-based efforts had not been accompanied by any new money for social services, several scholars suggested that Charitable Choice represented an attempt by a newly empowered Christian Right to "control the narrative"—to define what is to be considered genuinely religious for purposes of accessing limited government funds (Chaves 2001, Sullivan 2001). Under this view, the issue was not whether religious organizations should be receiving government funding but rather which religious contractors should be preferred (Sullivan 2001).

Opponents also questioned whether the congregations frequently identified as mainstays of the hypothesized Armies of Compassion really had the resources to provide social services. Research conducted by Mark Chaves (1999) at the University of Arizona cast considerable doubt on that assertion. Chaves mined the National Congregational Study to provide a wealth of information about American congregations, including information relevant to the question of congregational capacity to provide social services. His data suggested that most congregations are severely limited in their capacity to operate formal programs. Only 12 percent of the congregations in his study operated social service programs under their own auspices—that is, using their own staff and financial resources. It was far more typical to find congregations supporting programs delivered by others. Chaves found congregations to be adept at mobilizing small groups of volunteers to conduct well-defined, periodic tasks. His data suggested that churches and synagogues are particularly well-suited to providing short-term responses to immediate needs, and much less able to sustain long-term programs requiring consistent staffing and supervision. An earlier study (1997) by Susan Grettenberger, limited to United Methodist congregations in Michigan, had come to similar conclusions; Grettenberger found that congregations in her study provided services primarily in response to emergencies, and that they simply did not possess the necessary resources to implement programs requiring more sustained service delivery.

Finally, opponents noted the absolute absence of credible research either supporting or rebutting the assertion that faith-based organizations were more effective providers of antipoverty programming. Such research simply did not exist. If there was no new money, no evidence that the targeted organizations were more effective, and no evidence of discrimination, opponents asked, what was the real motivation for Charitable Choice?

RELIGIOUS ROOTS

These ostensibly secular arguments over comparative efficacy and discriminatory application of the law were firmly rooted in very different paradigms. Even the terminology chosen betrays the presence of conflicting worldviews: proponents undoubtedly chose the term *faith-based* rather than *religious* in an effort to be inclusive, but the notion that faith is the central defining feature of religiosity betrays a narrowly Protestant conception of religion and ignores the fact that many religious traditions emphasize works rather than belief.

The arguments about effectiveness, particularly, cannot be understood without reference to their roots in the very different religious beliefs about the nature of poverty. Americans who believe, with Marvin Olasky, that the poor "need the internal pressure to [as Booker T. Washington said] 'live honored and useful lives modeled after our perfect leader, Christ'" (Chernus 2001), will seek to end poverty through individual transformation, ideally achieved through religious conversion of the poor, but failing conversion, through inculcation of religious values. If poverty, in the classic fundamentalist formulation, is a result of individual moral inadequacy and the lack of proper values and internalized norms, then the remedy for poverty is moral regeneration and better values and norms. Religious liberals and longtime government partners like Catholic Charities, on the other hand, begin from the premise that "generally the poor are no more in need of religious instruction and worship than the rest of society" (Daly 2001; personal e-mail). They believe that poverty is predominantly, although not exclusively, a systemic social issue best addressed by job creation programs, educational reform, or similar structural approaches. They recognize that accomplishing structural change takes time, and that during the interim they have a religious duty to "feed the hungry and clothe the naked." In short, they believe, as a Baptist minister who heads up a large and highly successful welfare services organization in North Carolina puts it, "Most poor people have all the religion in the world. What they don't have is job skills" (Cleveland 2003).

Those who approach poverty through the Puritan paradigm see poverty as a personal failure, and thus sincerely believe that personal transformation is the only effective remedy. This leads logically to the belief that organizations failing to equate poverty with individual failures of values are not authentically faith based, whatever their purported religious affiliation. It also leads logically to their insistence on the importance of exempting religious contractors from compliance with antidiscrimination laws. This has undoubtedly been the most contentious issue raised by Charitable Choice, and opponents have strenuously objected to the use of tax dollars to pay people whose employment is subject to a religious test. Approaching the issue through a liberal, modernist paradigm, they see no reason that the religion of the person hired to ladle out portions at the soup kitchen, or teach computer skills at the job training center, should matter. If the employee can ladle or teach, his or her religious beliefs should be irrelevant. For those beginning from a Puritan paradigm, however, what is really being provided is spiritual improvement and instruction. Ensuring that those hired to transmit what are really religious values understand and agree with those values is critically important.

The same Puritan paradigm is responsible for perceptions of discriminatory treatment. When the administration issued a white paper purporting to detail the unnecessary barriers faced by religious contractors, welfare professionals were quick to point out that when rhetorical embellishments were discounted, the major barrier identified was a lack of capacity. Coming—as most did—from a modernist perspective, they argued that conditioning government contracts on demonstrated capacity by the bidder to provide the services involved is not only reasonable, but essential. Why would government prefer organizations with no relevant experience or credentials over those having such assets? These critics endorsed administration proposals for programs that would build capacity—government programs to provide training in grant writing, compliance, and similar skills needed by organizations wishing to contract with the government—but they were incredulous at the charge that conditioning a contract on the bidder's capacity to perform was discrimination.

Religious literalists, predictably, saw an entirely different issue. They were highly critical of contracting agencies' insistence upon professional credentials and compliance with professional norms, arguing for "elimination of arbitrary rules that allow, for example, the use of professional therapy but not pastoral counseling" (Lenkowsky 2001, 23). They saw the preference for professional credentials as arbitrary because they saw poverty as the result of individual value deficits. If the proper course of action is to supply the individual with better values, it seemed self-evident that pastors could do that just as well, if not better, than licensed social workers or certified job counselors. Since they saw no legitimate reason to require professional credentials, they saw the requirement as part of an effort to disadvantage faith-based contractors. What looked like a level playing field from the perspective of supporters looked decidedly tilted from the perspective of opponents, and vice versa.

The arguments over the church-state issues involved were similarly incommensurate. Those with more Puritan paradigms about the nature of liberty—those who believe that liberty is freedom to do the right thing—saw government efforts to avoid privileging religion as efforts to marginalize it. To them, this was one more area where liberals were misinterpreting the First Amendment in an effort to drive religion out of the public square. As reports began to surface that some of the new contractors had used tax dollars to purchase Bibles, and others had engaged in explicitly religious programming, modernists saw confirmation of their belief that Charitable Choice laws were primarily intended to breach the wall between church and state.

One of the most interesting arguments attributable to these contending worldviews arose among the literalists themselves. Social Darwinism not only emphasized individual responsibility for poverty, it opposed government attempts to ameliorate that poverty. On the one hand, this preference for private rather than collective solutions has led literalists to champion contracting out, which they inaccurately see as privatization.[1] Social Darwinists believe that the private sector is almost always more competent than government; if government is going to provide goods or services, it is thus infinitely preferable that it do so through a private intermediary. However, contracting out is not the same thing as private provision—government is still deciding what service to provide, dictating the terms on which the service is to be offered, identifying the recipients, and paying the bills. Recognizing that reality, several conservative religious leaders refused to endorse Charitable Choice and the Faith-Based Initiative, fearing that religious contractors would be seen as supporting government's responsibility to

---

[1] Actual privatization occurs when government assets are sold to private operators, who henceforth own and operate them and pay taxes on their earnings; in the United States the word usually means that the government delivers services through a surrogate, a third-party contractor.

provide for the poor, or worse, that religious organizations would be co-opted and secularized by the experience of partnering with government. (As one African-American pastor memorably put it, "With the government's shekels come the government's shackles.") That suspicion and reluctance may be another reason the anticipated Armies of Compassion failed to materialize. At this writing, despite all the political rhetoric pro and con, and despite significant and well-funded outreach efforts by the Bush Administration and several state governments, there has been little if any change in the composition of the pool of social service contractors (Kennedy and Bielefeld 2006).

Finally, it is important to recognize that many people supported or opposed Charitable Choice for genuinely secular reasons. Some Republican strategists hoped to make inroads into the African-American community by funding programs in black churches. Some welfare professionals hoped that new contractors, with new approaches and energies, would offer creative solutions to seemingly intractable problems. Some nonprofit scholars theorized that faith-based organizations might prove to be more holistic, and thus more effective. Critics of government expenditures for welfare hoped that volunteers would shoulder some of the tasks for less money, or at no charge—a prospect that critics also foresaw, and deplored as "load shedding." As important as the theological perspectives are to an understanding of this policy debate, not every participant is either a social Darwinist or a proponent of the Social Gospel. In Freud's classic phrase, "sometimes a cigar is just a cigar."

Chapter 8

RELIGION, SCIENCE, AND THE ENVIRONMENT

It might seem that issues of environmental protection, dependent as they are on hard scientific evidence and analysis, would be relatively unaffected by religiously rooted paradigms. And that is arguably the case; debates over environmental policy tend to be conducted within a largely Enlightenment framework. As a number of studies confirm, however, that does not mean that our religious worldviews do not affect our environmental policy preferences. While it is true that technical analyses of the nature and extent of environmental problems are unlikely to implicate embedded attitudes, the significance of the natural world and the degree of importance a culture assigns to its protection, the balance it strikes between resource conservation and economic productivity, or between individual and state responsibilities, are powerfully influenced by culture, as is the depth of a society's commitment to preservation of the natural ecosystem.

The influence of national religious cultures on "green politics and policies" was the focus of a 2001 study by David Vogel, at the University of California at Berkeley. Vogel surveyed the environmental policies of rich nations, dividing them into *light green* and *dark green* based upon differences in their commitments to environmental protection; he found that "much of public support for environmentalism is linked to values and preferences which have little or nothing to do with the actual physical scope or magnitude of environmental problems." After examining the cultural differences involved, he found a striking correlation between Protestantism and dark green environmentalism. (For purposes of his classification of countries, he notes that he considered all Americans to be Protestant.) Vogel is careful to note that correlation is not necessarily causation, and that "explicitly religious beliefs have not made an important contribution to the growth of contemporary public concern about the environment" (25). He speculates that these national differences grow out of Protestantism's apocalyptic vision and its "pervasive sense of moralism."

> There is within Protestantism, a religion which emerged as a reaction to the sensuous gratification-seeking behavior of the Medieval Church, a deep suspicion of self-indulgence and excessive consumption and a strong bias in favor of self-discipline. . . .
>
> For both Protestantism and dark green environmentalism, the ordinary person bears some responsibility for the fate of the world. The Protestant concept of stewardship finds its contemporary expression in an environmental politics which makes each person responsible for both nature and fate of the earth. Hence the relatively high salience of environmental issues in dark green countries and the high level of public interest in both nature protection and the global dimensions of environmental protection. (28–29)

Daniel Sarewitz, an environmental scientist, has concluded that the influence of value paradigms on those engaged in environmental science is inescapable, that scientific knowledge is not—and cannot be—independent of political context, but is rather "coproduced by scientists and the society within which they are embedded." After noting that even scientists who reach opposite conclusions on a question "share the old-fashioned idea that scientific facts build the appropriate foundation for knowing how to act in the world," he raises the obvious issue: how do we account for the wide, even radical, differences in supposedly science-based views? Is it because categorizing something as a problem demands a preexisting framework or paradigm that recognizes such things as problems? (2004)

It cannot be reiterated too often that the relationships between our religiously rooted cultural assumptions and our policy preferences are complex and nonlinear. Most contemporary American worldviews result from an ongoing and dynamic synthesis of basic Enlightenment and Puritan attitudes that have been enriched (or polluted, depending upon one's point of view) by successive waves of immigration, the pervasiveness of national culture, science, and technology, and accelerated globalization—by what Robert Bellah has called the "enormously powerful common culture in America . . . carried predominantly by the market and the state and by their agencies of socialization: television and education" (2002, 13). So it should not surprise us that—with one exception—American public attitudes about environmental protection are unrelated to their formal religious commitments. A number of studies have found that religious variables are "weak predictors" of environmental policy preferences (Boyd 1999; Hayes and Marangudakis 2000). The single exception is religious fundamentalists, who consistently express less support for measures to protect the environment (Tarakeshwar et al. 2000; Kohut et al. 2000).

CONFLICTING ENVIRONMENTAL WORLDVIEWS

Richard Hughes has defined American belief in "Nature's Nation" as one of the formative myths by which we understand ourselves. Thomas Jefferson, as a good Deist, grounded the Declaration of Independence in "the Laws of Nature and Nature's God."

> What Jefferson did not say is as important as what he said. He said nothing in the Declaration about Jesus, or the Trinity, or the church, or the Virgin Mary, or Moses, or Buddha, or Mohammed. He did not appeal to the New Testament, the old Testament, the Koran or to any other body of sacred Scripture. Instead, he rooted the American Revolution in the existence of a God, apparent to all human beings in nature, and in a moral order that he proclaimed as self-evident. (Hughes 2003, 53)

Hughes traces the Enlightenment construct of nature's God to a 1624 book by Edward Lord Herbert of England, who believed that the way to resolve religious strife was to look to nature for the fundamental truths that stood at the heart of all religious faiths. "By arguing for a religion grounded in nature and knowable through the powers of reason, Herbert helped give birth both to the Enlightenment and to English Deism" (48).

> How successful was this strategy? Immensely so. From Jefferson's day to this, many Americans have commonly claimed that it makes very little difference what particular religious faith one embraces, just so long as one believes in God and lives a good moral life. These are not the values of any particular religious faith such as Christianity, Judaism or Islam, much less the values of any particular Christian denomination. . . . Instead, these are the values of eighteenth-century Deism, made incarnate in the Declaration of Independence. (54)

The belief in nature's God has shaped American majority culture, but there is a highly influential minority counterpoint to the environmentalism—and ecumenicism—it encourages. Interestingly, that minority perspective arises not from the largely unconscious paradigms that shape the cultural zeitgeist, but from conscious and quite explicit religious commitments. This fact sets environmental policy preferences apart from the other policy areas explored in this book, and creates a political dynamic quite different from that driving many other policy debates.

END TIMES AND THE ENVIRONMENT

Dispensational premillenialism is perhaps the most important of the fundamentalist theologies that include belief in the *end times* and thus generate opposition to environmental protection efforts. As the *Christian Science Monitor* has reported, although fundamentalists represent a minority of Christians, "the interest in end-times prophecy has spread beyond their circles" (Lampman 2004). The theology behind the prophecy owes much of its acceptance to John Nelson Darby, a nineteenth-century British evangelist who taught that history unfolds in stages, called dispensations (Luo 2005). He also introduced the concept of the Rapture. Dispensationalists believe that the plagues and catastrophes predicted in Revelation, known as the tribulation, will precede the return of Jesus, who will save true Christians from the sufferings involved by taking them suddenly to heaven—this is called the Rapture. He will leave everyone else to suffer the outpourings of God's wrath. Martin Marty has provided an excellent explanation of Dispensationalism in his masterful history of American religion, *Modern American Religion: The Irony of It All* (1893–1919).

The eminent journalist Bill Moyers described belief in the Rapture, and its consequences, in a speech (2004) accepting Harvard Medical School's Global Environment Citizen Award.

> [O]nce Israel has occupied the rest of its "biblical lands," legions of the anti-Christ will attack it, triggering a final showdown in the valley of Armageddon. As the Jews who have not been converted are burned, the messiah will return for the rapture. True believers will be lifted out of their clothes and transported to heaven, where, seated next to the right hand of God, they will watch their political and religious opponents suffer plagues of boils, sores, locusts, and frogs during the several years of tribulation that follow. (2004)

If the Rapture is imminent, as many fundamentalists believe, environmental laws are, at best, beside the point. (Again, granting the premise, this is perfectly logical. As Dwight Moody, the famous revivalist, supposedly said, "Why polish the brass on a sinking ship?") With the immense popularity of Tim LeHaye's *Left Behind* books,[1] the popular influence of Rapture theology—if not actual belief in it—has grown dramatically. (A popular bumper sticker proclaims "In case of Rapture, this car will be unmanned"—much to the confusion of drivers unschooled in this particular theological theory.) Those who do accept

---

[1] This series of fictional thrillers is based upon the book of Revelation, the tribulations, and the Rapture. It has sold millions of copies, and brought these concepts to a wide audience, many of whom were previously unfamiliar with them.

the doctrine believe they need not worry about the environment "because God is going to take them away from it" (Lampman 2004).

Believers see increasing evidence that the end times are imminent. In the aftermath of Hurricane Katrina, the pastor of one of America's megachurches told his congregation that the hurricane, the tsunami that struck Southeast Asia in December of 2004, and the attacks of September 11, were among signs of "the times," indications that Jesus was about to return. He attributed the increase in the incidence of earthquakes as further evidence that the end times were nearing. Unfortunately for this part of his thesis, the United States Geological Survey has issued a publication pointing out that the frequency of earthquakes has not increased; what has increased is the ability of scientists to locate them, due to a greater number of seismograph stations and improved global communications (Brayton 2005). Brayton notes that the pastor's claim echoes those made by Hal Lindsay, author of the *Late Great Planet Earth*, in his 1997 book, *Apocalypse Code*. The book claims that earthquakes have increased in both frequency and intensity, "just as the Bible predicts" and claims that since the 1950s, each decade has seen significant increases, from nine in the 1950s, to more than 150 between 1990 and 1996 (2005).

There are several variations of end-times theology—at least four major systems and a number of minor ones—and there are significant theological differences among them. The total number of evangelical Christians who consciously accept all or part of any of these end-times beliefs is under 30 percent, if polls are accurate.

It is not simply explicit belief in end-times philosophy that affects religious conservatives' responses to environmental policies, however. Literalists' attitudes toward—and suspicion of—science are also implicated. Environmental science rests on evolutionary biology, the concept of continually evolving and changing ecosystems. As we have seen, for literalists, conceding the authority of the evolutionary thesis is anathema. Furthermore, environmental issues can be highly technical, and the science involved is frequently contested. Much as in the creationism and intelligent design debates, literalists have pointed to the incomplete nature of scientific explanations as evidence that science itself rests on a flawed understanding of the nature of authority, and they have seized upon areas of uncertainty to mount scientific challenges to assertions about the causes—and even the reality—of such environmental phenomena as global warming. As Sarewitz notes, "[T]hose holding different value perspectives may see in the huge and diverse body of scientific information relevant to climate change different facts, theories and hypotheses relevant to and consistent with their own normative frameworks" (2004, 389). In other words, in so large a body of data, components can be assembled and interpreted in different ways, suggesting different perspectives on the nature of the problems and solutions. The existence of large amounts of data capable of being interpreted through different frameworks allows those who begin with an acceptance of the end times to make common cause with those holding the less explicit religiously rooted belief that government should not regulate economic activity, as well as with those whose personal economic interests lead them to oppose environmental regulation. The existence of competing arguments all of which claim to be based on science adds to public doubts about the proper policies to be pursued, doubts held even by people genuinely interested in protecting the quality of the environment.

Finally, the argument over environmental regulation implicates another important religious belief, that God gave mankind dominion over the earth. A widely quoted fundamentalist high school text, *America's Providential History*, contains the following passage: "[T]he secular or socialist has a limited resource mentality and views the world as a pie . . . that needs to be cut up so everyone can get a piece. . . . The Christian knows that the potential in God is unlimited and that there is no shortage of resources in God's earth" (Moyers 2004). Literalists and modernists both claim to be guided by the passage from Genesis in which God told Adam that he put him in the garden to "till it" and to "keep it." For literalists, this passage provides evidence that the material world is intended to be subordinate to the needs of humans. "Because nature is wild," explains Nina George Hacker in Concerned Women for America's Family Voice, "we [humans] were given the authority to 'subdue' it for life's necessities" (Berkowitz 2001). An "Election Message" issued by Dr. James Dobson and Focus on the Family in 2004 contained the following paragraph:

> Natural Resources: God put human beings on the earth to "subdue it" and to "have dominion" over the animals (Gen. 1:28). . . . The Bible does not view "untouched nature" as the ideal state of the earth, but expects human beings to develop and use the earth's resources wisely for mankind's needs (Gen. 1:28; 2:15; 9:3; 1 Tim. 4:4). . . . We believe the ethical choice is for candidates who will allow resources to be developed. . . . (MacQuarrie 2005)

MODERNIST PROTESTANTS AND THE ENVIRONMENT

Modernist Protestant theologians, needless to say, take a quite different approach to the biblical concept of stewardship. The same year that Focus on the Family published its "Election Message" (2004), the National Council of Churches published "Christian Principles in an Election Year." That document included the statement: "The earth belongs to God and is intrinsically good. We look for political leaders who recognize the earth's goodness, champion environmental justice, and uphold our responsibility to be stewards of God's creation." Perhaps the best summary of liberal Protestant beliefs about environmental policies was issued early in 2005 by a group of theologians convened by the NCC, and signed by representatives of the Presbyterian Church USA, the Greek Orthodox Church, the Christian Methodist Episcopal Church, the Evangelical Lutheran Church, and a number of theology professors and ethicists representing various Christian educational institutions. The statement, entitled "God's Earth is Sacred: An Open Letter to Church and Society in the United States," identified both an environmental and a theological crisis, and proposed the methods through which both must be addressed. The statement began with the following preamble:

> We have listened to a false gospel that we continue to live out in our daily habits—a gospel that proclaims that God cares for the salvation

of humans only and that our human calling is to exploit Earth for our own ends alone. This false gospel still finds its proud preachers and continues to capture its adherents among emboldened political leaders and policy makers.

Asserting that Christians "are obliged to relate to Earth as God's creation in ways that sustain life on the planet," the statement continued by identifying eight norms that should guide Christians and others on a new environmental path: justice, sustainability, bioresponsibility, humility, generosity, frugality, solidarity, and compassion. The text emphasized the signers' belief that committing a crime against the natural world is a sin, and that it directly contests the "conviction that humans can master the earth." It lamented that "we have . . . distorted our God-given abilities and knowledge in order to ransack and often destroy ecosystems and human communities rather than to protect, strengthen and nourish them."

In the early 1990s, liberal Protestants joined with other religious groups to form the National Religious Partnership for the Environment. In addition to the National Council of Churches, the Partnership includes the U.S. Catholic Conference, the Coalition on Environment and Jewish Life, and the Evangelical Environmental Network. The partnership has commissioned scholarly studies on faith and the environment while attempting to provide clergy and lay people with tools for effective involvement in environmental issues. It has also launched public policy campaigns. The reason for such educational efforts was explicitly addressed by Dr. Bob Edgar of the National Council of Churches in a speech delivered in 2003:

> Does it matter to anyone else what faith says about the environment? I would say unequivocally Yes! It matters because of the power of religious ideas to shape life on earth including strong effects on the natural world. It is our religious worldview that tells us what value to place on the natural world and according to what values we may use Earth's precious resources and myriad species. What other sphere is so comprehensive as religion, affecting every aspect of life? Other fields and

disciplines tell us much about pieces of our world, but their scope is limited. . . . Unless the power of religious faith is tapped, I believe that the environmental movement will fall far short of its goals, to the detriment of us all. But this is *not at all* to say that religion should serve the goals of the environmental movement. There is something deeper here that says that care of creation is essentially a spiritual, moral and ethical issue. We can move from the religious ground of our being to gather the scientific, environmental, and social expertise needed to protect and heal creation and to make alliances with mature environmentalism. The moral and spiritual vision is primary, while the science is necessary but not sufficient.

The last two sentences are a succinct statement of the fundamental difference between the worldviews of literalist and modernist Protestants: literalists dispute the validity and authority of science to the extent that is inconsistent with their interpretation of the Bible; modernists accept the value of science as a tool, and its authoritative nature within its provenance, but insist that it be used to advance a broader ethical and moral framework informed by religion.

There is growing evidence that, in this particular policy arena at least, many, if not most, evangelicals agree—at least to some extent—with the modernists' approach. This is partly due to the strength and pervasiveness of the environmental paradigms that characterize the broader culture, and partly to the fact that denominational affiliation is a very inexact proxy for the analytical categories *literalist* and *modernist*. Whatever the explanation, however, it would be highly inaccurate to characterize all or most evangelical Christians as antienvironment. Despite their continued suspicion of the *paganism* of environmental activists, a growing number of evangelicals join with modernists in viewing stewardship of the environment as a responsibility mandated by God. In 2005, the *Washington Post* reported on the issuance of an "Evangelical Call to Civic Responsibility" by the National Association of Evangelicals, an organization representing thirty million members. The call emphasized "every Christian's duty to care for the planet and the role of government in safeguarding a sustainable environment." The statement—which was distributed to fifty thousand member churches—warned members against abusing the "creation of which we are a part." It also noted, in a significant passage, that government regulation of environmental matters is necessary and appropriate, "because clean air, pure water and adequate resources are so crucial to public health and civic order" (Harden 2005). Whatever doctrinal differences may exist between denominations, the available evidence strongly suggests that Vogel's observation about the "deep green" correlation with Protestant political cultures was accurate: the worldviews of an overwhelming majority of Americans include a belief in the importance of environmental stewardship and conservation.

OTHER RELIGIOUS TRADITIONS

In the United States, official pronouncements of both Jews and Catholics are almost uniformly supportive of public and private efforts to protect the environment. There is a millennial tradition in Judaism, but it has been interpreted in a fashion that makes it substantially different from the Protestant millennial tradition. Judaism teaches that "our life-affirming actions produce the reality of a messianic future" (Spiegel 2005). To illustrate this belief in the importance of "life affirming actions," rabbis often quote a midrash (teaching) attributed to Rabbi Yochanan ben Zakkai; the midrash translates as "If you have a sapling in your hand, and someone says to you that the Messiah has come, stay and complete the planting, and then go to greet the Messiah" (Spiegel 2005).

No central authority speaks for American Jews, but the Jewish community includes a substantial number of environmental organizations and activists. The Coalition on the Environment and Jewish Life (COEJL) serves as a national coordinating office for the Jewish environmental movement. Founded in 1993, the coalition is comprised of twenty-six national Jewish organizations spanning the spectrum of American Jewish religious and communal life. It supports a broad range of environmental education and advocacy efforts in the American Jewish community.

American Catholics often cite a 1977 message issued by Pope Paul VI, on the Fifth World-Wide Day of the Environment. The message tied the church's historic concern for the poor to the necessity of environmental stewardship.

> This consciousness of the environment around us is more pressing today than ever. For men who have the means and the ability to construct and ennoble the world about them can also destroy it and squander its goods. Human science and technology have made marvelous gains. But care must be taken that they are used to enhance human life and not to diminish it. Human effort has brought forth much wealth from the earth. But this wealth should not be squandered superfluously by a small minority nor selfishly hoarded for a few at the expense of the rest of mankind in need . . . this Day of celebration of the environment we live in should also be a day of appeal to all of us to be united as custodians of God's creation. It should be a day of rededication to the enterprise of preserving, improving and handing over to future generations a healthy environment in which every person is truly at home. (Pope Paul VI, 1977)

However, not all American Catholics have read the pope's statement as a mandate for environmental regulatory activity. One, Fr. Robert Sirico, CSP, a Catholic priest who heads the Acton Institute for the Study of Religion and Liberty, was instrumental in drafting the antienvironmental Cornwall Declaration. The declaration was issued in 1999, and "sought to counter established faith-based environmental initiatives by Catholic, Jewish, evangelical and especially mainline Protestant bodies" by arguing against a government role and for a "compassionate conservative" approach. "The Cornwall signatories epitomize the current trend in political coalition building on the Christian Right, as conservative evangelicals join rightest Catholics like Fr. Frank Pavone and John Neuhaus, and a few conservative Jews such as Rabbi Daniel Lapin" (Public Eye 2005). Groups like the Cornwall signatories, however, represent only a small minority of American Jews and Catholics. In the United States, Catholics and

Jews must be counted as part of the large majority of Americans who—whatever their differences on the details—are generally supportive of government efforts to protect the environment and conserve resources.

THE EXPLICIT DIMENSION

To this virtual unanimity of doctrinal religious opinion supporting environmental protection must be added the evidence of numerous public opinion polls, showing that by significant margins, Americans—whatever their denominational affiliation or lack thereof—hold worldviews that lead them to support measures to protect the environment. Indeed, the level of support and the intensity with which some green groups express their ecological concerns have led some observers to suggest that for some people, environmentalism itself may be becoming a religion. "Many evangelicals are nervous about pantheism, or what Calvin Beisner calls 'biological egalitarianism,' which, he argues, slights the humans who should dominate the rest of nature" (Marty 2005a). Despite these and other concerns, support for what some call "creation care" is widespread. There may be arguments about the proper methods to employ, or the relative costs and benefits of particular legislation, but rarely are there arguments disputing the importance of protecting America's natural environment. This is one policy area where the polarization on goals that characterizes so many other debates is largely absent.

This lack of polarization raises an obvious question: why hasn't such overwhelming public support been translated into government action? Contrary to what we might expect given the strength of public opinion, Congress regularly passes legislation relaxing environmental safeguards, and just as routinely rejects policies to encourage energy conservation. Many environmental activists trace this disconnect to 1981, when James Watt—then Secretary of the Interior—made a widely quoted speech to Congress in which he said that protecting natural resources was unimportant because Jesus Christ's return was imminent. "God gave us these things to use. After the last tree is felled, Christ will come back" (Scherer 2005). The public furor over Watt's testimony led to his firing, and for a number of years following his termination, if public officials held similar views, they have been less forthright about them.

The attack on environmental regulation subsequently reemerged, however, and that reemergence has been especially dramatic since 2000. This inconsistency between the general public's demonstrable policy preferences and official action is a function of the beliefs of those who make the rules—the members of Congress and various administrative appointees charged with making and enforcing the laws. Scherer notes that in 2003, most of the 231 legislators who received an average approval rating of 80 percent or higher from Christian Right advocacy organizations received a score of 10 percent or less from the League of Conservation Voters. While it is easy to argue with the fairness of calculations issued by such political rating systems, which are intended to "stir up" partisans, it is clear that the lawmakers most likely to be favored by literalist Christian organizations are those who are also least likely to support pro-environmental measures. Furthermore, some of these legislators have been among the most powerful members of Congress since 2000: in the Senate, they include Majority Leader Bill Frist, Majority Whip Mitch McConnell, Republican Policy chair Jon Kyl, and Republican Conference chair Rick Santorum. In the House of Representatives, they include the Speaker, Dennis Hastert, and the Majority Whip and interim majority leader, Roy Blunt (Scherer 2005).

Perhaps the most influential antienvironment lawmakers during this period have been Tom DeLay of Texas, who served as House Majority Leader until criminal indictments forced him first to step down from that position and then to resign from Congress entirely, and Senate Environment and Public Works Committee chair James Inhofe. The religious basis of other lawmakers' votes may be arguable, but these two legislators have been quite explicit about the beliefs that motivate their efforts. DeLay has often said that he wants Congress to "march forward with a biblical worldview" (Perl 2001). Inhofe, who has argued for policies on the basis that "God says so," and who told an interviewer that "I don't believe there is a single issue we deal with in government that hasn't been dealt with in the Scriptures," has called global warming "the greatest hoax ever perpetrated on the American people" (Scherer 2005). While it would be a mistake to discount the influence of campaign contributions from industries affected by environmental regulations, congressional hostility to environmental regulations clearly has an explicitly religious dimension. Both the underlying worldviews and the conscious beliefs of those who make and enforce our laws are inevitably reflected in those laws, and at least in the environmental arena, lawmakers' explicit religious commitments have trumped evidence of broad public support for regulation.

THE INTERSECTION OF SCIENCE AND WORLDVIEWS

It would be both inaccurate and unfair to divide all participants in environmental policy debates into opposing categories labeled *religious* and *scientific*. As noted previously, with the exception of those holding conscious, literalist commitments, most Americans want to do what is necessary to prevent further degradation of the natural world. Few of us, however, have a sufficient understanding of the science supporting various proposals to make informed judgments about their probable efficacy. This is where conflicting worldviews do matter, because our willingness to consider any particular proposal reasonable will be affected by our attitudes toward government, science, and the economy.

Furthermore, scientists are not immune from the effects of their own value commitments. As Sarewitz has written:

> [T]he growth of considerable bodies of scientific knowledge, created especially to resolve political dispute and enable effective decision making, has often been accompanied instead by growing political controversy and gridlock. Science typically lies at the center of the debate, where those who advocate some line of action are likely to claim a scientific justification for their position, while those opposing the action will either invoke scientific uncertainty or competing scientific results to support their opposition. (2004, 386)

Despite occasional charges of academic dishonesty, accusations that this group of scientists or that has "sold out" to (choose one) corporate interests or left-wing ideology, it is highly unlikely that serious scientists are promoting research results they know to be false. They are simply framing their questions and arriving at their conclusions—as we all do—through the lenses of their individual worldviews.

Even where science has achieved consensus on the reality and/or severity of a problem, policy makers—viewing those problems through their various frameworks—will frequently disagree on the best way to solve the problem. Again, it should be emphasized that much of that disagreement is the honest result of analyses conducted through the frameworks of particular value structures. Lawmakers whose worldviews tend to favor collective action will opt for policies giving government more control over emissions, fuel efficiency standards, and the like; those who place more trust in the efficacy of market mechanisms will support tax incentives and other "carrots" in lieu of regulatory "sticks." Both approaches may be motivated by genuine commitment to the goal of finding the most effective way to protect the environment. We do not advance the cause of political consensus and responsible government policy by assuming that everyone advocating views with which we disagree is either corrupt or a religious zealot.

Chapter 9

SIN AND CRIME

There has been substantial research by criminal justice scholars on the relationship—or lack thereof—between religiosity and criminal behavior. Researchers have explored the effectiveness of prison ministries; religious efforts to counter drug addiction, prevent juvenile delinquency, and remake or rethink prisons; and the connections between religiosity and lawful behavior in general. There has been considerably less attention paid to the more basic questions with which this book has been occupied: how different cultural paradigms, rooted in religious belief, affect construction of our social world, including the threshold question of how a society defines the acts it considers criminal and thus subject to state sanction.

DEFINING CRIME

By definition, crime is behavior that a particular society has chosen to condemn and punish. Some actions have been considered criminal by most societies at most times: murder, rape, and robbery come immediately to mind, but even these are highly dependent upon social norms and cultural definitions. Killing in self-defense is generally not considered murder. Legal definitions of and sanctions against rape have evolved over time as attitudes about gender roles have changed, and rape laws still vary widely among societies. Other crimes are more clearly affronts to particular cultural norms at particular times. In our Puritan past we have outlawed heresy, absence from church, drunkenness, conducting business on Sunday, and similar *unchristian* behaviors (as well as nonexistent ones like witchcraft). Until relatively recently, suicide was a capital offense in many states, as illogical as that may seem. As social norms have changed, the use of the coercive power of the state to enforce particularistic piety has come to be seen as illegitimate, but there is still a substantial tendency of Americans to conflate criminal and *sinful* behaviors. Secular arguments over criminal justice policy often grow out of the ongoing tension between our Puritan and Enlightenment paradigms. We may see this most clearly in the debates over *consensual* or *victimless* crimes like gambling, prostitution, and substance abuse. Consensual sodomy remained a criminal offense in fourteen states until the Supreme Court's 2003 ruling in *Lawrence v. Texas*.

Support for such measures is grounded in America's Puritan history—the belief that the government's task is to build the City on the Hill, and that the police power of that government must therefore be deployed to elevate and protect the public morality. America has a long history of criminalizing nonconforming behaviors, although that history has been subject to the ebb and flow of other intellectual currents. As Morone has noted, "although Christian fundamentalists have played a critical role in framing the American moral debate, many voices—from almost every political quarter—[have] amplified the sermons about spiritual decline. . . . The message boiled down to this: our society has abandoned the morals that once guided us. And there will be hell to pay" (2003 454, 455).

The modernist worldview, by contrast, is rooted in quite different assumptions about the purpose of government, assumptions reflecting the Enlightenment commitment to individual moral autonomy, and the necessity of limiting state power. In the famous libertarian construct, the state is justified in interfering with an individual's action only when that action harms the person or property of a nonconsenting other. This approach still leaves considerable space for arguments about the nature of harm and what constitutes meaningful consent. Does the wide availability of pornography "pollute" society, thus harming all of us, especially children? What about violence? Would decriminalization of drugs amount to a tacit endorsement of the right to use them, and if so, would that encourage added abuse leading to crime? Can the government penalize people who do not buckle up on the grounds that failure to do so will lead to higher insurance rates for everyone? Once criminal behavior is defined as that which causes harm, even those who approach state power through an Enlightenment framework must agree on the nature and degree of harm sufficient to justify state intervention. Furthermore, since most Americans hold worldviews that have been influenced by both Puritan and Enlightenment perspectives, we often find it difficult to agree on those crucial definitions.

To complicate matters further, literalists and modernists will evaluate the criminal justice system differently, because they not only begin with quite different conceptions of the legitimacy of the police power, but with different conceptions of its purposes. Literalists, echoing the Puritans, place a high value on the symbolic importance of the legal system. Failure to criminalize a behavior is tantamount, in that view, to endorsing it. It is collective complicity in sin. There is a significantly aspirational element to law in the Puritan paradigm, and accordingly less emphasis on demonstrated efficacy. Modernists begin with a quite different concept of the goals to be achieved, seeing the system as a utilitarian effort to secure social order and protect persons and property with the minimum amount of interference in activities that do not threaten that order. Modernists thus tend to disapprove of laws passed to send a message, and instead bring their general reliance upon science and empirical evidence to bear on questions of effectiveness and enforceability. We can see this dynamic rather clearly in arguments about the criminalization of consensual sexual behaviors like sodomy. Modernists point out that such laws are essentially unenforceable, that they tend to be applied—when applied at all—arbitrarily, and that they thus reduce respect for the rule of law. Literalists find these arguments quite beside the point. They believe that the absence of such laws will be read as acceptance of the behavior, which they condemn as unbiblical and/or immoral.

The argument about sodomy laws is one of those areas where the religious roots of a policy dispute are clear. But less visible religious paradigms about the propriety of government sanctions, the purposes of law, and the nature of culpability and social harm permeate the criminal justice system. Conservatives who charge that the system *coddles* criminals rest that assertion on fundamental premises about individual culpability and human nature. There are striking parallels to the arguments over social welfare discussed in chapter 7: modernists argue for more systemic approaches, and point to research indicating that structural and social environments influence criminal behavior; conservatives scorn social approaches that they believe diminish personal responsibility, arguing (as Ronald Reagan repeatedly did), "Don't blame society; blame the sinner" (Morone 2003, 454).

Arguments about relative social and individual responsibility for bad behavior owe a great deal to attitudes about human nature derived from Calvinism and the doctrine of original sin. Sometimes, the relationship is quite explicit; in *Justice That Restores*, Charles Colson argues that government's primary task is to restrain sin, and he founds that argument on belief in original sin—a belief he says was abandoned in the Enlightenment.

> In the area of criminal justice, for example, the most significant harm wrought by the Enlightenment in displacing the Christian worldview was that of saddling us with a view of humankind that was not only wrong, but wrong in such a way as to guarantee us centuries of ineffective law enforcement, with all the human suffering that involves. As I've said before, I don't mean to imply that sinful humanity somehow got everything right up until the Enlightenment. Most of the failed and flawed criminal justice policies of this past century, to which the high crime rates and burgeoning prison systems of our countries stand as towering monuments, can be traced to a wrong view of human nature, a wrong answer to the second great worldview question, "Who are we and why are we in the mess we are in?"

Later, Colson concludes,

> But to say that the law should reflect God's order; to say that government serves to restrain sin is to presuppose sin. And it is precisely on this point that the two great worldviews contending for our allegiance in the world today, secular naturalism and biblical theism, clash most dramatically. They represent utterly antithetical viewpoints and lead to dramatically different under-standings of how government should function to preserve order and promote justice. (2001,15–16)

Colson's characterization of the conflict between worldviews is entirely accurate. Of course, most Americans do not hold pure versions of either worldview; most of us have incorporated elements of both.

Puritan and Enlightenment paradigms can also be seen in the recurring arguments over due process guarantees. A breach of legal duty by police or prosecutors that leads to a dismissal of charges or to the reversal of a conviction will be seen as "letting criminals off on a technicality" by those approaching the issue through a Puritan paradigm, and as a method of controlling the power of the state and ensuring the fairness of the system by those using an Enlightenment framework. Literalists will tend to emphasize proper results over impartial processes—ends over means—and define justice as punishment of the wrongdoer. If some corners must be cut in order to achieve the just result, it may be regrettable but sometimes it is necessary. Modernists place greater emphasis on the importance of limiting state power and ensuring the integrity of the process; they begin with a greater willingness to see an occasional wrongdoer escape punishment if they can thereby reduce the risk of unfair imprisonment of innocent individuals. Fourth Amendment issues of search and seizure often display this conflict; in arguments over drug testing in public high schools, for example, literalists will argue that students who have nothing to hide should not object to random testing, while modernists will argue that government should be required to demonstrate a sound reason (individualized suspicion) for choosing to test a particular student.

Criminal justice policy debates are conducted primarily—although certainly not exclusively, as the quotation from Colson attests—in the language of the Enlightenment. So efforts to ban adult bookstores or adult nightclubs will be based upon arguments that their presence generates criminal activity, rather than upon the sinful nature of the business, whatever the real impetus for those attempts. Alcohol and drug prohibition efforts are supported by assertions that drinking or drug use leads to criminal acts. Prostitution is said to increase transmission of sexually transmitted disease, and so forth. Unfortunately, such justifications have often not withstood empirical scrutiny. In one study of the effects of adult businesses, for example, researchers concluded:

> We find that the presence of an adult nightclub does not increase the number of crime incidents reported in localized areas surrounding the club (defined by circular areas of 500- and 1,000-foot radii) as compared to the number of crime incidents reported in comparable localized areas that do not contain such an adult business. Indeed, the analyses imply the opposite, namely, that the nearby areas surrounding the adult business sites have smaller numbers of reported crime incidents than do corresponding areas surrounding the three control sites studied. (Linz et al. 2004, 69)

There is a large criminal justice research literature considering the effects of drug prohibition, and a substantial consensus that most criminal activity associated with drug traffic is a result of prohibition, not the abuse itself. (Much the same phenomenon accompanied the national experiment with alcohol prohibition; following repeal of the Eighteenth Amendment, murder rates declined precipitously.) Proponents of legal prostitution argue that, if preventing disease were truly the goal, laws would punish violation of health regulations rather than practices deemed immoral. They point to Nevada, where prostitution is legal but regulated and the health of sex workers is monitored. In some areas, research is mixed or inconclusive, but in others, it is quite compelling. Our continued resistance to policy changes based upon such evidence is more likely to be a function of underlying worldviews inconsistent with that evidence—not just our religious paradigms, it is important to recognize, but similarly ingrained attitudes about class, race, and social status—than a result of thoughtful analysis of the effectiveness of the particular policy in achieving its stated purpose.

RELIGION AND THE GOOD SOCIETY

As we have seen in previous chapters, Puritans believe that social order and law are possible only in a society where most citizens are, if not Christian, at least religious. This conviction undergirds policy preferences in a number of areas: education, law, social welfare, and especially criminal justice. Belief in the social utility of religion is at the heart of ongoing battles over school prayer and is the foundation of faith-based social programs and prison ministries. Policymakers routinely assert that religious people are happier, more likely to marry, less likely to have children out of wedlock, less likely to be juvenile delinquents or adult criminals, and less likely to engage in other antisocial activities. Unfortunately, this confidence in the social utility of religion not only begs the question whether coerced religious expression would be equally useful, but it is not supported by research.[1] To the extent that studies have found a correlation between religious commitment and lawful behavior—that is, a negative relationship between religiosity and social deviance—it has varied by denomination, type of offense, and social context (Evans et al. 1995). Some researchers argue that any positive effects are likely to be the results of familial supports, social bonding, and socioeconomic factors rather than religious belief per se, while others find positive effects even after controlling for those variables (Johnson et al. 2001). Still others have found a relationship between religion and adolescent alcohol use, but not between religion and adolescent crime (Rodell and Benda 1999). This is an area where

---

[1] The belief in the *utility* of religion arguably displays the adopting of at least some of the perspectives of enlightment utilitarianism. The notion that religion must be justified by reference to its usefulness as a tool of social control raises intriguing questions—questions that go well beyond the purview of this discussion, however.

methodological challenges are significant, and different researchers come to different conclusions based in part upon the way they define and measure both religious commitment and illegal activity.

Correlation is not the same thing as causation, of course, and studies suggesting that highly religious cultures may be less healthy than more secularized ones must also be viewed with that caveat. In a 2005 article in the *Journal of Religion and Society*, Gregory Paul notes the widespread belief that religion is important for social health, and the accompanying concern that the doctrine of evolution—by undermining belief in God—is detrimental to social cohesion and civic virtue. He writes, "In the United States many conservative theists consider evolutionary science a leading contributor to social dysfunction because it is amoral or worse, and because it inspires disbelief in a moral creator" (2). Noting his surprise "that a more systematic examination of the question has not been previously executed since the factors required to do so are in place," Paul proceeded to look at cross-national indicators of social health, religious belief, and acceptance of Darwinian science.

> With surveys showing a strong majority from conservative to liberal believing that religion is beneficial for society and for individuals, many Americans agree that their church-going nation is an exceptional, God blessed, "shining city on the hill" that stands as an impressive example for an increasingly skeptical world. But in other developed democracies religiosity continues to decline precipitously and avowed atheists often win high office. (4)

Contrary to popular expectation, Paul found a correlation between higher rates of belief in a creator and higher rates of homicide, juvenile and early adult mortality, STD infection rates, teen pregnancy, and abortion. He found the least theistic nations to be the least dysfunctional on these dimensions, and found no democracy where strong religiosity and widespread rejection of Darwin co-existed with societal health. There are many possible explanations for America's status as an outlier on these measures: greater diversity, the immense role that racial bias continues to play in our society, and the relative youth of the country itself. Whatever the causes, however, Americans' greater religiosity has clearly not correlated with greater social health.

RELIGIOUS WORLDVIEWS AND SPECIFIC POLICIES

Religion and religiously rooted worldviews intersect with the criminal justice system at many different points. The growing pluralism of America's religious landscape presents new challenges to policing, much as language and other cultural differences do. Nancy Ammerman has written about one such challenge: the tragic confrontation by federal law enforcement officers and the Branch Davidians in Waco, Texas. The strategies chosen by the FBI displayed total incomprehension of the worldviews of apocalyptic believers, and it obviously never occurred to the authorities that there might be religious scholars who could assist them in handling the problem more effectively. As Nancy Ammerman described the attitudes of the law men, "They saw no reason to try to understand [Koresh's] religious beliefs, indeed thought them so bizarre as to be incomprehensible by normal people. . . . People in positions of public service have perhaps come to believe that religion is not a part of the culture about which they have any need to be conversant, whether or not they themselves are believers" (Ammerman 1995, 2). The different paradigms held by law enforcement officers and those who violate the law are rarely this obvious, although they emerge from time to time; bombings of abortion clinics and murders of doctors providing abortion services are an example. Far more common are the different attitudes about the legitimacy of law, the use of force, and the purposes of the police power—differences that are fostered by different religious cultures.

Punishment

Worldviews shape our initial classification of behaviors as either lawful or criminal. They affect our beliefs about human nature, and they heavily influence our attitudes about the appropriate use of the police power. They also dictate how we perceive the purpose and appropriateness of punishment. Penal philosophies tend to fall into three broad categories based upon different beliefs about the purposes to be served by collective punitive mechanisms: retributive, utilitarian, or redemptive.

Retribution is sometimes confused with vengeance, but the two are not synonymous: retribution is certainly focused upon punishment, but it includes concerns about proportionality of the offense and the sanction, and consistency in the application of the sanctions. Most systems based on retribution discount the likelihood of rehabilitation and place primary focus on the operations of penal mechanisms and institutions. Utilitarianism is a product of Enlightenment philosophy and the social contract: in return for giving government a monopoly on the legitimate use of coercive power, government undertakes to ensure the public safety. An effective justice system will administer only so much punishment as is necessary to the achievement of that result and will employ methods that are empirically demonstrated to be effective. Utilitarian systems stress punishment that is appropriate to the severity of the offense, prompt, and—if not inevitable, which would be the ideal—highly likely, believing that these elements are most likely to achieve deterrence, which is a major goal of a utilitarian system. Redemptive approaches are sometimes called *restorative justice*. They begin with an emphasis on forgiveness, hope, and earned redemption. The catechism of the Catholic Church contains what may be the most apt description of this approach: it provides that the punishment should "redress the disorder caused by the offense. When this punishment is voluntarily accepted by the offender, it takes on the value of expiation" (2006). Faith-based programs and prison ministries tend to fall within this model.

There are literally thousands of books and a copious academic literature on each of these penal philosophies, and this truncated description certainly cannot adequately describe them. Nevertheless, it is possible to see the influence of religiously rooted cultural worldviews even in their broad outlines. Sociologists studying punishment view cultural norms as an important aspect of their scholarship. As one scholar has noted,

> Today, cultural analysis is a prominent feature of writing in this field. Writers pay close attention to the role of culture in the shaping of pun-

ishment, and to the cultural consequences of penal practices. Not the least reason for this shift was the realization that culture encodes and is encoded by economic and political forces, and that the analysis of culture is not a distraction from the study of penal power's controlling effects but is, on the contrary, a vital component of such study. (Garland 2004)

There is relatively little research on the influence of religion on policy preferences related to prisons and punishment, but the research that has focused on this question has found literalists to be more supportive of retribution and more punitive in general. They are more likely to support capital punishment and more likely to favor harsher prison conditions and longer prison sentences (Unnever et al. 2005). Applegate, Cullen, Fisher, and Vander Ven have found that, "People interpreting the Bible literally and people perceiving God as punitive tend to favor harsher courts, harsher treatment of juvenile offenders, capital punishment for both adults and juveniles, and retribution" (2000, 723). Religious modernists who emphasize more forgiving elements of the biblical text, and who envision God as loving and compassionate, were found to be more supportive of rehabilitation and treatment, and significantly less punitive in their views. This finding is consistent with the significant role played by many liberal Christians and Jews in prison reform efforts over the years. One of the very first efforts to establish a "modern" prison was in Philadelphia, in 1790, where Quakers were instrumental in establishing the Walnut Street Jail. The term *penitentiary* is said to have originated with the Quaker concern with penitence as an essential element of reform.

Rehabilitation, Redemption, and the Constitution

Prison ministries are a long-standing feature of American correctional institutions, where they raise thorny constitutional issues. The nature of the dilemma is illustrated by the testimony of literalist advocates of religious interventions: they are convinced that religion is necessary to moral behavior, and are thus very clear that the only way to help teenagers on drugs, or prisoners, is through religious conversion. A quotation from Jack Cowley, national director of operations for The InnerChange Prison Fellowship Ministry, is illustrative. According to Cowley, "We see crime as a result of sin and therefore we know that a relationship with Christ can heal people." Unlike faith-based organizations providing social services, most prison ministries have explicitly religious doctrines as the primary content of their programs: acceptance of Jesus and the primacy of biblical precepts and morality.

Prison Fellowship Ministries, one of the most prominent of the prison programs, describes itself as "Christ-based" and its vision as "That God's kingdom will be manifested as the redemptive grace and peace of Jesus Christ are experienced by those impacted by crime." The organization's Web page argues that crime is fundamentally a moral and spiritual problem that requires a moral and spiritual solution, and asserts that "offenders do not simply need rehabilitation; they require regeneration of a sinful heart." As Mark Earlry and Jim Tonkowich wrote (in an article about the InnerChange Freedom Initiative in *Liberty Magazine* [2003]),

> What we need in our correctional system is an opportunity for hearts to be transformed, not simply for people to get some job skills. What Prison Fellowship provides in InnerChange Freedom Initiative is not only skills, but hearts that have been transformed through the love of God and the power of the Gospel of Jesus Christ. And this is of great benefit to prisoners, their families, their victims, their communities and, ultimately, our whole society.

Prison programs like InnerChange have religious conversion as their primary purpose. Funding for such programs is thus funding for religion and—under decades of First Amendment jurisprudence—constitutionally prohibited. In 2003, Americans United for Separation of Church and State filed suit in the Southern District of Iowa, challenging InnerChange over a religious program conducted in Iowa's Newton Correctional Facility. The complaint alleged that inmates who participated in the program were housed in a separate unit in the prison, where they were immersed in twenty-four-hour per day Christ-centered Bible-based programming conducted by InnerChange employees, who were required by policy to be Christian. Tax dollars were used to support the program and to pay a portion of the salaries of InnerChange employees, and inmates who volunteered to participate received special privileges—keys to their cells, private bathrooms, and access to computers.

Americans United made an entirely modernist argument: preferential treatment by government based solely upon religious belief violates constitutional guarantees of religious liberty. The Enlightenment beliefs incorporated in the First Amendment forbid privileging some religions over others, or religion over nonreligion. Whatever the merits of the program, it is inconsistent with a basic foundation of American law. InnerChange responded from a literalist perspective, which accords more importance to ends (inculcating religious virtue) than means (obeying the niceties of First Amendment jurisprudence). The Federal District Court, predictably, ruled for Americans United and against the InnerChange program's defenders. The case is being appealed, but it is hard to imagine that the literalists will prevail. If the program is ultimately ruled unconstitutional, the literalists will undoubtedly view that result as part of the marginalization of religion—the ejection of religion from the public square that they see as a reality of contemporary American life. Modernists will respond that the public square remains open to all; that what the literalists have been denied is preferential treatment by the public sector. Both sides will be bemused by the other's failure to understand the situation.

Capital Punishment

With the exception of arguments over faith-based programs, the role of religious worldviews in attitudes toward prison policies is considerably less visible than the religious dimension of arguments about capital punishment. Religious modernists (joined by many—but certainly not all—literalist Catholics, who start from different premises than literalist Protestants in this area) often ground their positions on very explicit theological beliefs about the sanctity of life and the nature of justice. "An eye for an eye" is met by "vengeance is mine, saith the Lord." In addition to beliefs about the sanctity of life, religious and secular modernists who oppose the death penalty generally argue that capital punishment has not been found to have a deterrent effect, that it is much more costly than incarceration, that our federalist system makes imposition of the death penalty highly arbitrary, that the inevitable fallibility of the system means that innocent people are executed, and that the United States is the only Western democracy that continues to impose capital punishment. The utilitarian worldviews of those making these arguments is quite clear: if the purpose of a penal practice is to deter others from committing similar offenses, then evidence that the practice does not have that effect is reason to abandon it. Similarly, if the costs incurred outweigh the benefits, it is time to reassess. Unequal application of the penalty is unjust in a system founded upon belief in equality before the law, and fosters public resentment and racial tensions. The execution of innocent people is the ultimate injustice. America's continued imposition of capital punishment not only makes us an outlier in the Western world, but complicates law enforcement efforts to cooperate with other countries to apprehend criminals and terrorists, because many of those countries will not extradite detainees to a jurisdiction where they will face the death penalty. The bottom line, say the modernists, is that capital punishment does not serve the purposes of justice and should be abandoned in favor of life in prison.

Literalists find none of these arguments persuasive. They also ground their policy preferences on a belief in the sanctity of life, but believe that it is precisely because of that sanctity that justice is required, and justice is "a life for a life, an eye for an eye, a tooth for a tooth." To each of the other objections to capital punishment raised by the modernists, they also bring a quite different perspective. They respond to the rather overwhelming evidence that the death penalty does not deter others from killing by pointing to the undeniable fact that it prevents the person who is executed from killing again. Since the greater costs of capital punishment are largely attributable to the availability of a lengthy appeals process, they argue that "streamlining" and limiting appellate review will achieve two goals: it will reduce the costs of executing wrongdoers, and it will make justice swifter. Acknowledging that some errors will inevitably occur—some innocent people will be executed—many death penalty proponents consider it an unfortunate side effect of justice, much as occasional infections resulting from public immunizations are an unfortunate side effect of ensuring the public health. Literalists are actually offended by the argument that America should consider the practices of other countries when making decisions about our domestic laws—their firm belief in American exceptionalism leads them to the position that taking account of international legal practices is an affront to American sovereignty.

The Drug War

Proponents and opponents of capital punishment bring incompatible paradigms to that debate, and the foregoing discussion demonstrates the ways in which those paradigms cause them to talk past each other. Both points of view are internally consistent, but their consistency flows from vastly different premises about the nature of justice and the proper purposes of government. Much the same dynamic can be seen in American drug policy disputes. There is an enormous amount of legal, sociological, medical, and criminal policy research on the causes of drug addiction, the comparative efficacy of efforts to battle substance abuse, and the costs and outcomes of prohibition. Most of that research is sharply critical of America's war on drugs.

Most opposition to the drug war is rooted in a very utilitarian argument: drug prohibition does not work. In 1988, the United States government spent 3.6 billion dollars directly on the drug war. In 1999 it spent over 17–17.9 billion, according to the Drug Enforcement Agency's own figures. These amounts do not include the ancillary costs of extra police officers, prison construction and operation, or extra courts. These expenditures have not affected addiction rates; aside from marijuana use, which tends to fluctuate, America's addict population has remained virtually unchanged. Worse, as sociologists and economists (notably Milton Friedman) have documented, most criminal activity stemming from drug trafficking is a direct result of prohibition, without which it would be far less profitable. Indeed, criminal justice scholars emphasize the negative impact of prohibition on public safety. In *Drug Crazy* (2000), author Mike Gray documented the similarities between the war on drugs and America's failed experiment with alcohol prohibition. The most striking data he provided was a chart overlaying the U.S. murder rate with the dates of prohibition and the drug war. Immediately following the end of prohibition, murders plummeted. They did not spike upward again until we got serious about the drug war.

If our goal is to reduce the number of people who abuse drugs, we have ample evidence that increased criminal sanctions have not accomplished that, and are unlikely to do so in the future. Against that failure, critics weigh the enormous social and fiscal costs involved. Civil libertarians complain that the drug war has spawned abuses by law enforcement; that in their zeal, authorities often ignore the rights of suspects. African Americans contend that the drug war is more accurately characterized as a war on black America, that despite ample evidence that most drug abuse occurs in white suburban and rural communities, enforcement efforts are virtually all concentrated in black urban areas. Doctors complain that the zealousness of the drug war has prevented even the clinical study of the ameliorative effects of marijuana for certain ailments. And lawyers, judges, and law enforcement officers concede that there is little sense in the legal distinctions drawn between abuse of many legal medications and illegal, *scheduled* drugs, or between alcohol and marijuana. In fact, studies consistently show a much higher link between violent crime and alcohol than between violent crime and cannabis. As Kappeler, Blumberg, and Potter have reported, "The only drug for which a clear causal link with crime has been established is alcohol—a legal drug." They go on to note that "[w]hile there is no causal link between drugs and crime, the same cannot be said for drug laws" (2000, 155).

Finally, modernists argue that drug abuse, like alcoholism and smoking, is fundamentally a public health problem, and that we should treat it as a public health problem rather than through the criminal justice system. They charge that spending billions of dollars to throw nonviolent people in prison wastes tax dollars, distorts the criminal justice system, and decimates our inner cities. And, they remind us, it also doesn't work.

Literalists, as we have seen, come from a quite different perspective and begin with a different set of priorities. They want to reduce drug abuse, but they also want to create a society where the law reflects a collective commitment to morality. Laws should thus send a message about what morality looks like. Furthermore, their views of human nature are grounded in their belief in original sin. This leads very logically to a conviction that people will behave badly unless restrained by strong state enforcement of social norms. They believe that decriminalization of drugs will inexorably lead to increased abuse of those drugs—that in the absence of sanctions, most people will sin. Similarly, efforts to substitute treatment for punishment are seen by literalists as efforts to evade personal responsibility, to coddle wrongdoers and blame society rather than the sinner. Proposals to decriminalize marijuana, or to permit its medicinal use, meet resistance from the literalist tendency to view policies as stark, all-or-nothing choices between good and evil.

SUMMING UP

Attitudes about the criminal law are not rooted exclusively in these religious paradigms, of course. Like all other policy disputes, criminal justice policies in America are affected significantly by regional, ethnic, racial, and gender differences, and by ideological positions unrelated to religious culture. But a full understanding of the religious roots of these arguments, and partisans' resistance to expert evidence inconsistent with their worldviews, requires recognition of the religious perspectives that play so large a role in shaping American attitudes toward crime and punishment. As Kenneth J. Meier has written in "Drugs, Sex, and Rock and Roll," the politics of sin are particularly difficult.

> Compromise is not a viable strategy because that implies compromising one's deeply held values and because support is often perceived to

be greater than it actually is. This suggests that policy failures will be expensive failures, because the moderating influence of incrementalism will be absent in policy design. Expertise has no value because the issues grow out of conflict between core values; salience and simplicity trump expertise in such situations. (2001, 27)

Chapter 10

GOD AND COUNTRY, US AND THEM

The incomplete (and occasionally incoherent) synthesis of Americans' Puritan and Enlightenment worldviews is particularly confounding in the foreign policy arena. If our Enlightenment-rooted reliance on science and empirical evidence has been the predominant influence on national attitudes about the natural environment, religiously rooted moral paradigms have just as decisively provided the context within which we approach foreign policy. Conventional wisdom categorizes foreign policy preferences as either *realist* or *Wilsonian idealist*, but a fair reading of American history suggests that these are relative terms for characterizing approaches all of which fall within a decidedly Protestant moralistic worldview founded in no small part on a belief in American exceptionalism. David Gelernter, an unabashed and self-defined patriot, has written that "Americanism is in fact a Judeo-Christian religion; a millenarian religion; a biblical religion" (2005, 2). While American religiosity is neither the undifferentiated force nor the unalloyed good that Gelernter seems to believe, he is undoubtedly correct in identifying the largely religious paradigm that frames America's approach to foreign policy.

Of course, in foreign affairs as in domestic policy disputes, it is not always easy to trace the roots of conflict, or to distinguish between religious and temporal disputes. As the eminent historian Walter McDougall has written:

> In sum, the interplay of religion and politics has been and remains more complicated than conventional wisdom suggests. In some cases, apparent religious conflicts—from early modern times to the Northern Irish and Bosnian strife today—can be interpreted as familiar turf battles in which religious prejudice has played the role of a "force multiplier," inspiring greater zeal and sacrifice from the masses. By the same token, the origins and outcomes of apparent political conflicts—from the Crimean and Russo-Japanese wars to the recent war in Afghanistan—were powerfully influenced by religion. It was Napoleon, after all, who recognized that "In war, the moral is to the material as three is to one." . . . [O]ur notions of history are skewed by the tendency of Western intellectuals to think in dialectical terms. Thus, we set realism and idealism, or secularism and religion, against one another as if they were mutually exclusive. In fact, the most profound students of Christian moral theology from Thomas Aquinas to Niebuhr argued that whatever is "unrealistic" (hence contrary to natural law) cannot by definition be moral! Applied to statecraft, this means that to expect utopian results from diplomacy and war is inevitably to invite immoral consequences. . . . A truly moral approach to statecraft, therefore, takes human nature as it is, respects limits, and acknowledges the contingency of all human creation . . . there is no virtue in stupidity. (1998, 3)

McDougall's insight is important: American realists and idealists do not represent a conflict between amoral pragmatism and moral principle; they are advancing arguments about policy that are equally rooted in morality and religious culture, but they are drawing different conclusions—often based on differing analyses of the facts—about where that morality lies. Although today's "neoconservatives have often been supported by those elements of conservative evangelicalism with a robust, militaristic, and nationalistic sense of America's purpose in the world" (Thomas 2005, 25), partisans in these conflicts often fail to fit comfortably into their expected categories in the hypothesized "culture wars."

Realists may thus include literalists who believe in original sin; Wilsonian interventionists can be found among both millennialists and modernist social gospelers. David Gelernter to the contrary, there is no single Judeo-Christian approach to Americanism.

It seems more accurate to suggest that the uneasy and imperfect melding of Puritan religious worldviews with Enlightenment rationality, synthesized through our various national encounters with historical events, has given rise to a peculiarly American worldview, to what Roland Homet has called prevailing national attitudes and Richard Hughes has dubbed national myths, that profoundly influences American foreign policy preferences. Homet categorizes those attitudes as Triumphalism (including "the white man's burden" and various apocalyptic beliefs), Beneficence (or *liberal humanitarian imperialism*), and Modesty (realism and humility) (Homet 2001). As we have previously seen, Hughes has identified myths of "The Chosen Nation," "The Millennial Nation," and "The Innocent Nation," among others. Those attitudes and myths are a product of our national self-image and the (largely Puritan) narratives we have constructed to describe America's place in the world. Our national stories have informed a passionate nationalism that some critics argue is "the most powerful religion in the United States" (Marvin and Ingle 1996).

OUR STORIES, OURSELVES

Political leaders use what Rogers Smith has called *stories of peoplehood* to win support for a particular vision of America's identity and purpose. These stories are necessary because political communities are rarely, if ever, organic or natural; leaders cannot rely only on the use of coercive force, but must articulate a vision of communal identity—persuasive stories—if they are to forge such political communities

> [S]uch community-building narratives are always comprised of three types of elements: economic stories, which promise that membership will prevent economic exploitation . . . political power stories, which promise protection against coercive abuses and a share in the collective power of a strong political community . . . and "ethically constitutive"

stories, stories that present membership as an expression of traits that are somehow intrinsic to who members are, in ways that are ethically valuable. (Smith 2005, 3)

As Smith reminds us, stories of peoplehood inevitably have implications for foreign policy.

America's stories embody many of the religiously rooted paradigms discussed previously: a world divided into good and evil; a world in which the United States is *called* to be the City on the Hill; a world where capitalism is God's preferred economic system.[1] (Feminists also are quick to note the biblical patriarchal foundations of our concepts of authority and national self-image.) The elements of our self-image that Richard Hughes, Roland Homet, and many others have identified operate to structure our perceptions of, and responses to, world events: Samuel Huntington (2002) has gone so far as to suggest that the attacks of September 11 mobilized Americans' self-identification as a "Christian Nation." If that claim seems exaggerated, it is certainly true that our various interpretations of the obligations imposed by our chosenness shape our approach to multinational institutions and unilateral action, as does our persistent belief in America's innocence. Our national stories are important and their effects are by no means all negative; they are a covenant between our self-image and our obligations as citizens, and the "glue" holding an increasingly diverse people together. But they are also susceptible to many meanings. Like the Bible, America's constituent documents and national history teach different lessons to different readers. As James Traub has recently noted, foreign policy debates are "not so much the familiar one[s] between unsentimental realists and Wilsonian idealists as between doctrinal absolutists and empiricists" (2005, 8).

---

[1] In an article in *Christianity Today*, Eugene McCarraher engages in a withering diatribe against what he calls "the perverse religiosity of late-capitalist America" and argues that "civil religion—whose sectarian disputes are the 'culture wars'—defines redemption as inclusion in the capitalist market and pledges allegiance to what Philip Bobbit has called a 'market state.'"(1)

A "BIBLE" OF FOREIGN AFFAIRS

There is a copious literature on foreign policy, and many conceptual frameworks through which we might analyze the intertwined nature of our religiously rooted national mythology and our more empirically grounded strategic foreign policy decisions. One particularly useful approach has been outlined by Walter McDougall in *Promised Land, Crusader State: The American Encounter with the World Since 1776*. McDougall is a historian, and it is from a historical perspective that he divides American foreign policy into *Old Testament* and *New Testament* phases, the first phase running from 1776 until the 1890s, and the second dominating the years since. He underscores many of the same themes that Hughes, a scholar of religion, addressed in *Myths America Lives By*. McDougall believes that America has developed eight discrete foreign policy traditions since 1776, and he argues that none of those traditions has ever died—they all have contemporary adherents, and as he notes wryly, "several of them coexist uneasily within individual breasts" (xi). As he describes the phenomenon, "A democracy of many religious and secular faiths . . . is constantly at war with itself over matters of right and wrong, prudence and folly. In domestic policy, its battleground is the law; in foreign policy it is the hallowed traditions—the holy writ—that ought to guide its diplomacy" (4). Among the American foreign policy traditions that McDougall identifies as Old Testament are American Exceptionalism, Unilateralism, the Monroe Doctrine, and Manifest Destiny.

We have already seen that Americans' almost universal devotion to liberty often obscures the very different ways we define that term. As McDougall rather dryly notes, to the Puritans, rooted in the Reformation rather than the Enlightenment, liberty meant "freedom from Rome and Canterbury, no more" (18). To the Founding Fathers, liberty was freedom to live one's life free of government interference, consistent with respect for the equal rights of others. Americans may have quite different pictures of what liberty looks like, but we have historically agreed on our commitment to it. To a somewhat lesser extent, we have seen ourselves as the chosen people, whose destiny is to lead others to a proper understanding of true religion, liberty, and enlightened self-government. A sermon delivered by Abraham Keteltas, a Massachusetts preacher, in 1777, was an early, common expression of that (still potent) belief. "Our cause is not only righteous but, most important, it is God's own cause. It is the grand cause of the whole human race. . . . The cause of the American Revolution is the cause of truth against error and falsehood, the cause of righteousness against iniquity, the cause . . . of benevolence against barbarity, of virtue against vice. . . . In short, it is the cause of heaven against hell . . . " (Hughes 2003, 35). In the years following the Revolutionary War, such rhetoric became part of the American story. It is important to note, however, that until much later, this mission to lead the world was not understood to be a mandate for action; America was to lead by example, not force of arms. Our Puritan forebears saw America's role as that of a "light unto other nations." The Founding Fathers, products of the Enlightenment, were intent upon giving the new country's government only so much power as necessary to defend the new nation, but not enough to endanger liberty at home. Neither view was compatible with foreign adventurism. "The foreign policy powers of the executive branch were the shield, sword and lawyer's brief for American Exceptionalism; they were not themselves an expression of it" (McDougall 1997, 28).

The presence of two large oceans separating the new country from others was seen as fortuitous; it meant that America could forge its own destiny, that it did not need to put its trust in alliances and allies. McDougall quotes from a speech by George Washington:

> Our detached and distant situation invites and enables us to pursue a different course. . . . Why forgo the advantages of so peculiar a situation? Why quit our own to stand upon foreign ground? Why, by interweaving our destiny with that of any part of Europe, entangle our peace and prosperity in the toils of European ambition, rivalship, interest, humor or caprice?" (1997, 39).

The new country would be able to make decisions free of the encumbrances of treaties and other international constraints; it would be free to concentrate on domestic liberty (however conceived). As Hamilton argued, limiting American efforts abroad and insisting on national self-determination was required both by morality and self-interest. But if America was to remain independent, avoid "entangling alliances," and act unilaterally to advance its own interests, the United States needed to protect its own sphere of influence. We would not meddle in the affairs of Europe, but we would also find it necessary to ensure that Europe did not encroach upon our hemisphere—hence the enunciation of what came to be called the Monroe Doctrine. That doctrine revolved around three principles, each of which was consistent with American exceptionalism and unilateralism: no new colonization, no transfer of existing colonies, and no reimposition of colonial rule. Monroe was careful to underscore the nonaggressive nature of this doctrine.

> Our policy in regard to Europe, which was adopted at an early stage of the wars which have so long agitated that quarter of the globe, nevertheless remains the same, which is, not to interfere in the internal concerns of any of its powers; to consider the government *de facto* as the legitimate government for us; to cultivate friendly relations with it, and to preserve those relations by a frank, firm and manly policy, meeting in all instances the just claims of every power, submitting to injuries from none. (quoted in McDougall 1997, 71)

Consistent with these sentiments, for many years American administrations resolutely resisted the impulse to intervene in the internal affairs of other nations, even when sympathetic to the ideals of one side in the conflict.

If the young Republic pursued prudent self-interest abroad, at home things were getting more complicated. As Richard Hughes notes, the Great Awakening had changed the way Americans conceptualized the millennium. They began to see the coming "golden age" as a time when Americans would exercise their "unalienable rights to life, liberty and the pursuit of happiness." "Put another way . . . an affirmation of human rights largely displaced the expectation of the rule of God."

> The transition from the sovereignty of God to the sovereignty of the people with their unalienable rights marked a radical shift in the thinking of the American populace. Most of all, it tells us that the old Puritan dream of a distinctly Christian state no longer controlled American expectations. In its place stood a new vision of liberty and democratic self-government, a vision generated not by Puritanism, but by the Enlightenment. (Hughes 2003, 105)

By the mid-1840s, Hughes tells us, the United States had developed a "full-blown civic faith" that nourished the doctrine of Manifest Destiny. It was through that doctrine that America's millennial role was changed from providing an example—from being the City on the Hill that would be a "light unto nations"—to the view that God had chosen America to embrace a destiny. That manifest destiny included the right to extend influence not just through example, but through force. It "absolutized the myth of America as the Millennial Nation" (Hughes 2003, 107). The term itself came from a frequently cited speech by an influential editor named John L. O'Sullivan, in 1845. O'Sullivan wrote of America's "manifest destiny to over spread and to possess the whole of the continent which Providence has given us for the development of the great experiment of liberty. . . . It is a right such as that of the tree to the space of air and the earth suitable for the full expansion of its principle and destiny of growth" (1845). Manifest Destiny began with the American West, where it informed the policies of Andrew Jackson, and led to the virtual extinction of Native Americans and to the war with Mexico, among many other consequences. But it did not end there. Drawing on social Darwinism and the white man's burden, it justified a number of imperialist adventures as God's plan. Manifest Destiny continues to echo in contemporary pronouncements; in 1997, the Project for the New American Century issued a statement of principles calling for the United States to "shape a new century favorable to American principles and interests" and declaring its mission to "make the case and rally support for American global leadership." There are innumerable other examples.

In the wake of the Civil War, the United States had become a world power, thanks to enormous population growth, continuing industrialization, and improvements in mass transportation that facilitated the shipping of foodstuffs and other trade goods. However, these changes also made continued detachment from the rest of the world more difficult, and the temptations of benevolence greater. The Civil War also seemed to be evidence that benevolent intervention can have positive results, supporting the argument that armed conflict is sometimes necessary in order to liberate others from evil systems. Evidence of a shift in foreign policy emphasis, a change to New Testament doctrines, could be seen in 1898; Cuba was embroiled in a war to gain independence from Spain, and President McKinley requested authority from Congress to protect American interests in the area. Congress responded with a joint resolution recognizing Cuban independence and authorizing the use of force against Spain. The resolution expressly disclaimed any interest in annexing Cuba, and justified intervention not on the basis of the Monroe Doctrine or the protection of American interests, but—in the words of one senator, "for humanity's sake." McDougall dates the policy he calls "Progressive Imperialism" from that time. "[A] newly prideful United States began to measure its holiness by what it did, not just by what it was, and through Progressive Imperialism committed itself, for the first time, 'to the pursuit of abstractions such as liberty, democracy or justice'" (1997, 121). The stage was set for Wilsonian idealism, sometimes called liberal internationalism.

The various perspectives on Woodrow Wilson fill volumes, and political scientists, historians, and foreign policy experts continue to explore and debate his legacy. There is considerable consensus on Wilson the man—he was patrician, convinced that God had chosen him, contemptuous of "lesser races," and a vocal critic of the limitations imposed on the executive branch of government by separation of powers. Wilson embraced progressive imperialism and apparently believed that a foreign policy based only on self-interest was unworthy. Wilsonian idealism drew much of its strength from the belief that America's righteousness implied American power—and duty—to refashion the world. In this belief, Protestant millennialism was reinforced by Enlightenment optimism about the human capacity to understand and remake the world.

The Depression, and then the Japanese attack on Pearl Harbor, dampened and tempered the arrogance of that idealism, paving the way for a new emphasis on realism in foreign policy. But even in trying times, the country never completely abandoned idealism—Roosevelt's support of the United Nations, clearly influenced by Wilson's devotion to a League of Nations, and Truman's moral appeal for the Marshall Plan, offer evidence that it remained alive and well in our foreign policy. Nevertheless, the Wilsonian brand of idealism was increasingly tempered with healthy doses of realpolitik. Thus the emergence of the Soviet Union and the reality of a world divided by what Winston Churchill dubbed "the iron curtain" ushered in a new strategy: the policy of containment.

Containment had elements of all of the prior "isms"—it began, as American policies are wont to do, with the battle between good and evil, in this case, the battle between liberty and collectivism. Strategically, it hearkened back to the older belief that the American example would ultimately be more powerful—and not incidentally, more prudent—than arms taken up in a preventive war. But it also included the idealist's belief that Americans' liberties both required and depended upon the extension of a similar liberty to others, and that America had a duty to protect weaker nations from falling to stronger ones. That idealism led to the final "New Testament" story" that McDougall identifies: the doctrine of Global Meliorism, the belief that Americans have a moral mission to make the world a better place. It is distinguished from Wilsonian Idealism, in McDougall's view, because "Wilson just hoped to make the world safe for democracy; Global Meliorists aim to make the world democratic" (174). The most visible twentieth-century product of Global Meliorization was Vietnam.

There are obviously many other theoretical constructs through which we might analyze the historical evolution of American foreign policy, but the ones used by McDougall in his meticulously researched volume have the virtue of recognizing the theological and cultural context within which our foreign policies developed, and thereby illuminating the complexity of current policy debates.

FOREIGN POLICY IN THE TWENTY-FIRST CENTURY

What does this history tell us about contemporary foreign policy debates? For one thing, it underscores prior observations that—whatever our partisan takes on particular issues—we tend to conduct our arguments in shades of black and white. America is irredeemably evil, or America is all good. Countries with which we have disputes represent an *axis of evil*. Terrorism is evidence that *they* all hate us for our freedom, or it is evidence that we have systematically misunderstood and/or mistreated others. Such extremes are, to put it mildly, unhelpful. As David Gress has noted,

> The American political and cultural landscape at the year 2000 is torn between two incompatible ideas: one, that the West is globally triumphant and that the future of the world will be one of Westernization, in which all societies and cultures converge on a democratic and capitalist norm, with McDonalds in every town and Disney videos in every home. The other is that the West is an evil culture of exploitation, patriarchy and environmental degradation, a legacy of Eurocentrism that has been abolished in America by feminism and multiculturalism, and that certainly neither has nor deserves to have any future. (1998, 2)

James Lindsay, vice president director of studies at the Council on Foreign Relations once noted that when people act out of a certainty of moral rectitude, it is a very short step to sanctimony. In the wake of 9/11, President George W. Bush—paraphrasing Matthew 12:30—declared "Those who are not with us are against us." This is a classic example of America's impatience with nuanced arguments about good and evil, our historic tendency to cast conflicts in apocalyptic terms, and our firm belief that we are God's chosen people. Literalists and modernists alike mounted absolutist arguments in the wake of 9/11—a number of literalists saw the attacks as God's punishment for assorted sins, from tolerating homosexuality to countenancing abortion; many modernists were equally adamant that the tragedy was an inexorable result of American imperialism and our failure to address all of the legitimate grievances of Arab populations.

The attacks of 9/11 dealt an enormous psychic shock to most Americans; despite years of similar assaults on other nations, including many of our European allies, and despite prior attacks and attempted attacks on American ships and bases and even on the twin towers themselves, most Americans had simply believed that this country was somehow exempt.

GLOBALIZATION

Absolutism is a particularly unhelpful approach to international relationships in a rapidly shrinking world. The realities of globalization have presented policymakers with a number of unprecedented challenges, many of which have operated to intensify existing conflicts between Americans' most deep-seated convictions. On the one hand, our commitment to market economics requires that we support measures to ensure international stability and governing institutions with sufficient authority to regulate trade and mediate commercial disputes when they arise. On the other hand, our insistence on unilateralism and our reflexive recoil from any "entanglements" that might erode our absolute sovereignty makes us wary of treaties and multilateral undertakings and institutions. In a 2003 address to the Emory University School of Law, former president Jimmy Carter despaired of the possibility of the United States ever ratifying the U.N. Convention on the Rights of Children—a convention that has been ratified by every country except Somalia, which has no effective government that can ratify it. Carter was equally critical of the decision to pull out of the Kyoto Protocol; in his address, he focused particularly on the need to understand the cultural, the social, and especially the religious opposition to these and similar cooperative measures (Marty 2005).

Since the end of the cold war, there has been a renewed interest among foreign policy scholars in the questions Carter posed at Emory. Many sociologists and historians have wondered what took so long. As David Gress has written, "You can't explain major change by last year's or even last century's wars and elections" (1998, 1). Arguing that the distinction between domestic and international issues has become irrelevant, Gress points out that "America is no longer a country apart, whose condition can be studied in isolation. The critical demarcations of today are not national borders, but the lines of confrontation that separate traditionalists from liberals, fundamentalists from secularists, individuals from collectivists, libertarians from statists, and they run through and across all countries" (1998, 1). Furthermore, our encounters with global pluralism have plunged us into the same challenging dialectic we have experienced in our ongoing domestic encounters with diversity. It is well to recall, as Peter Berger reminds us, that there is not a single phenomenon called globalization; rather, there are alternative globalizations that open the possibility of alternative modernities. "Put simply: It is very unlikely that over time most of the world will look like Cleveland."

> Modernity fosters pluralism. There is no great mystery about this. It is the result of the breakdown of isolated cultural communities, as people and ideas move freely and massively across all cultural borders. And pluralism has one very important consequence: It undermines the taken-for-granted status of beliefs and values, a process that affects religion as any other component of culture. This does not mean that people *give up* beliefs or values, but rather that these are now *chosen* rather than taken for granted. (Berger 2004; emphasis in original)

What characterizes our era, according to Berger, is not that there is too little religion, but that there is too much—and the competition created by this robust religious market is arguably the central cultural challenge of globalization.

The implicit challenge of global institutions to our worldviews helps explain the near-hysteria of some attacks on globalization and multinational agreements in general, and to the United Nations in particular. A publication of an organization called Probe Ministries is illustrative. An article on "Globalism and Foreign Policy" begins with the assertion that a small but powerful group of internationalists is attempting to create a world society. It goes on to assert that the three institutions "standing in the way" of that goal are "the traditional family, the Christian Church, and the national government." The author makes it clear that "Christians who believe in God's salvation through faith in Jesus Christ, alone stand in the way of globalism and one-world government" and asserts that the public schools are being used as instruments in this assault on Christian tradition. The article concludes by urging readers to combat "global education" in the schools, and by singling out curricula on International Studies, Multicultural and International Education, Global R.E.A.C.H. (Respecting our Ethnic and Cultural Heritages), and others as threats to the American way of life (Anderson 1994).

Most policy disputes about America's proper relationship to other nations, or to international bodies like the United Nations, are not motivated by this sort of "black helicopter" mentality, of course. But elements of this particular worldview are more pervasive than some of us would like to believe. Opposition to international institutions is often based upon the concern that such institutions undermine American sovereignty and threaten our ability to be a redeemer nation, and upon the perception that the United Nations, in particular, is engaged in advancing a liberal social agenda, especially in the areas of women's rights and population policy. "The inherited unilateralism of the anticommunist right, opposition to the U.N.'s perceived social agenda, and biblical prophecy combine to create a movement resolutely opposed to multi-lateralism" (Oldfield 2004). Other common attitudes fostered by American culture and history also complicate questions of international engagement: our historic unilateralism, growing out of the security and isolation offered by two large oceans; our millennial fervor; and our persistent belief in our own righteousness have all influenced the worldviews of even the most pragmatic realists. While French, German, and English national identities have undergone considerable "Europeanization," a process that has facilitated development of the European Union, the

United States has continued to construct its identity around the belief in American exceptionalism, "which is used to justify the U.S. claim to benevolent global hegemony built on American values" (Bohne 2004).

Christian Zionism and Middle East Conflict

In a nation of immigrants, it is not surprising that Americans who retain emotional and cultural ties with their countries of origin would attempt to influence American opinion and official policies affecting those countries. Rather obvious examples are Latino Americans who support changes in immigration laws, and the influence of Cuban émigrés on policies toward Castro's Cuba. Similarly, American Jews have a long history of personal and organizational support for Israel. It is important to recognize that, although the Jewish community in America remains virtually unanimous in supporting Israel's security and right to exist, it is anything but monolithic in support of any particular Israeli policy. (Similarly, current Cuban attitudes toward Castro are less monolithic than in the past.) In this, American Jews mirror the considerable divisions between hawks and doves in Israel. Israeli hawks get far more uniform support from America's Christian Zionists, who have no such ethnic and historical ties with the State of Israel, and whose policy preferences for dealing with the Middle East are quite explicitly theological in nature.

Scholars have traced Christian Right support for Israel's hawks to the late 1970s, but note that it has gained considerable momentum since that time, with criticism of the Palestinians and support for very hardline Israeli policies a staple in Christian Right media. That support is closely related to prophetic concerns; "In the words of Christian right author John Hagee: 'Israel is the only nation created by a sovereign act of God, and He has sworn by His holiness to defend Jerusalem, His Holy City. If God created and defends Israel, those nations that fight against it fight against God'" (Oldfield 2004).

If anything, the attacks of 9/11 have confirmed the view of literalists that Israel is on God's side while the Arab nations are manifestations of the anti-Christ. In February of 2002, the Christian Coalition sponsored a "Symposium on Islam" at which speaker after speaker declared that Muslims want to kill Christians. According to a report in *Arab News*—admittedly, not necessarily the most reliable source of such information—some even compared Islam to Nazism. Less dubious in its authenticity was evangelist Franklin Graham's characterization of Islam as an "evil religion," and his efforts to convert Muslims, which have been widely reported by the American media. Graham's prominent role at George W. Bush's 2000 inauguration ceremonies was thus seen by many Arabs as confirmation of the United States' clear bias against them.

Christian Zionism is rooted in end-times theology, which teaches that the State of Israel is central to God's plan for the end times. As an article in the *Christian Science Monitor* explained, "Dispensationalists are also called Christian Zionists, and since the 19th century have supported the 'regathering of the Jews' in the Holy Land, which they say is an essential step toward the end times. It also says the temple will be rebuilt on the Temple Mount, where the Muslim Dome of the Rock now stands" (Lampman 2004). The return of the Jews to Israel is a necessary condition for the return of Jesus, and for that reason it is strongly supported by believers in the end-times. This recent solidarity with the Jews is not, however, of the "let's hold hands and sing Kumbaya" variety; the Jews return is seen as the second chance God is offering them to accept Jesus. Those who fail to take advantage of that offer will burn in hell after believers have been raptured.

In a country where the general population is much more focused upon domestic than foreign policy, organized minorities can have a disproportionate effect on policy decisions. In much the same way that the Jewish community, the Cuban-American community in Florida, and many other highly focused constituencies have from time to time exercised policy influence out of proportion to their numbers, Christian Zionists have been quite successful in generating U.S. support for Israel's hawks. When President Bush called upon Israel to pull back from the Jenin refugee camp in 2002, Christian Zionist organizations generated over one hundred thousand e-mails to the White House; the president "never said another word in public" (Lampman 2004).

Just Wars and Faith-Based Crusades

George W. Bush has used religious language to a greater extent than any previous president. In a study of presidential use of religious rhetoric, Rogers Smith asserts that Bush uses biblical references and authority to justify specific policy positions, unlike Ronald Reagan and other prior presidents who used religious language for more general and inspirational purposes. Smith quotes liberally from Bush's speeches to prove his point; one example he chooses is the president's address to the nation in the wake of 9/11. While noting his admiration for much in the speech, he finds other passages quite troubling. As he notes,

> [T]he President identified Al Qaeda and Osama bin Laden as the perpetrators of the attacks and Afghanistan's Taliban regime as their protectors, and he declared them the first targets in a new "War on Terrorism." He argued that America was "called to defend freedom" in this way and he concluded, "The course of this conflict is not known, yet its outcome is certain. Freedom and fear, justice and cruelty, have always been at war, and we know that God is not neutral between them." . . . The theologian Caryn Riswold has expressed concerns about this speech that are largely consonant with my own. She argues that Bush's language inescapably suggests that his call to arms is "justified by God." . . . She concludes that the speech "stakes a claim that America is the favored nation under God, and presents subtle justification for violence that begs for question, challenge, and serious criticism. It communicates a religious worldview that justified its veiled threat for holy war, equating patriotism with faith in a God who is not neutral. The presidential address was a religious response, presenting a retribution theology as national policy." . . . (Smith 2005)

Bush followed this speech with several others, notably his 2003 State of the Union address, which was replete with biblical language and allusions, and a speech later that year to the National Endowment for Democracy, in which he said, "Liberty is both the plan of Heaven for humanity, and the best hope for progress here on earth" and spoke of America's "mission to promote liberty around the world." In his speech accepting the Republican nomination in 2003, he stated that Americans "have a calling from beyond the stars to stand for freedom," and in his second inaugural address (2004), he asserted that the "success of liberty in other lands" should be the centerpiece of American foreign policy—a task he characterized as "the calling of our time."

Many of these biblical references to calling and mission have gone unrecognized as explicitly religious by more secular Americans, and some critics have suggested that the president was simply speaking—in code as it were—to his political base. Whatever the motives, both his language and policies represented a significant break with historic American foreign policy and its far more modernist theological roots. J. Bryan Hehir (2005) has traced that alternate tradition to the Treaty of Westphalia in 1648, a treaty that ended the bloody and religious Thirty Years War, and was intended to move the world beyond the seemingly interminable religious warfare that had ravaged European politics. Michael Walzer, perhaps the most eminent living authority on just-war theory worries that the hard-won just war tradition might be replaced by faith-based warfare.

> There is an alternative tradition, a medieval rival of just war, which has not been wholly supplanted: the crusade, the holy war, the jihad. All these words describe a faith-based struggle against the forces of darkness and evil, which are generally understood in explicitly religious terms: infidels, idolaters, the antichrist. In the West, especially after 9/11, we are a little leery about holy wars. (2004, 2)

Just war theory addresses two different questions: when is a resort to war justified, and what means of conducting war are morally acceptable? Many scholars believe the roots of the theory can be found in St. Augustine; whatever the merits of that contention, religious doctrine has clearly played a major role in its development. Just war theory is not pacifism, but rather a rebuttable presumption against the use of force that can be overcome if the following criteria are met.

- There is just cause, defined as the use of force to correct a grave public evil (for example, a massive violation of the basic rights of whole populations) or in defense;
- Comparative justice requires it. That is, in order to rebut the presumption against the use of force, any injustices suffered by one party must significantly outweigh injustices suffered by the other;
- Only duly constituted public authorities—i.e., sovereign states—may use deadly force or wage war;
- Force may be used solely for the purpose of the just cause that initiated it; correcting the wrong initially suffered, not for material gain. (This is sometimes called *right intention*.)
- There must be a reasonable probability of success. Arms should not be used in a futile cause or in a case where disproportionate measures are required to achieve success;
- There must be proportionality. The overall destruction expected from the use of force must be outweighed by the good to be achieved.
- Finally, war must be the last resort; it may be used only after all peaceful and viable alternatives have been seriously tried and exhausted.

Obviously, whether these criteria have been met will often be a matter of considerable debate, even among people who share a worldview. Many critics of the Bush administration have argued that the "war on terror" is misplaced and counterproductive, and many more argue that the war to achieve regime change in Iraq cannot be justified. In contrast, the war in Afghanistan is generally seen as a proper exercise of power. While every war has generated criticisms, it is instructive to look at the administration's justifications for the war on terror and the Iraq war through this just war lens, which is rooted in equally theological but quite different understandings of human nature and the deity than those upon which these particular efforts have been based.

War or Crime?

Nowhere is the American tendency to cast conflicts in absolute terms more striking than in the so-called war on terror. The attacks of 9/11 constituted a real blow to an American psyche that had been nurtured by both Enlightenment optimism and Puritan confidence in our special relationship with God. Certainly, most people—both in the United States and abroad—felt we were justified in striking back at Afghanistan, a state that had clearly harbored and abetted the terrorists. The broader war on terror, by contrast, runs into both just-war and realist objections. Just-war requirements of just cause are certainly met; this is an effort undertaken in self-defense. Similarly, our intentions are proper. The problem is that terrorists, by definition, are not state-sponsored. They are rogue individuals—international criminals—and, under just-war theory, not proper objects of warfare. This is also one of the key objections of realists, who fear that the use of war terminology creates conceptual and strategic problems, distorts the nature and effectiveness of antiterrorism efforts, and makes it far more difficult to forge cooperative efforts with other nations to root out the perpetrators. Realists argue that terrorists must be classified as international criminals, and that a criminal justice paradigm is a far more accurate—and useful—framework for describing the conflict. Terrorism has occurred throughout human history (although, as the saying goes, one man's terrorist is another man's freedom fighter); to characterize such acts as war is to confer a "warrior" status that elevates perpetrators, and initiates a state of war that by definition can never end. Furthermore, as Enlightenment libertarians point out, the existence of a state of war has historically been used by governments to amass new powers, excuse curtailments of civil liberties, and justify state behaviors that citizens are loathe to allow in times of peace. All of these arguments, which seem eminently reasonable to Enlightenment modernists and foreign policy realists, are met with incredulity by those who see Islamic terrorism as a threat of Armageddon that is fundamentally different from, say, the religious conflict in Northern Ireland.

The War in Iraq

Criticisms of the war on terror are essentially rooted in concerns about the misuse of language and the strategic consequences of mischaracterizing the nature of a conflict that everyone agrees is real and must be pursued. The war in Iraq has generated far more troubling, more complicated—and arguably far deeper—divisions. The just-war criticisms are relatively obvious, and emerged immediately after President Bush announced his doctrine of preventive war—itself a quite significant departure from America's prior policies (if not always our behavior—think of Andrew Jackson). There was no just cause, because we were not acting in self-defense; instead, Bush's new doctrine explicitly justified the use of force based upon another country's perceived ability to harm us in the future. Since we had not suffered harm, we could not meet the requirement of comparative justice. And clearly, we had not gone to war as a last resort. The probability of success, and the question of proportionality, were also matters of perspective.

It would be highly inaccurate, however, to suggest that the Iraq war was solely the consequence of the zeal of "Christian Soldiers." Many so-called liberal internationalists supported the war and many in the Christian Right opposed it: Pat Buchanan comes immediately to mind. Frances Fukuyama reminds us that neoconservatives originally made their name by warning about "the dangers of ambitious social engineering" (Traub 2005, 8). Traub suggests that the debate is not so much "the familiar one between unsentimental realists and Wilsonian idealists as between doctrinal absolutists and empiricists" (2005, 8).

Certainly those who are arguing from explicitly moral perspectives include both liberals and conservatives. In his recent book, *At the Point of a Gun*, David Rieff argues that Iraq should make liberal interventionists question the policy of humanitarian efforts like those that led the United States to intervene in Kosovo. He reasoned that humanitarianism can too easily be used to justify military adventures such as the war in Iraq, and recognized that liberals and neo-cons alike belong to an *interventionist* family.[2] In a series of posts to the TPM Café Web log discussing Rieff's thesis (telling titled "A Wilsonian Family Quarrel?"), G. John Ikenberry suggested that the question for liberal interventionists is really far more difficult than the *either-or* construct suggested by Rieff.

> If we think that American power can and should be used to respond to human misery abroad, how do you make principled distinctions between the "good" use of American power in cases such as Kosovo and Haiti, and the "bad" use of American power in Iraq? . . . In effect, liberal interventionism—as a body of ideas and norms—does not have within it the ability to distinguish enlightened from despotic use of power. If you buy into liberal ideas to support good interventions, you lose your principled ability to oppose bad interventions. (Ikenberry 2005)

Ikenberry argues that liberal interventionism is not the same thing as liberal "internationalism," and that the central focus of the latter is how to create stability and order among liberal states—not to spread democracy.

> [T]he character and quality of the rules of international order is fundamental. Inside countries, rule of law is what separates constitutional democracies from autocratic or authoritarian regimes. At the international level, this is what separates American hegemony with liberal characteristics from hegemony with imperial characteristics. Unilateralism and multilateralism are not simply styles or methods of diplomacy; they are indicators of the basic logic of power within the global system. (2005)

---

[2] The accuracy of that assertion received further support from an unlikely conference of Christian conservatives and political liberals, headed up by a genuinely "odd couple"—Madeleine Albright, secretary of state in the Clinton administration, and Senator Sam Brownback, one of the most conservative Republican senators. The conference addressed global issues like sex trafficking, genocide, religious oppression, and prison brutality, and found substantial common ground and support for interventionism on those issues (Kristof 2005).

A later, unsigned post framed the proper idealist formula in classically Enlightenment terms.

> Intervention to stop genocide and mass murder, yes. Intervention to re-establish order in a collapsing state, or to prevent the disorder from spreading to surrounding states, yes. But interventions to change political systems so that they more closely approximate certain liberal or democratic ideals—no. . . . People will have to work toward their own preferred future, in accordance with their own political and social ideals.

Some of the rhetoric issuing from self-identified Wilsonians seems quite similar to that used by the Bush administration—without, however, the explicitly Christian references employed by the president. Nevertheless, there are significant differences: the liberal interventionists are far more supportive of international institutions and multilateral, rather than unilateral, action, and far less likely to advocate regime change or democratization in the absence of other compelling reasons for action.

If the arguments among Wilsonians tend to break down along philosophical grounds, the arguments among realists generally result from drawing different conclusions from the facts involved, and weighing the costs and benefits differently. Many realists who opposed George W. Bush's war in Iraq did so on purely prudential grounds, believing that it would increase, rather than reduce, terrorism, that it would complicate Middle East peace efforts, and that it might well result in the establishment of a series of Islamist states opposed to American interests. Many of those same realists had supported George H. W. Bush and the first Gulf War, both because the circumstances were different and the objectives were clear and limited.

Brent Scowcroft, who served as national security adviser to the first President Bush, puts it quite simply: "What the realist fears is the consequences of idealism." In an article in the *New Yorker* that included a wide-ranging interview with Scowcroft, Jeffrey Goldberg managed to distill the difference between the father's realism and the son's brand of idealism (which has sometimes been called "Wilsonianism with teeth").

"For most of the past hundred years, American foreign policy has oscillated between two opposing impulses: to make the world more like America, or to deal with it as it is" (Goldberg 2005, 60). In the interview, Scowcroft seems bemused by the conversion of old friends like Vice President Dick Cheney ("I don't know him anymore") and especially Secretary of State Condoleezza Rice. He recounts a dinner conversation that had turned to a discussion of the administration's (then) planned invasion. When the conversation turned heated, he reports that Rice snapped, "The world is a messy place, and someone has to clean it up." According to Goldberg, the remark stunned the other guests, and Scowcroft says he was "flummoxed by Rice's 'evangelic tone'" (Goldberg 2005, 59). Scowcroft's characterization of Rice's current attitude as *evangelic* is consistent, Goldberg reports, with speculation among her colleagues that her "conversion to the worldview of George W. Bush" is rooted in her Christian faith, "which leads her to see the world in moralistic terms, much as the President does" (59).

Realists, however, take the position that, in Stephen Cimbala's words, "America's armed forces are not an imperial policing force, nor are they a Red Cross. They are our kids, our students and our future. They should not be sent into harm's way unless a vital interest is at stake, the mission is clear, and a strategy for victory, both political and military, has been defined" (Daalder 2005).

At this writing, the outcome of this effort at rebuilding the Middle East and installing democratic institutions is unknown. But even if we are successful to some extent in grafting democratic processes on a culture that has not developed democratic habits, most Americans have concluded that it will not be worth the costs. The anger reflected in current public opinion polls is palpable, and it has worsened an already toxic political environment. There are widespread allegations that the administration sold the war with doctored and misrepresented intelligence reports, and that may certainly prove to be the case. It is worth considering an alternative to intentional deception, however. As we have learned, when evidence exists that is inconsistent with one's worldview, or paradigm, that evidence is often simply unseen. One of the dangers in electing leaders who are too invested in a rigid paradigm is that they will be unable even to see other perspectives. That is particularly true of leaders like President Bush, who came to the office with very little relevant experience or expertise. With due respect to Mr. Scowcroft, perhaps what the realist should fear most is the uninformed idealist.

PART IV

Living Together

Chapter 11

LIVING TOGETHER

The question we face is quite simple: What do we do? If our understandings of the nature of liberty and our very perceptions of reality are at odds, if our policy disputes are inescapably intertwined with our incompatible conceptual paradigms, how do we talk to each other? How do we live together? How do we forge a working political community and make coherent public policies? Can we ever hope to reconcile our "inner Puritans" with our Enlightenment rationalism?

Political philosophers have grappled with the nature of the good society for centuries. The ambitions of this book, and this chapter, are more modest: to begin a discussion that is sorely needed. There is general agreement that America needs a shared paradigm—a culturally endorsed mythos (what some might call a "civil religion"). The current conflict is over the form that such a civil religion should take. The Puritans, harking back to the Planting Fathers, want a national narrative that portrays America as an unequivocally Christian nation although they do not necessarily agree upon the form such a Christian nation would assume or the rules it would impose. The modernists want an open and tolerant polis where diversity and civility are prized and empirical evidence forms the basis for national policy decisions, although—again—modernists have competing notions about the content of social norms appropriate for a diverse society, and about what constitutes credible empirical evidence.

The argument I will make in this chapter is that we need a national narrative that overlaps—that is, is at least partially consistent—with both the Puritan and Enlightenment paradigms. This is hardly an original insight, and it is a product of my own, decidedly modernist, worldview. Nevertheless, in the next few pages, I will first defend the proposition that the only workable governing paradigm for America in the twenty-first century is a constitutionally constrained liberal democratic one; second, identify elements of a worldview that I will argue most Americans—Puritan and Modernist alike—already share; and third, offer suggestions for forging a consensus that respects, insofar as possible, both liberal democratic principles and the deep religious commitments of those who hold comprehensive, hegemonic doctrines. Before engaging in that task, however, it is only fair to make as explicit as possible the basic assumptions I bring to the discussion, and to acknowledge that those assumptions (inescapably) reflect my own worldview, and are open to debate on that score.

MY ASSUMPTIONS

The preceding chapters offer us much evidence for the proposition that our conflicting worldviews are virtually all religious as I have employed that term. That is, they are all based upon cultural traditions incorporating a particular religiously rooted telos or ontology. Characterizing our current polarization as a contest between religious and secular citizens is both inaccurate and highly misleading, and it hinders useful consideration of our civic dilemma. Any genuine discussion must begin with the recognition that even the most secular among us bring religiously rooted worldviews to public policy debates and the fact that we do so is both inevitable and legitimate. It is equally misleading to label all literalists *theocrats* or—worse still—to suggest that all evangelical Christians are the homegrown equivalent of the Taliban. If we are to engage each other in a genuine effort to find common ground, we all need to take a deep breath and stop labeling whole categories of our fellow citizens. The arguments I will make in the remainder of this chapter are offered in that spirit, and they are based upon the following premises:

- Failure to deal constructively with these deeply rooted and constitutive differences is not an option. There are, it seems to me, only three possible consequences of the intense struggle currently being waged for control of the national narrative: a prolonged and paralyzing inability to forge effective policies or elect leaders that most citizens can accept as legitimate; reaffirmation of liberal democratic values (including the value of equal respect for those with whom we disagree) as our governing paradigm; or control of the coercive power of the state by those few among the Puritans who really are intent upon building an American "City on the Hill" to the specifications of biblical law as they understand that law.
- While conflict—often impassioned—is inevitable in any society, prolonged, intense inter-group hostility and polarization are undesirable. Equally undesirable, and ultimately unsustainable, is the uniformity or conformity achieved by authoritarian regimes, or through the domination of some by others. That is, while suppression of conflict through the exercise of power may be preferable to open warfare, it is both less desirable and less likely to endure than a peaceful coexistence that respects the equal civil and human rights of others.
- Increased pluralism and contact with people who are racially, ethnically, religiously, culturally, and ideologically different is a fact of modern life. Such contacts will only accelerate; they are inescapable. Communication and transportation technologies and global economic realities make cultural isolation impossible. This inevitable feature of contemporary society will continue to threaten the "taken for granted" nature of our worldviews.
- Maintaining cultural traditions is important not just to individuals but to political communities. A nation with no normative

culture is untenable—its center cannot hold. It is also important that subnational communities (religious, ethnic, or other) be able to maintain their distinctive identities, insofar as those are meaningful and important to them, and that our national norms include accepting and adapting to the resulting diversity of American cultures and traditions. We require a shared national identity that makes room for those particularistic communities within a distinctive common culture we call American.

THE LIBERAL DEMOCRATIC PARADIGM

Liberal democracy has been defined as "a principle of political organization that accords individuals the freedom to navigate a course of their own design, constituted by self-elected plans and purposes" (Beiner 1996). William Galston (1991) has argued that liberal societies are characterized by a strategy that minimizes coercion, and Ronald Dworkin has defined liberal constitutionalism as "a system that establishes legal rights [to self-determination] that the dominant legislature does not have the power to override" (1995, 2). Liberal societies are not unrestrained democracies; actions desired by the majority are constrained by constitutionally imposed limits on the state—even when the action the state proposes to take is endorsed by a majority of its citizens. In *The Future of Freedom*, Fareed Zakaria has reminded us of the significant difference between pure democracy—defined simply as rule by the majority—and liberal democratic regimes, where fundamental liberties are protected from majoritarian passions by constitutional principles (2003). Classical liberal theory accords to individuals the broadest moral authority over their own lives consistent with the maintenance of public order. So long as individuals do not act in ways that harm the persons or property of others, they are to be free of state coercion. What constitutes harm, of course, is subject to debate. Those holding communitarian or Puritan worldviews often argue that the existence of pornography, for example, harms society as well as individuals. At a libertarian minimum, murder, theft, vandalism, and the like are widely seen to be among the actions properly prohibited and punished by the state.

Liberalism rests upon a view of the world that separates—as many cultures do not—the public from the private. Liberal theory distinguishes between the communal and the personal; with respect to communal behaviors, it further distinguishes between public activities that are governmental, and collective actions taken through voluntary associations, which are considered private. Although the historic distinction between public and private is being substantially eroded by a number of contemporary practices, including the growth of so-called third-party government (Kennedy 2000), the distinction remains a bedrock of liberal democratic theory. Even today, libertarians advocate for a return to the original liberal conception of the role of the state, one that strictly limits the role of government to the conduct of those relatively few activities requiring the use of state coercive powers: controlling crime, waging war, levying taxes, and enforcing private agreements (Boaz 1997). They would leave other activities of a communal nature to civil society, which is composed of churches, mosques, synagogues, arts organizations, private charities, and a multiplicity of other voluntary associations and nonprofit corporations (DeTocqueville 1835, 1956; Putnam 2000).

Having defined spheres of human activity in this way, Enlightenment liberalism fostered a definition of justice based upon a concept of *negative* liberty, a conception that accorded great importance to liberty and individual autonomy, which were in turn (as we have seen) defined as the right to be free of governmental constraint. The fact that economic or personal factors might operate to constrain autonomy as dramatically as any government edict was seen as unfortunate, but beside the point. The point was to limit government power.

This original understanding has been criticized as representing a cramped view of human rights and so strict a libertarian paradigm no longer describes American political reality. However, the importance of negative liberty and the high priority assigned to limitations on government power continue to inform modern liberal public policy and influence public attitudes. Legislative bodies in the United States have constantly struggled against the limits imposed on government in the

American system, often in pursuit of quite illiberal goals, and in other cases, in an effort to secure so-called positive or affirmative rights which were not included in the original U.S. Constitution. Civil rights is one example of rights that have been guaranteed not by the original Constitution, but by federal statutes and state statutory and constitutional provisions.

A negative approach to the exercise of public power positions government as a neutral arbiter among citizens who are legal equals. There are many problems with such a neutral system, not least the fact that it does not address systemic inequalities and does not recognize the absence of a level playing field. Indeed, there are many justice issues that simply fall outside the paradigm of negative liberty as conceived by the Enlightenment's liberal state. An even more fundamental problem is that—as we have repeatedly seen in the preceding chapters—neutrality is not experienced as neutral by those who hold totalizing doctrines. For such "seamless garment" believers, no system that fails to recognize the supremacy and impose the mandates of their own belief system can ever be legitimate, and such individuals pose a particular problem for liberal democratic systems.

Puritans are not the only ones who hold these totalizing doctrines. Within the Western liberal tradition, communitarians, like the socialists and communists before them, complain that state neutrality in the face of competing visions of the good inevitably places process above substance. Because it considers individual moral choice as a private rather than public concern, they argue that such a state fails to meet the universal and human need for meaning. They contend that liberal theory suffers from an impoverished vision of citizenship and community (Sandel 1996). Communitarians, Puritans, and other critics of liberalism take issue with the most fundamental commitment of liberal democracies: that persons should be free to set and pursue their own ends, in accordance with their own values. They argue instead that freedom, properly understood, is "freedom to do the right thing" and that political community, in order to be experienced and sustained as a true community, must insist upon a shared telos, a normative agreement on moral ends (Mulhall and Swift 1996; Sandel 1996). In this view, it is more important that those ends be morally correct than it is that they be freely chosen. To those of a less authoritarian disposition, a system of government neutrality and negative rights has one overriding virtue: it makes the use of power to enforce conformity largely illegitimate.

There is a reason that Americans tend to settle even our most deeply felt differences without bloodshed — a reason we are more likely to use the courts and the political process rather than force to settle our differences. (The Civil War remains a sobering reminder that this has not always been true.) An important part of that reason is that we have refused to insist on a *thick* common morality enforced by the state, and have instead opted for a *thin*, liberal consensus about a much more limited set of values. Basing a culture on such a "thin" consensus, however, is not tantamount to adopting a wholly procedural approach to the exercise of state authority. As I argued in chapter 6, liberalism does endorse ends: liberty, individual autonomy, equality before the law, and tolerance. Elsewhere, I have referred to the American Bill of Rights as a moral code (Kennedy 1997), because inherent in its hierarchy of rights and powers is a particular moral vision. Liberalism begins with respect for the value and uniqueness of each individual, and requires behavior consistent with that respect, notably tolerance for those who differ. Liberal political theory values a unity that can accommodate diversity (Kymlicka 1996) and affirms the belief that society is strengthened and enriched by a multiplicity of voices and a constant testing of moral and political theories. To allow the state to prescribe a particular moral code or to impose a significant measure of political uniformity would violate the conscience and insult the personhood of citizens and would engender resentments ultimately dangerous to continued social stability and civic peace.

Liberals also challenge the notion that human community must be defined politically. They assert that political communities, in common with religious communities, ethnic groups, professional or fraternal organizations, and any number of other associations that are meaningful to their members, are all — and inevitably — partial communities, and that their utility in promoting justice rests upon the fact that they provide maximum room for competing allegiances. Stephen Macedo has offered one of the best explanations of that thesis.

> Freedom-promoting social orders are, it appears, *pluralistic*; societies of partial allegiances in which groups endlessly compete with each other and with the state for the allegiances of individuals, and in which individuals loyalties are divided among a variety of crosscutting (or only partially overlapping) memberships and affiliations. . . .
>
> Liberalism needs community life, therefore, and it needs community life to be constituted in a certain way. Liberal statecraft should aim for a complex, cross-cutting structure of community life in which particular group-based allegiances are tempered by other, competing group allegiances and by a state representing a common, overarching, but partial, point of view that gives everyone something in common. (Macedo 1996, 255; emphasis in original)

It is important to recognize that a society and its government are not the same thing. Governments are mechanisms for collective action, and can certainly be a venue for the expression of social values and communal aspirations, but liberals warn that there is substantial danger in reposing ultimate moral authority in a coercive state. If the goal of political community is unity without uniformity and diversity without culture war, tolerance for the divergent lifestyles and diverse values of multiple communities is both a tool and an end. Liberal democrats also make another, more practical argument: there is no reasonable alternative to state neutrality, unless one wishes to use the state's coercive power to impose ends endorsed by the majority (or at least by a majority of those holding the reins of power) on unwilling minorities. John Rawls (1993) defends the liberal enterprise by positing an "overlapping consensus" of shared limited goals. The complex framework he establishes rests in part upon a central insight: every time you add a goal that government is to enforce, you introduce a new source of conflict. In the United States today, we have deep divisions over numerous such issues.

The right to enjoy the proceeds of one's own labor conflicts with taxation that redistributes money for social ends; the right of a woman to control her own body conflicts with the religious belief of many that abortion is murder; the right of government to wage war encounters the resistance of those who believe all wars to be immoral. As we have seen in the preceding chapters, there are many other examples. No government can avoid such conflicts, no matter how respectful of individual autonomy, but liberal democracies are obliged to minimize them by restraining the state from intruding too much into the realms that have been defined as private. The classic formulation of this principle is that with which this section began: government intervention is warranted only when one citizen threatens harm to the person or property of another (Nozick 1974). While the United States and the world's other liberal democracies have long since moderated that simple libertarian principle, often for reasons that are sound and even more often for reasons that are specious and worrisome, I would argue that it is a formula with much to recommend it. As Marc Stier has described the liberal strategy for avoiding conflict,

> Neutrality about the good is, for liberals, also central to their strategy for preserving internal peace. Liberals hold that we can reduce political and social conflict if we place certain matters beyond the bounds of political decision-making. Extreme and dangerous political conflict, the kind that leads to civil wars, results when governments prevent some citizens from pursuing ends of fundamental importance to them. When governments respect our rights, though, people are free to make decisions for themselves about these matters. Thus conflict about divisive issues is prevented. This strategy of avoidance is one of the prime ways in which liberals hope to keep the peace. Of course, some people may be frustrated because they cannot attain their own ends by using the power of the state to restrict what other people say and do. The liberal expectation, however, is that people would rather have their own freedom protected than interfere with the freedom of others, if only because they recognize that an illiberal regime might at some point turn against them. (Stier 2000, 3)

The liberal democratic idea, the concept of a limited state having a *social contract* with its citizens, was a product of the Enlightenment. While there were certainly differences of emphasis and disagreements on details, it was the vision that animated the worldviews of America's founders, and it was the basis of the American constitutional system. It reflects a morality that continues to exert enormous influence over the opinions and values of contemporary American citizens.

A SHARED AMERICAN WORLDVIEW

The obvious question raised by everything in this book thus far is whether Americans share enough values, enough of an *overlapping consensus* to constitute a sufficient national paradigm, or civil religion. I have said that I believe the answer to that question is yes. If I am incorrect, if there is simply no common ground upon which Americans can build, the only alternative is the domination of some by others. If the glass is half-full, however, rather than wholly empty, what—to extend the metaphor—is in that glass?

Richard Hughes says that the American Creed begins with the passage in the Declaration of Independence that "[w]e hold these Truths to be self-evident, that all Men are created equal, that they are endowed by their Creator with certain unalienable Rights, that among these are Life, Liberty and the Pursuit of Happiness" (Hughes 2004, 2). This was the genesis of the American narrative, what I have called elsewhere the American Idea. As we have seen, elements of that idea have always been contested, but generally, the nation has moved in the direction of more expansive, rather than more restrictive, applications. Equality no longer means "for white men." Contemporary Americans—literalist and modernist alike—prize their liberty to make choices that would have undoubtedly scandalized both the Planters and the Founders. For that matter, the values that I will argue Americans already share are admittedly far more likely to be shared in the abstract than in their application. Virtually all Americans will claim, for example, that they are committed to religious liberty; as we have seen, however, literalists define religious liberty far differently than do modernists, so it is always important to define the terms upon which we are said to agree.

It is also important to recognize that substantial or majority acceptance of a particular value is not universal acceptance, and that any workable polis must be able to deal fairly but effectively with those who dissent. Finally, we need to distinguish between the sorts of American myths identified by Hughes, and American values, which are different—albeit related. The former refers to our conceptions of American identity; the latter describes those elements of our national story that have become social norms integrated into our personal worldviews.

As with so many issues in these contentious times, advocates of various stripes argue that their particular agenda represents those values *really* held by most Americans. Google "American values" and you will get page after page of links to interest groups, partisan think tanks, and ideological "culture warriors"—and very little else. Academics and public intellectuals who bring their own worldviews to the definition of real American values also—unsurprisingly—reach different conclusions. (To read Alan Wolfe and Gertrude Himmelfarb at the same time is to invite cognitive dissonance.) In an effort to avoid ideology (my own and others), I base the following description of America's common norms on a study conducted on behalf of elementary and secondary school teachers and educators, in which parents of school-aged children were asked to identify the values that they wanted the schools to teach their children. The logic was rather simple: parents are unlikely to want their children taught values contrary to their own; and there is no reason to believe that questions asked for this purpose would be tailored to elicit any ideologically preferred result. (It also increases my comfort level to note that a number of other polls and surveys have reached similar conclusions.)

Public Agenda conducted such a study and published the results in 1998, under the title *A Lot to be Thankful For*. The researchers concluded that American parents—immigrants and native-born alike—were characterized by a clear-eyed patriotism, a belief in American exceptionalism that was nonetheless tempered by recognition of the nation's shortcomings. They wanted the schools to acknowledge those shortcomings, but not to dwell on them. The parents surveyed had "absorbed the principles" of the Bill of Rights (although they displayed very little concrete constitutional knowledge), and they believed in "personal freedom, tolerance toward others, and hard work." Bad citizens were most often described as those who were lazy and/or intolerant. Above all, according to the report, the parents who responded disapproved of strategies that encouraged divisiveness; in the words of the report, "The parents we surveyed fear division, not diversity." The study's authors concluded that there is considerable agreement on core American values: "The chief components of the American ideal—identified by very strong majorities of all groups—are individual freedom, opportunity and hard work, combined with a commitment to tolerance and respect for others" (Public Agenda 1998). These results support my own thesis that there is, in fact, a core set of American norms, internalized beliefs held by large majorities of the nation's citizens, that constitute an American creed. Certainly, Hughes's observation that the words of the Declaration of Independence are at the center of that creed has ample support in both polling data and sociological research. My own reading of that data and research suggests that the following five values are a component of most Americans' worldviews, whether those worldviews are predominantly Puritan or modernist.

- Americans believe strongly in equality, defined as equal treatment and fair play. Very few of us are egalitarians who believe in equality of results, but most of us really do believe in equality of opportunity—the "level playing field" is a favorite metaphor—and once we are convinced that a particular practice or situation operates to make that playing field uneven and the game unfair, we will try to remedy the problem.
- Despite all the evidence to the contrary, Americans really do believe in tolerance. Over and over, citizens in this country have demonstrated a "live and let live" attitude very consistent with our Enlightenment libertarian origins. Most of us agree with Thomas Jefferson's famous formulation that, "It does me no injury for my neighbor to say there are twenty gods or no God. It neither picks my pocket nor breaks my leg" (Jefferson 1782, 184). One component of that tolerance is a belief in civility, the

distaste for divisiveness that was so marked an outcome of the Public Agenda survey.

- Americans believe in individual rights and choices—and in individual responsibility for those choices. We are, for good or ill, among the most individualistic cultures on earth. If that insistence upon individualism complicates efforts to provide effective and coherent social welfare, if it sometimes demonizes as lazy many who are simply unfortunate, if it has sometimes supported a distressingly superficial consumerism, it has also fueled our formidable economic progress and reinforced our overwhelming belief in the individual's inalienable right to choose what to think, how to live, how to love, and how to pray. Americans take their right to make such choices as an absolute given; even our Puritans, who are so often unwilling to extend the same liberties to their neighbors, take for granted that they are entitled to them.
- Americans really do believe in the rule of law, although as we have seen, there is considerable dispute about much that the rule of law entails, and much ignorance about such constitutional principles as separation of powers and the role of the judiciary. But there is wide agreement that all citizens should be treated equally before the law, that no one is above the law, including (or perhaps especially) elected officials, that individuals have the right to dissent from policies they disapprove of, and to express that dissent peacefully without fear of official retribution. Americans believe in playing by the rules, and they expect those rules to be fair and fairly applied.
- Finally, I would submit that Americans by large majorities believe in the value of science and empirical evidence. As we saw in chapter 8, wide majorities of Americans of all religious categories support environmental protection measures; that support is clearly premised upon acceptance of scientific warnings that we are damaging the environment. If we did not overwhelmingly trust science, proponents of intelligent design

would not insist upon that theory's scientific validity. If we did not value objectivity and evidence, there would be no need for pundits to spin their analyses (or fabricate facts) to buttress their political preferences. If hypocrisy is the homage vice pays to virtue, there is ample evidence that facts, objective truth, and empirical evidence are widely considered virtuous.

The question we face is whether those areas of agreement are enough. Can we reasonably hope to build a meaningful, cohesive national political community on so small a cultural base? Without racial, religious, ethnic, or even cultural homogeneity, can an allegiance to these principles provide Americans with a sufficient national story, a shared mythos strong enough to create unity from our diversity?

The challenges we face are formidable: when the taken-for-granted elements of our cultural paradigms are subject to daily assault by new ideas, new ways of seeing and being, it is only natural to react with fear, and in today's America, that fear is palpable. Fear makes us cling ever more tightly to that which we see as threatened and makes rational analysis much harder to achieve. It reinforces our (already pronounced and very American) tendency to ignore ambiguity and complexity, to see issues as stark choices between right and wrong, good and evil. One of the least-used phrases in the American political vocabulary is *it depends*.

In 1994 Harvard professor Robert Kegan published a provocative book, *In Over Our Heads*, in which he compared the evolving complexity of a child's mind to similar stages in the conceptual growth of adults over generations. Kegan believes that human intellectual development is in part a response to the changing demands of social environments, and that the intellectual skills required for living a coherent life in modern Western societies are quite different from those required by simpler, tribal cultures. We become more complex as the demands of our environment require such complexity, but the process is very uneven. Kegan identified five clusters of intellectual capacities, each constituting a discrete stage of human mental development. He concluded that dealing successfully with the complexities of contemporary Western culture requires stage four skills—and that most of us are still at stage three.

Other social analysts might describe our current situation as a time of paradigm shift, while historians would undoubtedly remind us that we are not the first generation to experience upheaval and deep divisions. Whichever analytic lens one might prefer, describing a situation (or arguing about the correct description), however important the insights such analyses might yield, is not the same thing as solving—or at least addressing—a problem. And one area of almost universal agreement is that the problem is real.

As difficult as it will be to rise above our current antagonisms, however, Americans also have a wealth of resources to draw on. We should not take for granted the almost unfathomable generosity, goodwill, and fundamental fairness of the American public. Think back to the outpouring of solidarity and genuine kindness in the wake of 9/11 and Hurricane Katrina. Look at the hundreds and thousands of voluntary organizations working to make a positive difference in their communities. Look at the burgeoning numbers of interfaith and interracial organizations and their efforts to genuinely understand differences and find common ground. For every Pat Robertson praying for the death of Supreme Court justices, there are pastors, priests, rabbis, and imams from all points on the religious spectrum emphasizing messages of humility, love, and acceptance. We do not go into the battle for this nation's soul unarmed.

THREE NOT-SO-MODEST PROPOSALS

What can Americans do? Each of us will answer that question in different ways, but I suggest consideration of three steps toward a calmer, more productive national discourse.

First, Civic Education

Everyone talks about education—it's like the weather—but the reason most of us start there is because education is widely seen as a pivotal, absolutely essential element of any solution to our civic woes. For purposes of this discussion, however, I mean something that is both more and less than what goes on in the nation's schoolrooms. Americans are woefully, embarrassingly ignorant of the history and premises of our constitutional system. A poll a few years ago by the Constitution Center concluded that Americans revere the Constitution, but have absolutely no idea what is in it. (Much, I suspect, like the Bible.) One of the unfortunate consequences of that profound ignorance is that constitutionally required state neutrality is often seen as bias favoring those on the other side of the argument. So failure to allow government to shut down a "dirty" bookstore or remove an allegedly indecent book from the local library is seen as an endorsement of smut; failure to prevent a Klan rally is decried as promoting hatred; allowing students to pray around the flagpole before school is trumpeted as evidence of the erosion of separation of church and state. Without a basic understanding of the limits on state action and majority preferences imposed by the Constitution, citizens misunderstand both the role of the judiciary and context and meaning of their decisions.

A recent example from my own state of Indiana is illustrative: our state legislature was opening sessions with very exclusionist Christian prayers. (One even included a sing-along of "Take a Little Walk with Jesus.") The local ACLU represented several plaintiffs—including such ungodly folks as a retired Methodist minister, a devout Quaker, and a Catholic active in his parish—and sued, asking for an order that prayers offered in that venue be nonsectarian and inclusive. The federal judge (the son of a widely respected local minister) ruled, in accordance with an unbroken and unambiguous series of precedents,[1] that if official prayers are to be offered, they must be genuinely nonsectarian. There was an immediate outcry by supporters of specifically Christian prayer,

---

[1] While state-sponsored prayer is generally constitutionally forbidden, the Supreme Court allowed a limited exception for legislative prayer. In *Marsh v. Alabama*, the Court noted the "settled tradition" of such devotions, and the fact that adults—who could choose to be present or not—constituted the audience for such prayer. Nevertheless, the Court ruled that prayers in such venues must be genuinely inclusive (critics would say generic) and could not be specific to any particular religious tradition, nor be offered in the name of particular deities.

alleging that their free speech rights had been infringed by liberals and atheists waging war on Christianity. The judge's integrity was impugned; the Speaker of the House labeled the ruling (which was entirely predictable, given the absolute lack of any contrary case law) "intolerable and outrageous."

When most citizens do not understand the rules, they are susceptible to arguments that those rules have been broken. The use of so-called wedge issues by politicians pandering to various constituencies is enabled and abetted by widespread public ignorance of very basic constitutional principles. It is not necessary that citizens be constitutional scholars, or that they agree with prior court interpretations of constitutional principles, or even that they agree with the principles themselves. But it is critical that they understand them. There is a constitutional distinction between individual expression and government speech, and failure to understand that very elementary distinction fuels dissent and distrust. In this case, an insistence that government be neutral, that it follow the rules, was experienced as an assault on Christianity.

We desperately need civic education in this country. Certainly, our public schools should do a better job of teaching the Constitution and Bill of Rights, but it is both unfair and inadequate to place the burden on our beleaguered public schools alone. We need the broadest possible national conversation about our constitutional roots, a balanced, historically accurate conversation that explicitly acknowledges the contributions of both the Planting and Founding Fathers, and explains the basic architecture of our constitution. We need civic forums, movies, television specials, Internet sites—if we can devise a game show or even (forgive me) a reality show that transmits constitutional competence, we should do so.

Both Puritans and modernists have much to gain from such education. For the Puritans, especially, one of the most galling features of our current discourse is their perception that the government neutrality required by the Constitution is equivalent to disrespect for religious conviction. The Indiana legislative example is instructive: many devout Christians interpreted the court ruling as a statement that they could no longer pray in authentically Christian terms, rather than as the (considerably more limited) proposition that government could not act to favor one religion over others. If our polity understood neutrality as neutrality, if there were a widespread recognition that such rulings are not endorsements of particular views, but are simply determinations that government has exceeded its (limited) authority, feelings of being disrespected would be considerably ameliorated. Furthermore, by teaching modernists to distinguish between genuine assaults on the Establishment Clause and the equally important protections afforded by the Free Exercise Clause, broader public education about the Bill of Rights should ease the modernist perception that Establishment Clause liberties are under assault, and ultimately reduce the number of legal challenges to practices that are important to Puritans and protected under Free Exercise or Free Speech doctrine.

Civic education would perform another service: it would fully and accurately acknowledge the contributions of both the Planting and Founding Fathers. Today, widespread historical ignorance abets those in both camps who have a vested interest in disinformation. So we see fabricated—or at best, distorted—history from Puritans and modernists alike: the Puritans insist that the Founders were all pious Christians who understood themselves to be writing a Constitution for a specifically Protestant culture, while modernists insist the Founders were all Freethinkers and Enlightenment rationalists whose decision to draft a secular Constitution was an effort to free the new country from the superstitions of the Old World. An honest civic education would stress the importance of religion to the early settlers, and its continued relevance to the context within which our Constitution was drafted. It would acknowledge the godless nature of the federal Constitution, but it would also acknowledge that the constitutional silence on religion was prompted as much by political considerations as philosophical commitments, and that the document's secular nature was offset by state constitutions that established religion.

Finally, an adequate civic education would help citizens understand the importance and consequences of the Fourteenth Amendment, which some scholars call America's second founding. Too often, I pick up our local newspaper and read a letter to the editor beginning "I just read the First Amendment, and it says Congress shall make no law . . . that doesn't mean our [state legislature or school board] can't [require prayer, declare that this is a Christian state]." Partisans are certainly entitled to debate states' rights and local control, but those arguments should at least begin with an understanding of the historical evolution of our constitutional system.

Above all, civic education should stress the common values that have shaped and been shaped by this history: individual liberty and responsibility, legal equality and fair play, unity within diversity. It will acknowledge our differences, but will emphasize those common values that provide Americans with our overarching national identity. It will teach the children of Puritans and modernists alike that allegiance to those core common values is what we mean by patriotism.

Second, The Media

The mass media are everyone's favorite villain, and it is not my purpose to "pile on." Furthermore, in this era of accelerating and dramatic change, it is getting more and more difficult even to define what constitutes mainstream media. It is not my intent to engage in a broadside, or take sides in the perennial debate over media bias. Instead, I have a far narrower proposition. I believe it may be time to revisit and adapt some version of the Fairness Doctrine.

For those readers who do not remember it, the Fairness Doctrine required broadcast media using the public airwaves to make equal time available to all sides of a public debate. If an editorial was aired supporting a legislative proposal, opponents must be given the right to purchase time to state their position. If Candidate A bought time, the broadcaster could not refuse to sell time to Candidate B. The rule was justified by the fact that more people wanted to use the airwaves than the limited number of bandwidths allowed; the government awarded broadcast licenses on the understanding that successful bidders would use those airwaves *in the public interest*, and one part of the public interest was balance—

fairness. Once cable and other technologies vastly increased the number of available channels, the Fairness Doctrine was abandoned. Currently, just as privately owned newspapers and magazines cannot be forced to give equal time to all sides of an argument, we depend upon the sheer multitude of contending voices in the marketplace of ideas to provide any needed corrective to mistaken or unfair coverage.

Over the past twenty years, however, media ownership has become more and more concentrated, with the result that, increasingly, that multitude of voices is not the cacophony we envisioned, but an increasingly harmonious chorus conducted by a dwindling number of corporate *maestros*. This will not be an easy problem to solve, because we must be careful not to tread on the precious First Amendment principle of a free press. But there are very troubling indications that concentrated control is being exercised to crowd out disfavored messages. A couple of examples: in 2005, an Ohio billboard company that controls virtually all the billboards in that state allegedly refused to sell billboard space to an organization critical of a favored elected official. In 2004, in the month preceding the election, it was widely reported that a television network with stations in virtually every media market was preparing to air an hour-long show based upon the widely discredited "Swift Boat Veterans" attack on presidential candidate John Kerry. Only an energetic public campaign (presumably mobilized by Kerry partisans) forced the network to reconsider. There have been a growing number of similar incidents, on both sides of the political divide. Of course, in the Swift Boat case, the public campaign worked, vindicating a core assumption of the First Amendment: the way to counter bad speech is not suppression, but more speech. It is doubtful, thought, that such an effort would have been mounted in the absence of a heated political campaign and the availability of partisan resources.

If it is possible—and it may not be—to craft a law that both respects the First Amendment and requires those who effectively control a given media market to sell time to those who have contrary views, we should consider such a law. In the alternative, we must be vigilant to protect the Internet from efforts to regulate the blogs and Web sites that are increasingly the only competing sources of information in many parts of the country. Bloggers should have all the protections that other journalists enjoy, and we must vigorously oppose efforts to suggest that they should enjoy less freedom than more traditional media. If talk radio figures are protected by freedom of the press (and they are), surely bloggers are entitled to no less.

The benefits of a renewed commitment to fairness are several, and the beneficiaries—Puritan or modernist—will be different in different parts of the country. Americans believe in fair play, and no matter whether we are Puritan or modernist, we are offended when we are denied voice, denied the opportunity to have our say. There is considerable evidence that people who lose out in a debate are far less troubled by the loss if they feel they have been heard—if they believe the fight was fair. In some parts of the country, the media tends to be dominated by modernists, in others, by Puritans. (Of course, in virtually every part of the country, Puritans perceive bias favoring modernists, and modernists see bias favoring Puritans, no matter what the actual orientation of media outlets. Journalists will tell you this is the "nature of the beast.") Rather than engaging in the interminable argument about who is being favored and who is being shut out, we need to respect our fellow citizens enough to ensure that their position and point of view receives a fair hearing.

A very welcome consequence of such an approach would be a reduction in the number of people who are getting all their information from sources they have selected for compatibility. This *niching* of media—the growing numbers of Americans who visit only politically and culturally congenial Web sites, listen only to broadcast outlets and commentators who agree with them, and read only those newspapers and magazines that reflect their preferred point of view—is hugely problematic for democratic governance. So we end up with the "Christian Broadcasting Network" and "Air America," each talking only to its partisans. This situation reinforces the incommensurability of our respective realities and makes it much easier to avoid engaging opinions different from our own. It also encourages intemperate, even vicious, allegations about those who disagree—the sort of discourse that greatly troubles, and repels, thoughtful Puritans and modernists alike. Much of this degraded and polarized discourse can be traced to the lack of opportunity to rebut contrary views.

Third, Clean Up Government

This is related to the questions of voice and fairness, and is another case of "easier said than done," but there are encouraging signs. Democratic legitimacy is absolutely dependent upon the perception that government processes are fair and impartial. A fair process, as I am using that term, means at least the following:

- It is transparent. Citizens can see how rules are made. Secrecy is minimized, and claims of privilege reserved for matters truly affecting national security and the government's ability to function. While it is important that government be honest (see below), it is equally important that it be seen as honest, and that elected officials conduct themselves so as to minimize the opportunities for suspicion.
- Citizens have a real vote (voice). In most of the country, the right to create voting districts is considered part of the political spoils system, where the party in the majority gets to ensure the best possible outcome for itself. It has aptly been characterized as a system where the politicians choose their voters, rather than the other way around. Also in most parts of the country, presidential elections are conducted under a *winner take all* system that operates to disenfranchise voters; if you are in the minority (even if that minority is 49.9 percent) in your state, your vote simply does not count—the state's electoral votes are all awarded to the candidate receiving 50.1 percent. Add to that the drawing of grossly partisan districts, and you have a system that enrages those who are deprived of representation, leads to apathy and disengagement of others, and reinforces the perception that the deck is stacked against "us." Relatively simple

reforms—such as independent redistricting commisssions that are required to draw compact districts based upon population numbers and respect for geographic and political communities, or state statutes allocating electoral votes in accordance with popular vote totals, etc.—would go a long way toward healing resentments that are not the exclusive property of either Puritans or modernists, Republicans or Democrats.
- It is honest. Nothing breeds cynicism like fat, no-bid contracts, revelations of huge campaign contributions followed by passage of legislation favorable to the contributor, and a daily drumbeat announcing official misconduct and corruption. When people believe that justice is what is sold to the highest bidder, when they are convinced that they are powerless unless they are rich or otherwise connected to some powerful elite, they lose respect for the law and they lose faith in America.

There is a useful analogy here to a fair trial. Appellate courts often remind us that the Constitution does not guarantee litigants a right outcome, only a fair and impartial process. Mistakes will inevitably be made; all we fallible humans can do is ensure that the judge and jury are fair and unbiased, and that all reliable evidence is considered and weighed. Most Americans—Puritans and modernists alike—are willing to abide by laws they disapprove of, if they are confident that those laws were passed by fairly elected legislators who listened to all sides of the argument and voted on the basis of their best judgment. It is when we suspect that the contest has been rigged that we rebel.

Of the three actions I have proposed, I have the most confidence that this one will be achieved. America periodically goes through periods where our elected officials betray our principles—Teapot Dome and Watergate come to mind; there have been many others. If history is any guide, we will clean up the current mess as well—probably not completely, and certainly not forever, but mostly and at least for the time being.

TALKING TO EACH OTHER

If we can elevate the terms of the debate by increasing civic literacy, protecting the marketplace of ideas, and reestablishing respect for our governing institutions and constitutional tradition, we can vastly improve the possibility of meaningful conversations about our public policies.

In a free society, people will disagree. They will interpret facts differently; they will assign different priorities to different interests. They will continue to inhabit different realities. The goal is not a national paradigm shared in all its particulars. The goal is just enough common ground—just enough elements common to all of our paradigms—to serve as our shared civil religion, and to make genuine conversation and effective self-government possible.

BIBLIOGRAPHY

Ahlstrom, Sydney E. 1972. *A Religious History of the American People.* 2d ed. New Haven: Yale University Press.

Alexander, Jeffrey. 2004. "The Darkside of Modernity After the Axial Age: Tension Relief, Splitting, and the Problem of Grace" (February). http://research.yale.edu/ccs/research/working-papers/alexander-darkside.pdf.

Allport, Gordon W. 1954, 1979. *The Nature of Prejudice.* Boston: Addison-Wesley.

Amar, Akhil Reed. 1998, 2000. *The Bill of Rights: Creation and Reconstruction.* New Haven: Yale University Press.

Ammerman, Nancy T. 1995. *Armageddon in Waco.* Chicago: University of Chicago Press.

———. 1997. "Golden Rule Christianity: Lived Religion in the American Mainstream." In *Lived Religion in America: Toward a History of Practice.* Edited by David D. Hall, 196–216. Princeton: Princeton University Press.

Anderson, Kerby. 1994. "Globalism and Foreign Policy." *Probe Ministries.* http://www.probe.org./content/view/668/88.

Appenzeller, George W. 2004. "The Role of Culture in the Current Conservative Administration's Policy Decisions." Presentation to Policy Conference, Charleston, S.C., August 7.

Applegate, Brandon K., Francis C. Cullen, Bonnie S. Fisher, and Thomas Vander Ven. 2000. "Forgiveness and Fundamentalism: Reconsidering the Relationship Between Correctional Attitudes and Religion." *Criminology* 38 (3): 719–54.

Armstrong, Karen. 2000. *The Battle for God: A History of Fundamentalism.* New York: Ballantine Books.

Bailey, Michael E. 2002. "The Wisdom of Serpents: When Religious Groups Use Secular Language." *Journal of Church of State* 44 (2): 249–69.

Battalora, Jacqueline. 2005. "Making Difference: Antimiscegenation Law and the One Man One Woman Marriage Requirement." Paper delivered at annual meeting, Law and Society Association, June 3. Las Vegas, Nevada.

Beiner, Ronald. 1996. "What Liberalism Means." *Social Philosophy and Policy* 13 (1): 190–206.

Bell, Daniel M., Jr. 2004. "State and Civil Society." In *Blackwell Companion to Political Theology.* Edited by Peter Scott and William Cavanaugh, 423–38. London: Blackwell.

Bellah, Robert N. 2002. "The Protestant Structure of American Culture: Multiculture or Monoculture?" *The Hedgehog Review* (Institute for Advanced Studies in Culture) 4 (1): 7–28.

Bellah, Robert N., Richard Madsen, William M. Sullivan, Ann Swidler, and Steven M. Tipton. 1985. *Habits of the Heart: Individualism and Commitment in American Life.* Berkeley: University of California Press.

Berger, Peter L. 1967. *The Sacred Canopy: Elements of a Sociological Theory of Religion.* New York: Anchor Books.

Berger, Peter. 2004. "Religion and Globalization." Lecture, Boise Institute, Boston, Mass.

Berkowitz, Bill. 2001. "Anti-Science." www.theocracywatch.org/environment.htm.

Berlin, Isaiah. 1956. *The Age of Enlightenment.* Mentor Philosopher Series. New York: New American Library.

Bigelow, Gordon. 2005. "Let There Be Markets: The Evangelical Roots of Economics." *Harper Magazine* 310 (1860). http://www.mindfully.org/Industry/2005/Evangelical-Economics1may05.htm.

Boaz, David. 1997. *Libertarianism: A Primer.* New York: Free Press.

Bohne, Eberhard. 2004. "U.S. and European Security Strategies from the Perspective of National and European Identities." Paper presented at 2004 Transatlantic Policy Consortium Colloquium: *The End of Sovereignty? A Transatlantic Perspective.* September 9–11. Austin, Texas.

Borg, Marcus. 2003. *The Heart of Christianity: Rediscovering a Life of Faith.* San Francisco: Harper.

Boyd, Heather Hartwig. 1999. "Christianity and the Environment in the American Public." *Journal for the Scientific Study of Religion* 38 (1): 36–44.

Brayton, Ed. 2005. "Natural Disasters and the 'End Times.'" *Dispatches from the Culture Wars*, September 6. www.stcynic.com/blog/archives/2005/natural_disasters_and_the_end.php.
Butler, Jon. 1990. *Awash in a Sea of Faith: Christianizing the American People*. Cambridge, Mass.: Harvard University Press.
Cass, Ronald A. 2001. *The Rule of Law in America*. Baltimore: Johns Hopkins University Press.
Catechism, Catholic Church. www.vatican.va/archive/catechism/ccc_toc.htm (accessed December 19, 2006).
Chaves, Mark. 1999. "Religious Congregations and Welfare Reform: Who Will Take Advantage of 'Charitable Choice'?" *American Sociological Review* 6 (4): 836–46.
— — —. 2001. Interview by author. Chicago, Illinois, April.
Chernus, Ira. 2001. http://spot.colorado.edu/~chernus/Newspaper%20Columns/The%20Bush%20Aadministration/Olaskyand19th%20Century.htm.
Cleveland, Odell. 2003. *Tempting Faith*. http://ccr.urbancenter.iupui.edu/PDFs/Tempting%20Faith%20nr.pdf.
Colson, Charles. 2001. *Justice That Restores*. New York: Tyndale House.
Cotgrove, Stephen. 1982. *Catastrophe or Cornucopia: Environment, Politics, and the Future*. New York: John Wiley.
Cowing, Cedric. 1971. *The Great Awakening and the American Revolution: Colonial Thought in the 18th Century*. Chicago: Rand McNally.
Curry, Bishop Thomas J. 2003. "Religion and the Constitution Confounded: Treating the First Amendment as a Theological Statement." Lecture delivered at the University of Chicago, March 14. http://marty-center.uchicago.edu/webforum/092003/commentary.shtml.
Curtis, Susan. 2001. *A Consuming Faith: The Social Gospel and Modern American Culture*. Columbia: University of Missouri Press.
Daalder, Ivo. 2005. "A Wilsonian Family Quarrel." *TPM Café*. http://tpmcafe.com/story/2005/11/1/10058/1863.
Dalai Lama, The. 2005. *The Universe in a Single Atom*. New York: Morgan Road Books.
Dane, Perry. 1996, 1999. "Constitutional Law and Religion." In *A Companion to Philosophy of Law and Legal Theory*. Edited by Dennis Patterson, 113–25. Malden: Blackwell.
Davidson, James D., Alan K. Mock, and C. Lincoln Johnson. 1997. "Through the Eye of a Needle: Social Ministry in Affluent Churches." *Review of Religious Research* 38 (3): 247–62.

DeTocqueville, Alexis. 1835. *Democracy in America*. Reprint, New York: Mentor Books, 1956.

DiIulio, John J., Jr. 2001. "Know Us by Our Works." *Wall Street Journal*, February 14 2001, A22.

Durbin, William A. 2004. "Science." In *Themes in Religion and American Culture*. Edited by Philip Joff and Paul Harvey. 293–326. Chapel Hill: University of North Carolina Press.

Durkheim, Emile, and Lewis A. Coser. 1997. The Division of Labor in Society. Reprint, New York: Free Press. Originally published 1933, Macmillan.

Dworkin, Ronald. 1995. "Constitutionalism and Democracy." *European Journal of Philosophy* 3 (1): 1–11.

Earlry, Mark, and Jim Tonkowitch. 2003. "The InnerChange Freedom Initiative." *Liberty Magazine*, September/October. www.libertymagazine.com/article/articleview/380/ (accessed December 19, 2006).

Eck, Diana L. 2001. *A New Religious America*. San Francisco: HarperCollins.

Edgar, Bob. 2003. "Faith and the Environment." Address to the Religion Communicators Council, Indianapolis, April 24, 2003. http:/www.ncc-cusa.org/news/03news49.html.

Egan, Patrick J., and Kenneth Sherrill. 2005. "Marriage and the Shifting Priorities of a New Generation of Lesbians and Gays." *Political Science and Politics* 38(2): 229–32.

Elazar, Daniel J. 1994. "The Political Subcultures of the United States." In his *The American Mosaic: The Impact of Space, Time, and Culture on American Politics*, 229–57. Boulder: Westview.

Evans, T. David, Francis T. Cullen, R. Gregory Dunaway, and Velmer S. Burton Jr. 1995. "Religion and Crime Re-examined: The Impact of Religion, Secular Controls, and Social Ecology on Adult Criminality." *Criminology* 33 (2): 195–224.

Farnsley, Arthur. (2003). Personal conversation with the author.

Fox, Jonathan. 2004. *Religion, Civilization, and Civil War: 1945 Through the New Millenium*. Lanham, Md.: Lexington Books.

Galston, William. 1991. *Liberal Purposes: Goods, Virtues and Diversity in the Liberal State*. Cambridge: Cambridge University Press.

Garland, David. 2006. "Concepts of Culture in the Sociology of Punishment." *Theoretical Criminology* 10 (4): 419–47.

Gatewood, Willard B., Jr. 1969. *Controversy in the Twenties: Fundamentalism, Modernism and Evolution*. Nashville: Vanderbilt University Press.

Gay, Peter. 1969. *The Enlightmenent: An Interpretation.* Reissued edition, 1996. New York: W. W. Norton.

Geertz, Clifford. 1973, 2000. *The Interpretation of Cultures.* New York: Basic Books.

Gelernter, David. 2005. "Americanism and its Enemies." *Commentary Magazine.* www.commentarymagazine.com/article.asp.paid=11901043_1.

German, James. 2004. "Economy." In *Themes in Religion and American Culture.* Edited by Philip Goff and Paul Harvey, 261–92. Chapel Hill: University of North Carolina Press.

Goff, Philip. 2004. "Diversity and Region." In *Themes in Religion and American Culture.* Edited by Philip Goff and Paul Harvey, 327–60. Chapel Hill: University of North Carolina Press.

Goff, Philip, and Paul Harvey, ed. 2004. *Themes in Religion and American Culture.* Chapel Hill: University of North Carolina Press.

Gold, Jonathan. 2001. "Searching in Vain for an Essence" *Sightings*, Martin Marty Center, University of Chicago Divinity School. December 6.

Goldberg, Jeffrey. 2005. "Breaking Ranks." *The New Yorker Magazine*, October 31. 54.

Gray, Mike. 2000. *Drug Crazy.* New York: Routledge.

Green, John C. 2004. "The American Religious Landscape and Political Attitudes: A Baseline for 2004." *Fourth National Survey of Religion and Politics.* Bliss Institute, University of Akron (March–May). Pew Forum on Religion and Public Life.

Gress, David. 1998. "The Idea of the West." *Watch on the West: A Newsletter of FPRI's Center for the Study of America and the West.* Vol. 1.5.

Grettenberger, Susan. 1997. "Churches as a Resource for Human Services and Social Capital Development: A Survey of West Michigan Conference of the United Methodist Church." Ph.D. diss., Michigan State University.

Guardian Unlimited. 2002. "Are We Hardwired For God?" http://books.guardian.co.uk/lrb/articles/0,6109,646445,00.html.

Gusfield, Joseph R. 1963. *Symbolic Crusade: Status Politics and the American Temperance Movement.* Urbana: University of Illinois Press.

Hackney, C. H., and G. S. Sanders. 2003. "Religion and Mental Health: A Meta-Analysis of Recent Studies." *Journal for the Scientific Study of Religion* 42 (1): 43–55.

Hall, Charles. 1997. "The Christian Left: Who Are They and How are They Different From the Christian Right?" *Review of Religious Research* 39 (1): 27–45.

Harden, Blaine. 2005. "The Greening of Evangelicals." *Washington Post*, February 6. A01.
Harris-Lacewell, Melissa. 2004. "Black Churches: Liberation or Prosperity?" *Sightings*. Martin Marty Center, University of Chicago Divinity School, October 14.
Hart, Gary. 2004. "When the Personal Shouldn't Be Political." *The New York Times*, November 8. "Opinion," p. 8.
Hatch, Nathan. 1977. *The Sacred Cause of Liberty: Republican Thought and the Millenium in Revolutionary New England*. New Haven: Yale University Press.
Hayes, Bernadette, and Manussos Marangudakis. 2000. "Religion and Environmental Issues within Anglo American Democracies." *Review of Religious Research* 42 (2): 159–74.
Hehir, J. Bryan. 2005. *Liberty and Power: A Dialogue on Religion and U.S. Foreign Policy in an Unjust World*. Washington, D.C.: Brookings Institution Press.
Henneberger, Melinda. 2005. "Overturning the Gospels." www.msnbcmsn.com /id/9342324/site/newsweek/print/1/displaymode/1098.
Hofstadter, Richard. 1964. *The Paranoid Style in American Politics and Other Essays*. Reprint, New York: Harvard University Press.
Holloway, Richard. 2003. Address delivered at Cheltenham, UK. May. http:://homepages.which.net/~radical faith/holloway/sixth%20paradigm. htm.
Homet, Roland. 2001. "The Wisdom of Serpents: Reflections on Religion and Foreign Policy." Unpublished paper.
Howe, Mark DeWolfe. 1965. *The Garden and the Wilderness: Religion and Government in American Constitutional History*. Chicago: University of Chicago Press. http://research.yale.edu/ccs/papers.html#alexander.
Hughes, Richard T. 2003. *Myths America Lives By*. Urbana: University of Illinois Press.
Hunsberger, Ruth Pederen. 2005. "The American Reception of Sigmund Freud." www.hunsberger.org/freud-america.htm).
Hunter, James Davison. 1991. *Culture Wars: The Struggle to Define America*. New York: Basic Books.
———. 2005. "Living with Uncertainty." *Commentary*, April 25, National Public Radio. Reprinted in *INSight*, Institute for Advanced Studies in Culture, Center on Religion and Democracy.
Huntington, Samuel. 2002. "The Classh of Civilizations Revisited." *New Prespectives Quarterly*, Center for the Study of Democratic Institutions 19.1: 1–4.

Hutchison, William R. 2003. *Religious Pluralism in America: The Contentious History of a Founding Ideal.* New Haven: Yale University Press.

Ikenberry, G. John. 2005. "A Wilsonian Family Quarrel." *TPM Café.* http://tpmcafe.com/story/2005/11/1/10058/1863.

Ingersoll, Robert G. 1983. *Best of Robert Ingersoll: Selections from His Writings and Speeches.* Edited by Roger E. Greenley. Amherst, N.Y.: Prometheus Books.

Jacoby, Susan. 2004. *Freethinkers: A History of American Secularism.* New York: Henry Holt.

Jefferson, Thomas. 1782. *Notes on the State of Virginia.* New York: Palgrove MacMillan; 2002 edition.

———. 1800. *The Writings of Thomas Jefferson* 1. Washington, D.C.: Issued under the auspices of the Thomas Jefferson memorial association of the United States, 1903–1904.

Johnson, Byron R., Sung Joon Jang, David B. Larson, and Spencer De Li. 2001. "Does Adolescent Religious Commitment Matter? A Reexamination of the Effects of Religiosity on Delinquency." *Journal of Research in Crime and Delinquency* 38 (1): 22–44.

Kahler, Miles, and David A. Lake. 2000. "Globalization and Governance." Paper prepared for the Annual Meeting of the American Political Science Association, Washington, D.C., August 31–September 3.

Kanagy, Conrad L. 1992. "Social Action, Evangelism, and Ecumenism: The Impact of Community, Theological, and Church Structural Variables." *Review of Religious Research* 34 (1): 34–50.

Kappeler, Victor E., Mark Blumberg, and Gary W. Potter. 2000. *The Mythology of Crime and Criminal Justice.* 3d ed. Prospect Height, Ill.: Waveland Press.

Kegan, Robert. 1994. *In Over Our Heads: The Mental Demands of Modern Life.* Cambridge, Mass.: Harvard University Press.

Kennedy, Sheila. 1997. *What's a Nice Republican Girl Like Me Doing at the ACLU?* Amherst, N.Y.: Prometheus Books.

———. 2000. "When is Private Public? State Action in an Era of Privatization and Government Contracting." Paper presented at Law and Society Association annual meeting, May. Miami Beach, Fla.

———. 2005. "Un-Evolved." *Indianapolis Star,* Op-Ed Page, April 18.

Kennedy, Sheila, and Wolfgang Bielefeld. 2006. *Charitable Choice at Work: Faith-Based Job Programs in the States.* Washington, D.C.: Georgetown University Press.

Kohut, Andrew, John C. Green, Scott Keeter, and Robert Toth. 2000. *The Diminishing Divide: Religion's Changing Role in American Politics*. Washington, D.C.: Brookings Institution Press.

Kraft, Charles H. 1980. "Conservative Christians and Anthropologists: A Clash of Worldviews." *Journal of the American Scientific Affiliation* 32: 142–45.

Kristof, Nicholas D. 2005. "Bleeding Hearts of the World, United!" *The New York Times*, November 6. "Opinion," p. 8.

Kuhn, Thomas. 1962. *The Structure of Scientific Revolutions*. Chicago: University of Chicago Press.

Kuttner, Robert. 2004. "An Attack on American Tolerance." *Boston Globe*, November 17. "Oped."

Kymlicka, Will. 1996. "Social Unity in a Liberal State." *Social Philosophy and Policy* 13 (1): 105–36.

Lambert, Frank. 2003. *The Founding Fathers and the Place of Religion in America*. Princeton: Princeton University Press.

Lampman, Jane. 2004. "The End of the World." *Christian Science Monitor*, February 18. 11–13.

Leege, David C. 1993. "Religion and Politics in Theoretical Perspective." In *Rediscovering the Religious Factor in American Politics*. Edited by David C. Leege and Lyman A. Kellstedt, 3–25. Armonk, N.Y.: M. E. Sharpe.

Leege, David C., and Lyman A. Kellstedt. 1993. *Rediscovering the Religious Factor in American Politics*. Armonk, N.Y.: M. E. Sharpe.

Lenkowsky, Leslie. 2001. "Funding the Faithful: Why Bush is Right." *Commentary* 111 (6): 19–24.

Leonard, Bill J. 1988. "The Modern Church and Social Action." *Review and Expositor* 85: 243–53.

Lilla, Mark. 2005. "Church Meets State." *The New York Times Book Review*, May 15. 39.

Linz, Daniel, Kenneth C. Land, and Jay R. Williams. 2004. "An Examination of the Assumption that Adult Businesses Are Associated with Crime in Surrounding Areas: A Secondary Effects Study in Charlotte, North Carolina." *Law and Society Review* 38 (1): 69–104.

Locke, John. 1689. *A Letter Concerning Toleration*. Translated by William Popple. www.mdx.ac.uk/WWW/STUDY/xlocketo.htm.

Lovejoy, David S. 1985. *Religious Enthusiasm in the New World*. Cambridge, Mass.: Harvard University Press.

Lowi, Theodore J. 1996. *The End of the Republican Era*. Norman: University of Oklahoma Press.
Luo, Michael. 2005. "Doomsday: The Latest Word If Not The Last." *The New York Times*, October 16. "Week in Review."
Macedo, Stephen. 1996. "Community, Diversity, and Civic Education: Toward a Liberal Political Science of Group Life." *Social Philosophy and Policy* 13 (1): 240–68.
Madison, James. 1964. *The Federalist*. #64. Modern Library College Edition. New York: McGraw Hill Humanities. Originally published in 1788.
MacQuarrie, Brian. 2005. "Dobson Spiritual Empire Wields Political Clout." *Boston Globe*, October 9. www.boston.com/news/nation/articles/2005/10/09/dobson_spiritual_empire_wields_political_clout/.
Marsden, George M. 1980. *Fundamentalism and American Culture: The Shaping of Twentieth-Century Evangelism*. Oxford: Oxford University Press.
———. 1991. *Understanding Fundamentalism and Evangelism 1870–1925*. Grand Rapids: Eerdmans.
Marty, Martin. 2005a. "Evangelical Ecologies." *Sightings*. Martin Marty Center, University of Chicago Divinity School, June 20.
———. 2005b. "Rights for Children." *Sightings*. Martin Marty Center, University of Chicago Divinity School, October 24.
Marvin, Carolyn, and David W. Ingle. 1996. "Blood Sacrifice and the Nation: Revisiting Civil Religion." *Journal of the American Academy of Religion* 64 (4): 767–80.
Mathisen, Robert R. 2001. *Critical Issues in American Religious History: A Reader*. Waco, Tex.: Baylor University Press.
Mazur, Eric Michael. 1999. *The Americanization of Religious Minorities: Confronting the Constitutional Order*. Baltimore: The Johns Hopkins University Press.
McCarraher, Eugene. 2005. "The Revolution Begins in the Pews." *Christianity Today*. http://www.christianitytoday.com/bc/2005/003/11.26.html.
McDougall, Walter W. 1997. *Promised Land, Crusader State: The American Encounter with the World Since 1776*. New York: Houghton Mifflin.
———. 1998. "Religion in Diplomatic History." *Orbis* Special Issue (Spring): 1–8.
Mees, Walter H., Jr. 2005. "Debating Darwin" *Sightings*. Martin Marty Center, University of Chicago Divinity School, September 8.

Meier, Kenneth J. 2001. "Drugs, Sex, and Rock and Roll: A Theory of Morality Politics." In *The Public Clash of Private Values: The Politics of Morality Policy.* Edited by Christopher Mooney, 21–36. New York: Chatham House, Seven Bridges.

Miller, Alan S. 1996. "The Influence of Religious Affiliation on the Clustering of Social Attitudes," *Review of Religious Research* 37 (3): 219–32.

Mills, C. Wright. 1959. *The Sociological Imagination.* Oxford: Oxford University Press.

Mintz, Steven. 1995. "The Promise of the Millennium." In his *Moralists and Modernizers: America's Pre-Civil War Reformers,* 16–49. Baltimore: The Johns Hopkins University Press.

Miyakawa, T. Scott. 1964. *Protestants and Pioneers: Individualism and Conformity on the American Frontier.* Chicago: University of Chicago Press.

"Monoculture?" *The Hedgehog Review: Critical Reflections on Contemporary Culture.* Institute for Advanced Studies in Culture (Spring): 7–28.

Monsma, Stephen V. 1996. *When Sacred and Secular Mix: Religious Nonprofit Organizations and Public Money.* Lanham, Md: Rowman & Littlefield.

Mooney, Christopher Z. 2001. *The Public Clash of Private Values: The Politics of Morality Policy.* New York: Seven Bridges Press.

Morone, James A. 2003. *Hellfire Nation: The Politics of Sin in American History.* New Haven: Yale University Press.

Moyers, Bill. 2004. "On Receiving Harvard Medical School's Global Environmental Citizen Award." December 1. www.commondreams.org/views04/1206-10.htm.

Mulhall, Stephen, and Adam Swift. 1996. *Liberals and Communitarians.* 2d ed. Oxford: Blackwell.

Niles, Franklyn C., and Erin G. McCammon. 2000. "Through a Glass Darkly: Assessing the Impact of Religious Identity and Private Devotionalism on Attitudes Toward Social Welfare Spending and Social Conservatism Among American Protestants." Paper delivered at the 2000 annual meeting of the American Political Science Association. September. Washington, D.C.

Noll, Mark. 1977. *Christians in the American Revolution.* Grand Rapids: Eerdmans.

Norris, Pippa, and Ronald Inglehart. 2005. *Sacred and Secular: Religion and Politics Worldwide.* Cambridge: Cambridge University Press.

Nozick, Robert. 1974. *Anarchy, State and Utopia.* Oxford: Blackwell.

O'Sullivan, John L. 1845. "The Great Nation of Futurity." *The United States Democratic Review* 6 (23): 426–30.

Oates, Mary J. 2003. "Faith and Good Works: Catholic Giving and Taking." In *Charity, Philanthropy, and Civility in American History*. Edited by Lawrence J. Friedman and Mark D. McGarvie, 281–300. New York: Cambridge University Press.

Oldfield, Duane. 2004. "The Evangelical Roots of American Unilateralism." *Foreign Policy in Focus*, March, 1–8.

Olsen, Marvin E., Dora G. Lodwick, and Riley E. Dunlap. 1992. *Viewing the World Ecologically*. Boulder: Westview.

Paul PP. VI. 1977. Message to the Conference on the Environment, Stockholm 1977: *Insegnamenti di Paolo VI*, 10 (1977): 607.

Paul, Gregory S. 2005. "Cross-National Correlations of Quantifiable Societal Health with Popular Religiosity and Secularism in the Prosperous Democracies: A First Look." *Journal of Religion and Society* 7. http://moses.creighton.edu/JRS/2005-11.html.

Perl, Peter. 2001. "Absolute Truth." *Washington Post*, May 13, W12.

PRA Public Eye.com. 2005. "The Environment." www.publiceye.org/magazine/v15n1/State_of_Christian_Rt-09.html.

Public Agenda. 1998. *A Lot to be Thankful For: What Parents Want Children to Learn about America*. www.publicagenda.org/specials/thankful/thankful.htm.

Putnam, Robert. 2000. *Bowling Alone*. New York: Simon & Schuster.

Raboteau, Albert J. 1999. *Canaan Land: A Religious History of African-Americans*. New York: Oxford University Press.

Rawls, John. 1993. *Political Liberalism*. New York: Columbia University Press.

Reimer, S., and J. Z. Park. 2001. "Tolerant (In)civility? A Longitudinal Analysis of White Conservative Protestants' Willingness to Grant Civil Liberties." *Journal for the Scientific Study of Religion* 40 (4): 735–45.

Rieff, David. 2005. *At the Point of a Gun: Democratic Dreams and Armed Intervention*. New York: Simon & Schuster.

Rodell, Daniel E., and Brent B. Benda. 1999. "Alcohol and Crime among Religious Youth." *Alcoholism Treatment Quarterly* 17 (4): 53–67.

Sandel, Michael. 1996. *Democracy's Discontent*. Cambridge: Harvard University Press.

Sarewitz, Daniel. 2004. "How Science Makes Environmental Controversies Worse." *Environmental Science and Policy* 7: 385–403.

Scherer, Glen. 2005. "The Rise of the Religious Right in the Republican Party." www.theocracywatch.org./environment.htm (accessed December 19, 2006).

Schlesinger, Arthur M., Jr. 1991. *The Disuniting of America*. Knoxville, Tenn.: Whittle Direct Books.

———. 2005. "Forgetting Reinhold Niebuhr." *The New York Times Book Review*, September 18, 2005. "Book Review."

Schwalm, Steven A. 1998. "The Assault on Christians by the Militant Homosexual Movement." *Family Research Council*. http://www.frc.org/podium/pd98j2hs.html.

Sider, Ron. 2005. "The Scandal of the Evangelical Conscience: Why Don't Christians Live What They Preach?" *Christianity Today*, January/February. http://ctlibrary.com/bc/2005/janfeb/e.8html.

Silk, Mark. 1989. "The Rise of the 'New Evangelism': Shock and Adjustment." In *Between the Times: The Travail of the Protestant Establishment, 1900–1960*. Edited by William R. Hutchinson, 278–99. Cambridge: Cambridge University Press.

Smidt, Corwin, ed. 2003. "Clergy as Political Activists." *Journal for the Scientific Study of Religion* 42 (44): 495–99.

Smith, Rogers M. 2005. "Providentialism, Foreign Policy, and the Ethics of Political Discourse." Unpublished paper.

Spiegel, Rabbi Aaron, e-mail to author, October 24, 2005.

Stark, Rodney. 2001. "Gods, Rituals, and the Moral Order," *Journal for the Scientific Study of Religion* 40 (4): 619–36.

———. 2005. *The Victory of Reason: How Christianity Led to Freedom, Capitalism, and Western Success*. New York: Random House.

Steensland, Brian, Jerry Z. Park, Mark D. Regnerus, Lynn D. Robinson, W. Bradford Wilcox, and Robert D. Woodbury. 2000. "The Measure of American Religion: Toward Improving the State of the Art." *Social Forces* 79 (1): 291–318.

Stier, Marc. 2000. "Principles and Prudence: Reconciling Liberalism and Communitarianism." Paper delivered at the 2000 Annual Meeting of the American Political Science Association, August 31–September 3. Washington, D.C.

Sullivan, Winnifred Fallers. 2001. Personal conversation with the author.

———. 2004. "The State." In *Themes in Religion and American Culture*. Edited by Philip Goff and Paul Harvey, 227–60. Chapel Hill: University of North Carolina Press.

Szasz, Ferenc M., and Margaret Connell Szasz. 1994. "Religion and Spirituality." In *The Oxford History of the American West.* Edited by Clyde A. Milner II et al., 75–77. Oxford: Oxford University Press.

Tarakeshwar, Nalini, et al. 2000. "The Sanctification of Nature and Theological Conservatism: A Study of Opposing Religious Correlates of Environmentalism." *Review of Religious Research* 42 (4): 387–404.

Thomas, Scott. 2005. "Review of *With or Against the World* by James W. Skillen." *Religion and Politics Newsletter* 22 (1): 25–29.

Tomasello, Michael. 1999. *The Cultural Origins of Human Cognition.* Cambridge: Harvard University Press.

Traub, James. 2005. "Everybody is a Realist Now." *The New York Times Book Review,* October 30. 7–8.

Unnever, James D., Francis T. Cullen, and Brandon Applegate. 2005. "Turning the Other Cheek: Reassessing the Impact of Religion on Punitive Ideology." *Justice Quarterly* 22 (3): 304–39.

Vogel, David. 2001. "The Protestant Ethic and the Spirit of Environmentalism: The Cultural Roots of Green Politics and Policies." Unpublished paper.

Walker, J. Brent. 2003. "Preserving the Legacy." *Liberty Magazine,* May/June. http://www.libertymagazine.org/article/articleview/352/1/67.

Walsh, Andrew D. 2000. *Religion, Economics, and Public Policy: Ironies, Tragedies and Absurdities of the Contemporary Culture Wars.* Westport, Conn.: Praeger.

Walzer, Michael. 2004. *Liberty and Power: A Dialogue on Religion and U.S. Foreign Policy in an Unjust World.* Washington, D.C.: Brookings Institution Press.

Weaver-Zercher, David L. 2004. "Theologies." In *Themes in Religion and American Culture.* Edited by Philip Goff and Paul Harvey, 5–38. Chapel Hill: University of North Carolina Press.

Weber, Max. 1904. *The Protestant Ethic and the Spirit of Capitalism; and Other Writings.* Edited and translated by Peter Baehr and Gordon C. Wells. Reprint, New York: Penguin Classics 2002.

Witte, John, Jr. 2000. *Religion and the American Constitutional Experiment: Essential Rights and Liberties.* Boulder: Westview.

Wolfe, Alan. 2005. Quoted in Martin Marty, "American Culture, American Religion," *Sightings,* Martin Marty Center, University of Chicago Divinity School, June 13.

———. 2001. "The God of a Diverse People." *The New York Times,* October 14, 13.

Wolfe, Alan. 1999. *One America After All*. New York: Penguin Press.
Zerubavel, Eviatar. 1997. *Social Mindscapes: An Invitation to Cognitive Sociology*. Cambridge: Harvard University Press.
Zakaria, Fareed. 2003. *The Future of Freedom: Illiberal Democracy at Home and Abroad*. New York: W. W. Norton.
Zimmerman, Jonathan. 2001. "Holy Pollers." *The New Republic Online*. http://magazines.enews.com/express/zimmerman112001.html.

INDEX

abortion, 2, 3, 4, 94, 106, 117, 118, 119, 170, 192, 217; Fourteenth Amendment, 67; *Rowe v. Wade*, 80
academic freedom, 80
Ahlstrom, Sidney, 41; church history, 23–24; and Puritan countercurrents, 27; Enlightenment origins, 38; Founding Fathers and religion, 47; patriotic spirits, 54
Allen, Ethan, 44
Allport, Gordon, 96–97
Al Qaeda, 197
American creed (*see* Hughes, Richard)
American exceptionalism, 26, 94, 177, 181, 185, 195, 219
American Revolution, 45, 59, 149, 186; and religious motives, 31
Ammerman, Nancy, 95, 96, 171
anti-Federalists, 51

Appenzeller, George, 98
axis of evil, 191

Bacon, Francis 38 (*see also* New Learning)
balanced treatment, 111
Beisner, Calvin; and biological egalitarianism, 159
Bellah, Robert, 10, 14, 77, 78, 149
Berger, Peter, 6, 8
Berlin, Isaiah, 40 (*see also* new learning)
biblical literalists (*see* fundamentalists)
Bill of Rights, 46, 51, 52, 66, 76; and religious clauses, 48; the Fourteenth Amendment, 67–70
black church, 62, 64, 93, 126, 146
Blunt, Ray, 160
Book of Mormon (*see* Smith, Joseph)

Boyles, Robert, 39 (*see also* new learning)
Brown v. Board of Education, 79, 123
Bryan, Williams Jennings, 14, 69, 72, 132
Buddhism, 8, 111
Bush, George W., 5, 84, 138, 191, 196–97, 203–4
Butler, Jon, 28, 33 (*see also* The Great Awakening)

Calvin, John, 117–18
Calvinism, 26, 128, 166; and terror of the laws, 30; naturalistic Calvinism, 69; Presbyterian model, 26
Calvinist, 35, 50, 60, 72, 75, 128, 129; Protestants, 35; Protestantism, 128
capital punishment, 173, 175–77
Carter, Jimmy, 192
Catholicism; and works-based religions, 9; anti-Catholicism, 24–26
Central American Free Trade Agreement, 2
Charitable Choice, 138–43, 145
Chaves, Mark, 141
Cheney, Dick, 204
Christianity; denominations, 21; conversion of slaves, 64; and evolution, 68; and economics, 136
Christian nation, 18, 21–22, 35, 38, 83
Christian Science (*see* Eddy, Mary)
Church of England, 25

Cimbalas, Stephen, 204
City on the Hill, 26, 50, 58, 68, 117, 119, 138, 164, 165, 184, 211
civic glue, 33
civil religion, 32, 34, 78, 184, 209, 218, 232
Civil Rights; movement 1, 79; Act, 80
Civil War, 1; Fourteenth Amendment, 50, and the black church, 63; aftermath, 184; economic consequences, 131
Columbus, Christopher, 23
Common Sense Realism, 41
communitarian, 126 (*also see* modernists)
conservative(s); religious conservatives, 6; Christianity, 22, 115; Protestants, 30, 73, 111, 136; and power of the state, 138; and environmental policies, 152; and Enlightenment principles, 52; and liberal-conservative division, 78
Colson, Charles, 166
Comstock Act, 75
Copernicus, 38
Cornwall Declaration, 158
Cowing, Cedric, 30 (*see also* The Great Awakening)
Cowley, Jack, 174
creationists, 74
cultural codes (*see* Bellah, Robert)
culture war, 75, 81, 84, 88, 89, 109, 110, 119, 124, 182; thesis, 19, 85, 86, 87; and the

Fourteenth Ammendment, 66; debates, 105; issues, 106
culture warriors, 108, 219
Curtis, Susan, 133

Dalai Lama, 111, 116
Darrow, Clarence, 14, 74
Darwin, Charles, 68
Darwinism, 67; Protestant conflict, 72–74
Deism, 27
Delay, Tom, 160
Descartes, 38 (*see also* new learning)
drug war, 2, 177–78
Durkheim, Emile, 15, 85

Earlry, Mark, 174
Eck, Diana, 84
Eddy, Mary, 77
Edgar, Bob, 155–56
Edwards, Jonathan, 28 (*see also* The Great Awakening)
Edwards v. Aguillard, 111
Eisenhower, Dwight, 18, 79
Elazar, Daniel, 89
Enlightenment; and The Great Awakening, 29; and new learning, 38–42; Common Sense Realism, 41–42; impact of, 42–44; liberal democratic solution, 49; constitutional framework, 51–52; and Puritan conflict, 50–53
Epperson v. Arkansas, 111
evangelical Protestants, 93, 126
evangelicals, 43, 47, 60, 68–69, 79, 95

faith-based, 9; initiatives 138–39, 158; secular arguments 140–42; roots of debate 142–46; social programs,169, 172, 174–75; warfare, 198; crusades, 197
Federalists, 51
Finney, Charles, 60
Founding Fathers; and new learning, 44, 46, 47, 49; distinction between Planting Fathers, 50, 113, 117, 185
Fourteenth Amendment, 46, 51, 52, 65–67, 119, 226
Fox, Jonathan, 108
Franklin, Benjamin, 45, 46
Freud, Sigmund, 77
Friedan, Betty, 80
Frist, Bill, 5, 160
fundamentalism; emergence of, 72–75
fundamentalists; modernists conflict, 74; and the Age of Reform, 109; and homosexuality, 114; environmental protections, 150–51; American moral debate, 164; the role of the state, 118, 120; economic arguments, 136–37, 143; and environmental protections, 150–51, 153; in the moral debate, 164

Galston, William, 212
Gay, Peter, 42
Geertz, Clifford, 10
Gelernter, David, 181, 183
Genesis, 110, 113, 153

Gilded Age, 69, 130–31, 133
Gladden, Washington, 132
Global Meliorism, 190
globalization, 149, 192–93
Gold, Jonathan; dialectic process, 6
Goldberg, Jeffrey, 203
Gore, Al, 84
Graham, Billy, 79
Graham, Franklin, 196
Gray, Mike, 178
Great Depression, 75, 136, 190
Green, John, 94
Gress, David, 191, 193
Grettenberger, Susan, 142
Gusfield, Joseph, 106

habits of the mind, 10, 12, 19, 88
Hall, Charles, 23
Hart, Gary, 99
Hastert, Dennis, 160
Hehir, Bryan, 198
Herberg, Will, 78
Hinduism, 8
Hocker, Nina George, 153
Hofstader, Richard, 109
Holloway, Richard, 21
holy experiment (*see* Penn, William)
Homet, Roland, 183
homosexuality, 13, 88, 97, 114, 116, 119
Hughes, Richard, 27, 53, 183, 184, 187; and the American Creed, 35, 218; the Chosen Nation, 54; and the Nature's Nation, 149

Hunter, James Davison, 12, 85–86, 99
Hunter, Samuel, 12, 85–87, 99
Huntington, Samuel, 12, 184
Hurricane Katrina, 88, 152, 223
Hutchinson, Ann, 27, 118
Hutchinson, William, 35
Huntington, Samuel, 12

individualists, 126 (*see also* fundamentalists)
Industrial Revolution, 15, 71
Inglehart, Ronald, 9, 16
intelligent design, 106, 111, 113, 152, 221
Ikenberry, John, 202
Iraq War, 2
Islam, 8, 110, 150, 196; divisions, 116
Israel, 151, 195, 196

Jackson, Andrew, 63, 188, 201
Jamestown, 24
Jefferson, Thomas, 1, 25, 45, 121, 149, 220
Judaism, 8; and works-based religions, 9
just-war theory, 198, 200; criteria, 199

Keeter, Scott, 94
Kennedy, John F., 79
Keteltas, Abraham, 186
King Jr., Martin Luther, 79–80
Kohut, Andrew, 94
Kraft, Charles, 17
Kuhn, Thomas, 10–11

Kultner, Robert, 100
Kyl, Jon, 160

Lambert, Frank, 28, 37 (*see also* The Great Awakening)
League of Nations, 190
Leland, John, 44
liberal(s); and Christianity, 22–23, 60, 74; Protestants, 30, 74, 79; theological liberals, 32; democratic worldview, 49, 120, 145, 215–17; conservative-divisions, 78; and the Enlightenment, 119; evangelical liberals, 127; democracy, 212; and social conflict, 217 (*also see* Stier, Marc)
Lilla, Mark, 110
Lindsay, Hal, 152
Lindsay, James, 191
Locke, John 40, 44 (*see also* new learning)
Lowi, Theodore, 52; and culture wars, 66–67

Macedo, Stephen, 216
Madison, James, 33, 45, 46, 65,
mainline Protestantism, 21, 22, 93, 95, 109, 158
manifest destiny, 61, 72, 185, 188
Mayhew, Jonathan, 32
Marsden, George, 14, 68, 69, 72–74, 109, 110
Martin, Marty, 58, 151
Mathisen, Robert, 31, 64
McConnell, Mitch, 160
McDougall, Walter, 182, 185

Meier, Kenneth, 179
Middle East, 195, 203
Miller, Alan, 13
Milton, John, 41, 44 (*see also* new learning)
modernists, 6, 7, 71, 72, 73, 74, 86, 87, 92, 110
Monroe, James, 22
Monroe Doctrine, 185, 187, 189
Monsma, Stephen, 140
Mooney, Christopher, 105
Moore, Judge Roy, 83, 88

negative liberty, 213–14
neoconservatives, 182, 201
New Israel, 27, 31, 53–54, 58
new learning, 38–42; and new religious thought, 44
Newton, Isaac, 39-40 (*see also* new learning)
Niebuhr, Richard, 54, 79, 109, 182
Noll, Mark, 33–34
North American Free Trade Agreement, 2

Olasky, Marvin, 143
O'Sullivan, John, 188

Paine, Thomas, 32, 44, 46, 68
paradigm, 5, 10, 35, 50; paradigm theory, 11; shifts, 14–15, 38, 87, 97
Parks, Rosa, 79
Paul, Gregory, 170
Pearl Harbor, 190
Penn, William, 25

people of faith, 53, 65, 109, 117, 119
Pickney, Charles, 48
pilpul, 110
Pippa, Norris, 9, 16
Planting Fathers, 38, 119–20, 209; distinction between Founding Fathers, 50, 113, 117, 185
Pope John Paul VI, 158
post-Enlightenment (*see* modernists)
Presbyterian, 33, 34, 70, 91
Progressive Imperialism, 189
Prohibition, 1; social gospel, 69
Protestant; conception of religion, 9; and the Protestant nation, 14, 18; individualism, 15, 43, 133; Reformation, 109, 128; political behavior, 93–95, 126
Protestantism; denominations, 21–22; and religious diversity in early America, 34–35, 42–43, 53; divisions, 23, 72–74; and the Social Gospel, 71–72; dark-green environmentalism, 148; and fundamentalism, 73; the Protestant nation, 14, 18
premillenialism, 73; dispensational, 150–51
Puritanism, 34, 57, 76; separatists, 24; American antecedents, 25; opposition to, 27
Puritans, 9, 77, 87, 89, 92; and human nature, 6; heritage, 6; colonial diversity, 25; worldviews, 26–28; and the Great Awakening, 29, 33, 34, 37–39; Enlightenment conflict, 50–53, 57–58, 67, 75; and culture wars, 79

Quakers, 25, 27, 34, 59

Reagan, Ronald, 166, 197
Rauschenbusch, Walter, 132
Rice, Condoleezza, 204
Redeemer Nation, 30, 194
Reformation, 15, 24, 43, 107
regime change, 203; and just-war theory, 199
Rieff, David, 201
religion; and public conflict, 7; and "habits of the mind," 10, 19, 88; faith-based, 9; works-based, 9; and science, 17, 113; civil religion, 32–34; voluntary affiliation, 52–53; the American west, 61–62; the defense of slavery, 63; and Darwinism, 67–70; and social health, 170
religious; freedom, 63, 79, 83, 88; liberals (*see* modernists); conservatives (*see also* Puritans) 67, 71; warriors, 109; liberty, 26, 45, 175, 218
Renaissance, 15; and new learning, 38, 43
Rehnquist, Justice, 111
Rhode Island (*see* Williams, Roger)
Robertson, Pat, 115, 223
Roosevelt, Franklin Delano, 75, 136, 190

same-sex marriage, 2, 4, 107, 114
Santorum, Rick, 160
Sarwitz, Daniel, 148
Scalia, Justice, 111
Schlesinger, Arthur, 14, 109
Scowcroft, Brend, 203–5
scientific method, 39, 40, 112
Scopes, John, 74 (*see also* Darwinism)
Scottish philosophy (*see* Common Sense Realism)
secularization theory, 16
separation of church and state, 24, 70, 92, 100, 108, 120, 174; early evangelicals, 43–44
Shiavo, Terry, 5
Sirico, Robert, 158
slavery, 27, 46–47; and the Second Great Awakening, 62–65; anti-slavery movement, 60
Smith, Adam, 41
Smith, Joseph, 60
Smith, Rogers, 183, 197
Sunday, Billy, 73
social Darwinism, 69–70, 130–31 (*see also* Darwinism)
Social Gospel, 22, 71, 72, 75, 130, 133–36, 146, 183
social contract, 34, 40, 172, 218
Stark, Rodney, 18
stem-cell research, 3
Stier, Marc, 217
Stonewall Inn, 80
stories of peoplehood (*see* Smith, Rogers)
Sullivan, Winnifred, 9

terrorism, 191, 197, 200, 203
The Great Awakening, 28–31, 35, 41; and individualism, 43
The Second Great Awakening, 59–60, 71; and slavery, 62–63
The Ten Commandments (*see* Moore, Judge Ray)
Thirty Years War, 198
Tonkowich, Jim, 174
Toth, Robert, 94
Treaty of Westphalia, 198
Truman, Harry, 190

Unitarianism, 27
United Nations, 190, 193–94
U.S. Constitution, 40

values, 6, 9, 16, 19, 22, 33, 34, 85–88, 94
values debate, 3; wedge issues, 4
Vietnam War, 80
Vogel, David, 147–48, 157

Walker, J. B., 100
wall of separation, 25 (*see also* Williams, Roger)
Walzer, Michael, 198
War on Terrorism, 197, 199, 200
Washington, George, 37, 46, 186
Watt, James, 159
Wicca, 8
Williams, Roger, 9, 25, 27
Wilson, Woodrow, 189
Winthrop, John, 25–26
Witherspoon, John, 35, 41
World-War I, 69, 70; and emergence of fundamentalism, 72–73

World War II, 75–77
works-based religions, 9
Wright, Mills C., 15

Zimmerman, Jonathan, 100
Zakeria, Fareed, 212
Zionism, 196